Global Jewish Plays

Global Jewish Plays

Five Works by Jewish Playwrights from around the World

Extinct

Heartlines

The Kahena: Berber Queen

Papa'gina

a People

Edited by

GLOBAL VOICES THEATRE

methuen | drama

LONDON • NEW YORK • OXFORD • NEW DELHI • SYDNEY

METHUEN DRAMA
Bloomsbury Publishing Plc
50 Bedford Square, London, WC1B 3DP, UK
1385 Broadway, New York, NY 10018, USA
29 Earlsfort Terrace, Dublin 2, Ireland

BLOOMSBURY, METHUEN DRAMA and the Methuen Drama logo are trademarks of Bloomsbury Publishing Plc

First published in Great Britain 2024

Cover design: Ayeola Whitworth
Cover artwork © Ayeola Omolara Kaplan

A catalogue record for this book is available from the British Library.

Library of Congress Cataloging-in-Publication Data
Names: Esses, Victor, writer of preface. | Global Voices Theatre, editor.
Title: Global Jewish plays : five works by Jewish playwrights from around the world / edited by Global Voices Theatre ; preface by Victor Esses.
Description: London ; New York : Methuen Drama, 2023. | Identifiers: LCCN 2023014755 (print) | LCCN 2023014756 (ebook) | ISBN 9781350383319 (hardback) | ISBN 9781350383302 (paperback) | ISBN 9781350383326 (epub) | ISBN 9781350383333 (pdf)
Subjects: LCSH: Jewish drama. | Jewish drama–Translations into English.
Classification: LCC PN6120.J4 G56 2023 (print) | LCC PN6120.J4 (ebook) | DDC 808.82/9921296—dc23/eng/20230726
LC record available at https://lccn.loc.gov/2023014755
LC ebook record available at https://lccn.loc.gov/2023014756

ISBN: HB: 978-1-3504-8331-9
PB: 978-1-3504-8330-2
ePDF: 978-1-3504-8333-3
eBook: 978-1-3504-8332-6

Series: Methuen Drama Play Collections

Typeset by RefineCatch Limited, Bungay, Suffolk
Printed and bound in Great Britain

To find out more about our authors and books visit www.bloomsbury.com and sign up for our newsletters.

Contents

Introduction

Global Voices Theatre (GVT) is a female and non-binary, immigrant-led theatre company, led by Lora Krasteva, Robin Skyer and Zhui Ning Chang. Established in 2018 after the successful mini-festival Global Queer Plays (alongside the eponymous anthology, published by the now defunct Oberon Books), GVT aims to diversify the UK theatre scene highlighting the vibrancy of written performance beyond the narrow Western canon that is taught and performed. Our mission is to amplify theatre and performance work by underrepresented global artists, to decolonise local theatre structures and advocate for international artistic practices, and to contribute to the professional development of artists across borders.

Since our first Global Female Voices event in April 2018 at the Arcola Theatre in East London, we have worked with forty-six writers and fourteen translators from all over the world, showcasing a total of forty-six plays never before performed in the UK. These plays were all selected via open calls: our core team, alongside the readers and curators in each event, have read over 450 texts from more than 100 countries, written in over sixty languages. We have curated Global Indigenous, Arab, Latin American and Black Voices events and have performed at the British Library, Rich Mix, the Roundhouse and, most recently, at Bush Theatre, who hosted Global Jewish Voices, the selection of plays you currently hold.

Since 2019 we have also produced a podcast, interviewing all the writers and translators who are based outside of the UK and often not able to attend the live events. This creates an additional space for the playwrights' voices and an opportunity for our audiences to delve deeper into the socio-political background of the plays. Both seasons of the *Global Voices* podcast (*Global Black Voices* hosted by theatre director Abigail Sewell, and *Global Jewish Voices* hosted by the event's curator, Victor Esses) are available via our website and anywhere you find your podcasts. We strongly recommend listening to the *Global Jewish Voices* episodes as companion pieces to the plays compiled here.

Our practice as a company was born from the desire to oppose the structural racism, classism, misogyny, ableism and xenophobia of the British theatre scene. We seek to explore alternatives, programming events in a more open, horizontal way; working *with* the people whose heritage is in focus rather than *for* them; and exploring each story further through conversation and debate. It felt radical to be an international theatre company focusing on translations and plays by marginalised creatives in 2018, and, unfortunately, it continues to be the case in 2023.

Given the success that we have seen in our previous work, with nine sold-out live events and well-received pay-what-you-can workshop series, we strongly believe in the appetite of audiences and artists for more. For bolder narratives that are experimental, different, exploring socio-political issues and focusing on communities side-lined by the mainstream. Our provocation to the British theatre establishment is this: if we can do it, so can you.

A crucial part of our practice is continuing to learn how to be better allies and advocates in dismantling oppressive structures, and this requires listening, honesty and critical reflection. We know that a commitment to educate ourselves and one another, to navigate an ever-complex and interconnected world, is hardly ground-breaking; and still, we have a long way to go. However, we hope that by making this principle an integral part of our work, others may join us.

It is our honour to help bring together this anthology, as a legacy to the incredible work that has gone into creating the plays and the event to showcase them for the first time in the UK. It is with incredible joy that we welcomed Methuen Drama's interest in publishing our latest selection of plays, helping us reach further than ever before, so many others can experience the breadth of possibility and potential in theatre and performance.

Lora, Robin, and Zhui Ning
https://globalvoicestheatre.com/
Facebook: Global Voices Theatre
Twitter: @GlobalVoicesTh

Preface

Before we ask the question 'What is Jewish theatre today?', perhaps we should consider: 'What is a Jew?' Jewish people are Ashkenazi, Sephardi, Mizrahi, Abayudaya, Bukharan and more. Upper-, middle-, and working-class; Zionists, anti-Zionists, and ambivalent. They are orthodox, reformist, conservative, revisionist, atheist, Christian, Muslim, Buddhist. Black, Arab, Asian, White and all the in-betweens, with differing views and identities (as the classic joke goes: two Jews, three opinions). Jews speak multiple languages – from Yiddish to Ladino to Hebrew to Judeo-Arabic dialects to Judeo-Persian to Bukharian to the ones in all the countries they live in. Jews are gay, straight, bi, fluid, non-binary, trans, cis, monogamous, married, polyamorous, unattached. There isn't one thing that defines all Jews, but the closest might be a history of migration.

Near the end of 2019 I attended 'Intermission', a weekend retreat – well, Sunday to Tuesday to avoid Shabbat – where several Jewish theatre-makers came together to discuss the growing antisemitism in the UK. The New York-based organisation Asylum Arts and writer/theatre maker Nick Cassenbaum hoped to create a Jewish artistic community to support each other in these challenging times, when antisemitism is weaponised politically and socially, and when wider society only hears from a small portion of Jews, lacking a wider understanding of different subjectivities. It felt like a good moment to acknowledge the complicated and cyclical nature of antisemitism, how it ebbs and flows between the perception and reality of both privilege and marginalisation within the establishment and in society as a whole.

What I had learned since arriving in the UK from Brazil in 2000, was that many British Jews didn't want to be 'out Jews'; they preferred to blend in to avoid feeling like outsiders. Jewish stories that gain commercial entertainment space tend to represent one specific horrendous unimaginable Jewish trauma of the twentieth century. More often than not they are also hetero American Ashkenazi-centric. Theatre is, or should be, the space where we can imagine better, where we can hopefully choose not to be *only* defined by our persecution and trauma. Where we can ask wider questions, and embrace intersections.

Thus, I was emboldened, in collaboration with Global Voices Theatre, to create Global Jewish Voices under the banner of their flagship model, as an afternoon of readings of extracts of international Jewish plays with the objective to open space, represent and surprise. To explore and celebrate all that we are, out loud.

In late summer 2021, we shared a call-out for plays all around the world, seeking original stories written by Jewish writers. They did not necessarily need to focus on Judaism. We wanted to see what was out there and what people wanted to share. Obviously we could never capture the extensive depth and nuance of every Jewish experience, but we wanted to connect with Jews living all around the world (not only in North America and Europe), people who spoke and worked and wrote in many different languages. We wanted to explore the multilayered nature of what it means to be Jewish, honouring lesser-heard Jewish voices. Highlighting the vastness of the Jewish experience was a way of showing the intersections and kinships of everyone who has ever felt like an outsider.

The reading process began, and we found ourselves engaged with a huge range of stories that venture far from what is usually staged here in the UK. It was truly exciting.

Sarah Waisvisz, a Jew of Dutch, French and Afro-Caribbean ancestry who grew up in Canada, submitted her play *Heartlines*. The piece tells the story of Claude Cahun and Suzanne Malherbe (aka Marcel Moore), a twentieth-century artistic queer couple who escape occupied Paris to Jersey (UK). It was poignant, intimate, a fun mix of cabaret, drama and historical storytelling that speaks of being non-binary when the word didn't exist; it speaks of queer love and resistance.

Philip Arditti's *Extinct* centres on a young Jewish man who takes part in the 2013 Istanbul protests. Initially to contest the urban development plan for Istanbul's Taksim Gezi Park, it later served to demonstrate against wider issues, such as lack of freedom of press and speech. The main character clashes with his conservative father, a Turkish Jew from a different era, the last generation to speak Ladino. Philip writes in English, not his mother tongue, like so many of us in the UK. I was moved and excited, it felt like a vibrant contemporary text.

Algerian playwright Berthe Benichou-Aboulker's *La Kahena: Berber Queen* was presented to us as a newly translated extract in English, along with its full original French version. Written in the 1930s, and the first published work by a female playwright in Algeria, the text sheds light on Berber Jews, who have since migrated around the world. A valuable addition, we're delighted that Jessica Benhamou translated the full text especially for this publication, its first ever complete English translation.

Of the North American submissions, L M Feldman's *A People* was an experimental, chaotic, hilarious, informative and thought-provoking journey. With an epic cast list, a cacophony of onomatopoeia, and references ranging from Moses to a homely Bubbe (grandmother in Yiddish), the play's gender-bending performance direction and queer feminist perspective felt apt and current, and we were all gripped.

How to then complete the selection? A beautiful text by Mizrahi playwright Hana Vazana Grunvald was the last piece of the puzzle. Hana grew up in Jaffa after migrating from Morocco. Her play, *Papa'gina*, spoke of the complexity of migration in Israel-Palestine, of the divide between Arabic and Hebrew, Israelis and Palestinians, from the personal perspective of an Arabic-speaking Jewish girl in her sexual awakening. Translated by Sivan Battat, it was bold and lovingly explored.

On 3 April 2022, we gathered at Bush Theatre in London for a day of exploration, connection, representation and future dreaming. The quality of the work by the cast and our directors – Julia Samuels, Kayla Feldman, Jessica Benhamou, Oscar Toeman, and Hetty Hodgeson – exceeded expectations, and the sense of community in the room was palpable. The work that Global Voices Theatre does is so open and loving and seeing those stories come alive on the main stage of this theatre was a triumph.

The panel discussion after, hosted by Lora Krasteva, included Stephen Bush, deputy editor of the *Financial Times* who had joined the Board of Deputies of British Jews to help address issues facing Jews of Colour; Dalia Fleming, who runs Keshet UK, an organisation that connects with Jewish institutions to help them welcome queer Jews and change the course of historical hostility; and myself. We spoke about the intersections of Jewishness and how we must make more space for these marginalised identities, about prejudices in society and our joys as Jews.

Through this work, we learned how rare these spaces are outside of synagogues or community centres in the UK, and that people were hungry for these stories. We aimed to create a space in the theatre landscape where Jews and non-Jews, artists and non-artists, could come together in a cross-cultural event, to experience joy and a sense of community.

So, 'What is Jewish theatre today?' There are particular traditions, embodied histories, traumas, moods, cultures, rituals, joys that make 'Jewish' an identity, and yet there are so many more that are rarely given a platform, or even acknowledged by the very people who live it. To understand what Jewish theatre is, we need to create space and opportunity to understand the complexities of our community, particularly as, sometimes, it's difficult to see oneself when one has so few reflections in society.

I will leave you with the plays in the next pages, and hope that the Global Jewish Voices event, podcast, and this anthology, open more conversations and welcomes more voices to come forward, to create and take space.

I'm so grateful for the support given by Bush Theatre, Asylum Arts and Arts Council England. To the longlist reading panel, the artists involved and audiences who came. And especially to Global Voices Theatre and Methuen Drama for making this space and understanding its importance. I hope that this anthology encourages others to explore their unique stories and histories.

Victor Esses

Victor Esses is a Jewish-Lebanese Latinx queer theatremaker and writer. His practice centres nuanced intersectional auto/biographical stories of belonging, resilience and intimacy. He has featured on BBC Radio 3's The Verb, Barbican's Fertility Fest and The Guardian's Audio Long Read. Curator credits includes: *We're Here!* (Battersea Arts Centre), *They Shall Not Pass* (Limehouse Town Hall). Writer/Performer includes *The Death & Life of All of Us* (Camden People's Theatre commission, Soho Theatre), *Unfamiliar* (Cambridge Junction, The Lowry, artsdepot); *Unfamiliar to Us* (Royal Docks commission); *Where to Belong* (Summerhall/Edinburgh Fringe, HOME Manchester, Chapter Cardiff, Oxford Playhouse). Performing includes: *Tunguska Event* (Whitechapel Gallery). *Where to Belong* is published by Methuen Drama (Oberon Modern Plays series).

www.victoresses.com

Extinct

Philip Ishak Arditti

The Playwright

Brought up in the Jewish community of Istanbul, Philip is an established theatre and TV actor based in London. *Extinct* is his first full-length play. Other writing credits include *English Kings* co-written with Nina Bowers (commissioned by Camden People's Theatre to be produced in November 2023). He has translated several plays into Turkish including *Tape*, *Facts* and *The Father*. He is in the 2022/23 cohort of the Soho Theatre Writers Lab. Philip sits on the Steering Committee of MENA ARTS UK and was part of the founding team of Arcola Theatre.

Synopsis

Istanbul. 2013. Yusuf, an idealistic twenty-year-old Jewish man, joins the activists protesting in Gezi Park. In pursuing both freedom and the love of a non-Jewish activist friend, Yusuf comes into conflict with his father and grandmother, who fear the backlash from authorities. In a play that shifts from intimate realism to fevered absurdist rallying call, Yusuf and his family are forced to confront their history of keeping silent, their desire for safety, and their buried revolutionary dreams.

Characters

Moris, *Sephardi Jewish, fifty*
Yusuf, *his son, twenty-two*
Carmen, *Moris's mother, eighty*
Kadir, *restaurant owner, thirties*
Devrim, *Kurdish protester, twenty-four*
A chorus of Protesters and Penguins

Time/Place

First week of June 2013 – during Gezi Park Protests.

Prologue

Spotlight on **Yusuf** *centre stage alone looking out, rabbit in the headlights. He can't move, what the fuck!? He doesn't understand why. A struggle with himself, with the world. . . his breathing heavy. He's about to speak but he can't. Blackout.*

A large tree.
It starts to move . . . slowly.
It's moving upwards.
It's being uprooted.
We can hear every fibre being torn from the ground where it has been rooted for centuries.

Scene One

Carmen*'s house on Lamartin Street, off Taksim Square, Central Istanbul. 1950s decorated living room. Sofa, armchair, dining table, cabinet with family photos on top. There's a large new TV. Mid-stage right is the entrance door. Upstage there's a corridor leading to the kitchen and Carmen's bedroom at the top. We can see the bed at the end.*

Yusuf *supported on* **Devrim***'s shoulder burst into the flat. They're out of breath and coughing, especially him. He violently retches through the first half of the scene.* **Devrim** *is high on adrenaline. They both are.*

Yusuf AHHHHHH! My eyes! AHHH! My throat!! AHHH!

Devrim FUCKING HELLLLLLL! WOW! I mean fucking WOW!

Yusuf . . . Oh my god . . . my . . throat is . . . burning

Devrim FUCK FUCK FUCK FUCK

Yusuf . . . Argh . . . I can't . . . breathe . . .

Devrim Fuck the police, fuck the state, fuck all those who have fucked us for all these fucking years.

Yusuf Yes . . . yes . . .

Devrim Fuck this regime of corrupt fucking gangsters

Yusuf definitely . . . I mean yes . . .

Devrim We are not going to let you destroy our trees and our park. We are not going to let you reshape this country according to some fucked up idea of what you think history is.

Yusuf . . . yes totally, I agree

Devrim Fuck your religion

Yusuf . . Wow OK . . .

Devrim Fuck your conservatism. We are not going away. We are here to stay. With our boobs, with our arses, with our trees, with our principles, with our progressive democracy and with our freedom!!!!

Yusuf *coughs.*

Devrim Go on, say it.

Yusuf What?

Devrim Say FUCK YOU with me!

Yusuf OK

Devrim Say it!

Yusuf fuck . . . you . . . (*Coughs.*)

Devrim Yeahhh! Let it out, let them have it.

Yusuf OK Yes Fuck you. . fuck you . . . fuck you . . . fuck you fuck you arghhhhhhhh FUUUUUCK YOU!

He collapses, coughing and retching.

Devrim Where's your spray?

Yusuf . . . haven't got it

Devrim and I gave mine to that poor old guy.

Yusuf I'll go and wash

Devrim That'll make it worse. Where's the kitchen?

She goes up the corridor. She comes back with a Borekitas, a glass of Subye (Pepitada), milk, half a lemon and some vinegar.

Devrim Ready for breakfast?

Gives the lemon to **Yusuf**.

Devrim Squeeze it and rub it on your eyes.

She takes out her scarf. Wets it with vinegar and milk.

Devrim Now rub this on your face

Then she drinks half the Pepitada.

Devrim Fuck my life what is this?! Here, have it, if this doesn't help you don't know what will.

He drinks it.

Devrim Better?

Yusuf Yes . . . Thank you

Devrim You got it bad.

Yusuf I know

Devrim You held your ground though

Yusuf Did I?

Devrim Oh yeah you were like that Tiananmen Square guy! Obviously they went for you

Yusuf I don't know what I was thinking.

Devrim You don't think when you protest.

Yusuf Yeah something else kicks in

Devrim Survival

Yusuf Fuck!

I can't believe they'd do that. That's . . . THE POLICE! Aren't they meant to protect us?

Devrim Is that a joke?! Where have you been all week? They're here to protect capital, to make sure nothing changes!

Yusuf I don't understand, we were sitting there, all peaceful, singing songs.

Devrim We had a grand piano on the main square of the country singing revolutionary songs to prevent them from illegally destroying the local park to build a shopping centre, in the shape of Ottoman Barracks! Pretty obvious they're not going to like it.

Yusuf I don't get it

Devrim Capital doesn't like songs. Capital doesn't like being told it can't build a shopping centre. Capital is a spoiled brat.

Yusuf Capital? Yes but on a simple human level, what was going on up there was amazing, the togetherness . . . I mean we didn't cause harm or make trouble.

Devrim You're very sweet. I hate to break it to you, but we're the enemy.

Yusuf Whose enemy?

Devrim We're like foreign invading soldiers wanting to occupy this country from the inside and, God forbid, make it more liveable. We're traitors!

Yusuf Oh my god!

Devrim Where do you live? You have to see it from their perspective. Just watch TV, any channel. Here.

She turns on the TV. Documentary on penguins. Changes the channel, same. They watch.

Devrim Point made

Yusuf Penguins?!

Devrim They're making us penguins.

Yusuf How?

Devrim Authoritarianism for dummies. Instead of reporting on tens of thousands of people braving violent police demanding justice, they're showing penguins braving the storms in Antarctica.

Yusuf That's . . .

She goes around the room pretending to be a penguin.

Devrim Come on. Come on! What are you waiting for? We're penguins!

Yusuf *laughs.*

Joins her.

They pretend to be Penguins for a while, chasing each other, referring back to the documentary for tips. Having fun. Their play gets bigger and louder as they get more confident.

Yusuf Stop! Stop!

Devrim What?

Yusuf I don't know. I'm not feeling great. Maybe it's the gas. What's going on?

Devrim What do you mean?

Yusuf My grandma is sleeping. I don't want to wake her.

Devrim You live here?

Yusuf We're staying here for a few days. It's her birthday.

Devrim Your grandma's?

Yusuf Yeah she's eighty, can you even imagine that?

Devrim Did she make that amazing drink?

Yusuf Pepitada . . .

Devrim What is that?

Yusuf It's a Jewish thing

Devrim Oh you're . . .

Yusuf Yeah

Devrim Cool. I'm Kurdish

Yusuf OK. That's great

Devrim Is it?

Yusuf I mean I think it's cool

Beat.

Yusuf You know that bus?

Devrim Which bus?

Yusuf The burnt one on the square. It's full of post-it messages. The overturned one in the middle of the square . . . I feel like that bus now. I am that bus. Do you know what I mean?

Devrim Yes! Yes! No actually, no I don't know, tell me more.

Yusuf Are we friends?

Devrim Yeah I'm your friend.

Yusuf I don't know you, you see!

Devrim We've never met?

Yusuf Not really

Devrim What do you mean?

Yusuf *That's* what I mean.

Devrim Ok.

Yusuf Like people don't know who they're connecting to/

Devrim Through the bus.

Yusuf YES! Through those post-it messages but it, it, it doesn't matter . . . AHHHHH! I feel like my brain is going to explode.

Devrim We're making something together

Yusuf YES that's exactly what I mean.

What are we making?

Devrim No! We're remaking

Yusuf What?

Devrim We're remaking each other! I'm changing you and you're changing me. Just now. We're talking and it's happening. Can you feel it?

Yusuf I think so

Devrim And we're remaking us. This country, our lives, and we're remaking the future.

Yusuf Future hasn't been made yet

Devrim Yes it has. Algorithms have written the future till eternity, the capital and this regime have it all worked out but, surprise surprise: we're here and we're changing that, that's why they hate us.

Yusuf What about the past?

Devrim What about it?

Yusuf There's so much suffering everywhere. You know my grandma, she's sad most of the time and my dad, he's . . . I don't know, they've suffered so much

Yusuf I know

Devrim Wish I could change that, but I can't

Devrim We can, we're doing that now

Yusuf Are we? How?

Devrim We're magician penguins and we are here to change whatever past you want changing.

Becomes a penguin again.

How can I help you sir?

Yusuf Hello!

Devrim What would you like changing? Something that happened in the past!

Yusuf I . . . I . . . oh fuck I had this terrible ice-cream just last week. I can still taste it, it was awful. Please could you change that?

Devrim Of course. Close your eyes. Bang! Done

Yusuf Yessss. Thank you, madam. Now you

Devrim Ok yes argh!

Yusuf Hello, mademoiselle

Devrim Hi yes! We're on the beach and I'm ten or something, my stupid sister pushes me in the sea again and again and I hate it. Change that please, Mr Magician Penguin.

Yusuf Let me see . . . got it! Here we go and bang! Done.

Devrim Thank you, Mr Magician Penguin. What do I owe you?

Yusuf NOTHING! You owe me nothing.

Devrim What else can I do for you?

Yusuf At school they didn't let me play football cause I was Jewish. Can you change that please? And my mum she went so early . . . but also my granddad who spent so much time in . . and the way my dad has been so . . .

Devrim Hey hey . . . Look at me. The police are moving in on the square but the world we created in the park in the last few days, that's not going anywhere, and every bit of that, people dancing, celebrating, being peacefully together, supporting each other is a world where your mum, your granddad, your dad, my dead uncle and the members of my parents' village that was burnt by the state before I was born and the Armenians who were massacred and the Greeks who were chased out of the country and the Roma who were discriminated and the lefties who were imprisoned and tortured and all the trans people who have been subjected to violent attack after violent attack and all the children who are abused and all the gay people who were raped and all the women who are killed by the men . . . All of that, we're creating a new world where all of that suffering, we share it. And there are so many of us, so many millions that when everyone has taken their share of that suffering, when everyone has taken a little bit of that pain, you will see that the weight that was in your chest will gently lift up into the air and lighten your heart and make space. That's right, we need to forget! Not remember. So we can make space for new memories. Space for you and me.

Yusuf Is this a dream? I don't want to wake up and find I've forgotten all this. I want to remember every single word. I don't want to forget any of this.

Devrim You won't

Yusuf Do you promise?

Devrim Yes

She leans in and they kiss.

They look at each other in silence.

They kiss again.

Yusuf What if . . .

Devrim What?

Yusuf I don't know. Couldn't something . . .

Devrim Go wrong

Yusuf How did you know what/

Devrim No, it cannot go wrong

Yusuf Fail?

Devrim Wipe that thought out of your mind.

Yusuf That's a possibility though, right?

Devrim Look at us, we're already won

Yusuf Have we? People are getting hurt. Didn't you see that woman in a white dress, all bloody, she looked terrified.

Devrim Whatever that is, thinking about it won't help.

Yusuf The protests are spreading to the whole country and as it gets bigger and bigger, they'll be coming harder and harder

Devrim Exactly. It's big, far bigger than this regime or even us. Look at the Arab Spring and the Occupy movements in the US and Europe, Syntagma Square in Athens, Podemos in Spain, Hong Kong . . . it's not about us, it's everywhere.

Yusuf Is it?

Devrim The truth is they decided to destroy our space and eradicate our trees. Capital is ruthless and will eat anything that gets in their way, so we have no choice. They chose us before we chose them

Yusuf Being careful could be a choice

Devrim You're still thinking like the old generation, we need to focus on winning, not failing. You know that saying, 'fail again, fail better': we're changing that too, to 'win again, win better'.

Yusuf Sounds good.

Devrim It will be good.

She kisses him.

Something is different.

Devrim What's wrong?

Yusuf Nothing

Devrim Are you worried?

Yusuf A bit . . . but I think it's fine.

Devrim Are you sure?

Yusuf Yes I am

Devrim You were like Superman out there.

Yusuf Yeah

Beat.

Yusuf What do we do now?

Devrim Spliff?

Yusuf I don't smoke

Devrim OK, Clark Kent. Let's go back out. Roam the streets, see what's happening.

Long silence.

Yusuf Let's go

They leave.

Scene Two

Yusuf *centre stage, rabbit in the headlights. He's looking for something . . . in the space, in his memory.*

Moris *is watching him.*

Moris Are you all right?

Yusuf I'm . . .

Moris Are you feeling better?

You look better.

What are you doing?

Yusuf I'm . . . trying to. . . .

Moris What?

Trying to what?

Trying to do what?

Yusuf I've lost . . .

Moris What have you lost?

Yusuf I've lost my . . .

Moris Your phone? Have you lost your phone?

Yusuf Yes I've lost my phone

Moris When did you last use it?

Yusuf I thought/

Moris Last night?

Yusuf Maybe

Moris Is that when you last used your phone?

Yusuf Yes

Moris Or this morning?

Yusuf Yes

Moris Well, which is it?

Yusuf Not sure

Moris You had a bit of a shock.

M takes his phone out and rings **Yusuf***. The phone is in* **Yusuf***'s pocket.*

Yusuf Oh . . . It's here!

Beat.

It was in my pocket the whole time.

. . .

I might get some fresh air.

Moris Where did you end up last night?

Yusuf Here.

Moris I mean before here, for the love of God!

Yusuf I was at the club.

Moris At the Jewish club?

Yusuf Yes

Carmen (*from inside*) Mosheee

Moris You didn't end up getting involved in the . . .

Yusuf No, no, of course not.

Moris Because you know . . . it's extremely dangerous

Yusuf Of course I know

Moris People getting hurt. And it's going to get worse, it always gets worse

Yusuf I might go for a short walk

Moris No. It's the lunch, the birthday lunch. That's why we're here.

Yusuf I just need to find/

Moris What the fuck do you need to find now?

Yusuf . . . Nothing, it's fine.

Beat.

Moris I don't know what you've been up to but you're unwell, Yusuf, and you need to rest.

Carmen (*off*) Mosheee!

Moris Don't go anywhere, please. She's eighty today, for God's sake! This might be the last . . .

Yusuf I get it

He leaves.

Yusuf *back to what he was doing at the start.*

Scene Three

Carmen *is working the dough with a thin long rolling pin (Oklava).*

Kadir *is restless.*

Carmen He'll be back soon, I think.

Kadir Not a problem.

Carmen Tea?

Kadir I just had one, thank you.

Carmen Drink?

Kadir At this time?!

Carmen Too early?

Kadir I don't . . . thank you.

Beat.

Carmen Fancy seeing you here at this hour.

Kadir I'm in the restaurant almost every day

Carmen Since you had the Prime Minister come for lunch, it gets busy down there.

Kadir Touch wood. Not disturbing you, I hope?

Carmen Your staff always help me with the shopping. But those rich, spoiled customers of yours/

Kadir You tell me if there's anything you're unhappy with.

Carmen I'm telling you now, they're rude.

Kadir Well . . . that's . . . You know the customer is always . . .

Carmen I know money has its way. I'll be gone soon anyway

Kadir What? Are you moving?

Carmen Not long now, I'll be off to the next world.

Kadir Oh I see

Silence.

Kadir Is Yusuf staying here as well?

Carmen They like to come over for my birthday. It's a little tradition.

Kadir Of course. Is he . . .

Carmen Married? No, he says he's too young, can you imagine? He's twenty-two!

Kadir I was gonna say, sleeping.

Carmen I should think so, he doesn't get up till/

Kadir Goes to bed late, does he?

Carmen Don't they all!

Beat.

Kadir You still work the dough yourself, ha?

Carmen You can't get quality thin pastry in the area anymore . . . it's all turned into coffee shops.

Kadir Well, working iron doesn't rust.

Carmen So they say

Kadir It's true! You don't look your age one little bit

Carmen Thank you for the compliment but I don't believe you one little bit.

They laugh.

Kadir Nothing's changed here; you're still like a speargun.

Looking around the flat, at the furniture.

Is this new?

Carmen Ha, ha! Don't make me laugh. I've had it upholstered seven times in fifty years. Krikor, the old Armenian, he can make everything look new.

Kadir Such fine work, he is a master.

Carmen I prefer IKEA, but it's too far to go.

Kadir It's an investment!

Carmen Who wants to pay money for an old chair like that?

Kadir Oh it's very popular these days.

Carmen I wouldn't know

Kadir Particularly in this area. They call it vintage.

Carmen You mean antique?

Kadir And they use it on TV. They'd give you quite some money to rent this flat for filming.

Carmen This old flat?

Kadir Exactly what they're looking for, as if time had stopped.

Carmen I wish it would.

Kadir Well the world is moving fast, things are changing all the time . . . not many are keeping the old ways.

Carmen I'm only good for stories. A tragedy, ending in death no doubt

Kadir Don't say that. You had a good life

Carmen I had a life

Kadir *looks at a photo on the wall.*

Kadir You look happy in this one. Everyone does

Carmen Oh that was . . . bring it close, yes, that's our wedding party!

Kadir In the country?

Carmen No! That's just here in the park, central Istanbul!

Fetch me my glasses, there.

You see, he's not very happy.

Kadir Uncle Shmuel? Before prison?

Carmen Oh yes, I was a hippy! Before that was a thing. I insisted we go to the local park for a wedding photo. He didn't like the idea, but I got my way. All my sisters are still here, you see.

Kadir You look beautiful. Where are they now?

Carmen This is Mathilde, she went to Egypt and then to France. This is Luiza and Perla, they went to Argentina, and Sarah went to Israel.

Kadir You're the only that stayed

Carmen I would never leave

Kadir You have family all over the world, you could go anywhere you like

Carmen As far as I'm concerned, this is the most beautiful city

Beat.

Kadir And this?

Carmen That's Elza.

Kadir The Jewish woman who was stabbed

Carmen Yes.

Kadir You were close friends

Carmen Put it back.

Silence.

I can tell Moris to call you when he comes.

Kadir I don't want to take any more of your time.

Carmen Oh I have nothing to do, you're the businessman.

He makes to go.

Carmen I know what you're after. The flat, you want to buy it.

Kadir It's not that

Carmen You dad promised me I could die here. I hope you will keep his word.

Kadir That's not why I'm here. I wouldn't dare disturb your peace. You and my dad were close, through all those years. I couldn't forget that.

Carmen I'm sorry

Kadir The situation is complicated, everything that's happening outside is . . . making it all very difficult, for everyone.

Carmen What do you mean?

Kadir I want you to know I'll do my best to look after you, just as my dad did.

Carmen He was a decent man, they don't make them like that anymore.

Long silence.

Kadir I better get going

Carmen I'll tell Moris you came by.

Kadir Sure. I just wanted to say . . .

Carmen What?

Kadir Somebody broke into the restaurant last night. Looks like they had the key to the building. I'll be changing the locks.

He leaves.

Scene Four

Devrim *is sitting.*

Moris *pacing.*

Moris A shock?

Devrim No

Moris You said a shock

Devrim Did I?

Moris What kind of a shock?

Devrim I think I said . . . a bit of a shock

Beat.

Moris What kind of a bit of a shock?

Devrim Is he/

Moris *leaves.*

Comes back shortly.

Devrim Is he sleeping?

Moris How do you divide shock into bits? What bit are we talking about? Is it a sudden, sharp kind of bit/ or is it

Devrim There's no need for alarm

Moris That's an alarming thing to say.

Devrim It's going to be fine.

Beat.

Moris Was it an accident?

Devrim Is he sleeping?

Moris An attack?

Devrim No accident, no attack. Is he/ sleeping

Moris What then? You must know

Devrim A reaction . . . maybe/ something

Moris To what?

Devrim A mixture of things

Moris What things?

Devrim I'm not sure I have all the answers you want.

Carmen (*off*) Moshe!

Moris No you don't

Beat.

Moris *goes up the corridor.*

Comes back shortly

Moris Who are you?

Devrim Is he sleeping?

Moris I said/ who are . . .

Devrim Everything is going to be fine.

Moris Stop saying that

Devrim He is . . .

Moris What?

Devrim Strong.

Moris He's a kid, you both are. Last night, what happened?

Devrim You should ask him.

Moris Does it look like he can answer?

Devrim Perhaps I should leave.

Moris Where are you going?

Devrim Sorry, but that's none of your business.

Moris I find you here with my son in a feverish sweat, muttering like a madman and then collapsing on the floor, I'd say it's very much my business

Beat.

Devrim 2-chlorobenzylidene malonitrile

Moris I beg your pardon.

Devrim 2-cholorbenzy – You're upset and I understand.

Moris What did you just say?

Devrim I'm not looking for a fight. There's plenty of it out there.

Moris You said/

Devrim We're on the same side

Moris What side are you talking about?

Devrim You're Jewish, aren't you? We've got similar troubles

Moris What do you know about my troubles?

Devrim I want your son to be fine.

Beat.

Moris Are you threatening me?

Devrim No

Beat.

Moris Is that a drug? 2 cloro – Did you give him drugs?

Devrim No.

Moris Are you a prostitute?

Devrim WHAT?!

Moris Is it money you want?

Devrim WHAT THE – I'm going

Moris How long have you known my son?

Devrim I said, step back.

Moris Do you even know his name?

Devrim Step back I said.

Moris Where were you last night?

Devrim Calm down, old man!

Moris What did you do to him?

Devrim Nothing. *I* did nothing to your son.

Moris What is my son in that state?

Devrim PEPPER GAS, tear gas! I don't know, OK? Might be the chlorobenzylidene malonitrile. CS2. It's got side-effects. We inhaled it in the street, it was all over. *I* did nothing to your son. Blame the police, the government. They use state violence and – you are hurting my arms. Let me go or I'll scream.

Moris You're a protestor?

Devrim I'm a citizen

Pause.

Moris You should leave.

Devrim I can go now, can I?

Moris It's dangerous here for you.

Devrim Clearly

Moris Not me. The downstairs restaurant, it's a front for secret police.

Devrim The fresh pasta place?

Moris It's a front. You should go.

Devrim Are you telling me secret state agents are working early hours turning dough into colourful fresh pasta?

Moris Morning shift starts at 8. You really should go

Devrim I'm not running

Silence.

Devrim I want to talk to him

Moris That's out of the question

Devrim It's important

Moris I'll pass on your number

Devrim I can wait.

Moris No. I doubt he'll wake up before lunchtime.

He gives her his phone, she enters her number. Gives it back to him.

She considers her options.

Devrim Something's happened

Moris What?

Devrim He is . . . changing . . .

Moris Changing?

Devrim He started/

Moris What?

Carmen Mosheeee

Moris What did he do?

Devrim He needs to come back.

Carmen Mosheee.

Moris What did he do?

Devrim Let me stay.

Moris NO! You have to go.

Devrim Tell him, please.

Moris Don't come back.

Devrim *exits.*

Beat.

Moris *alone for a while, taking it in.*

Then rings a number on his phone. No answer.

Scene Five

Yusuf *watching the penguin documentary. Phone rings. He answers.*

Yusuf Hey.

Watching TV. You?

I am. You didn't come back?

. . . .

I am just here

. . .

I know . . . I felt the same

. . . Later?

. . .

I'm not sure . . . I'm sorry

No, nothing

I'm just . . .

I don't think I can.

Here?

Don't know if that's a good idea

Helloo . . . helloo

Puts the phone down.

He lies down on the floor.

A penguin appears halfway up the corridor.

Scene Six

Carmen Where are you?

Moris I'm here

Carmen I was calling.

Moris I didn't hear

Carmen Why?

Moris I didn't

Carmen You don't care

Moris Of course I do.

Carmen You're here but you're not here, just like your dad after he came out of prison.

Moris I've been here far more than he has.

Carmen Where's Yusuf?

Moris Sleeping

Carmen What are you doing?

Moris Just thinking.

Carmen Why did you lie to me?

Moris When?

Carmen You said you didn't hear me

Moris I didn't

Carmen You're lying now

Moris Mum, please

Carmen What's wrong?

Moris There's nothing to say, I was just

Carmen I needed you. Was it more important than that?

Moris Somebody called and I had to take it. What did you need me for?

Beat.

Carmen Fucking nightmares.

Moris Mum, please don't swear

Carmen I feel like I've been in a washing machine.

Moris Was it . . .?

Carmen I don't want to tell you. It's awful.

Moris Get it off your chest, it helps

Carmen It's pointless. The same things again and again. How many times do I have to go through it, Moshe?

Moris Was it Dad?

Carmen Not just

Moris Elza?

Carmen Yes Elza, of course Elza. I should never have told him/ to go to her funeral.

Moris Mum, you can't/ go over it again . . .

Carmen I knew how angry he was, that he would mess things up.

Moris You have to let it go

Carmen It's not me, it's my mind, my heart. Every year it's the same. And now with everything that's happening outside . . . it's worse. I'm not you. I can't just draw a curtain over it all, as if it never happened.

Moris It was so many years ago.

Carmen But it was the cause of everything

Moris Of course it wasn't

Carmen If he hadn't been out there at Elza's funeral, making a mess and protesting, he'd never have gone to prison

Moris That's. Not. True.

Carmen How would you know, you weren't even there?

Moris Dad told me himself

Carmen He got blacklisted after that, they had their eye on him after that

Moris Mum, please.

Carmen Tell me honestly. What's happening outside . . . is it anything to do with . . .

Moris It's nothing to do with the community. Jews are not involved.

Carmen And Yusuf?

Moris What about him?

Carmen He came back so late last night? The racket in the living room, surely you heard that.

Moris He was at the club, he assured me he was.

Carmen We have to be careful, Moshe. He can't get involved. That would be . . .

Moris He's not going to

Carmen You have to tell him the whole truth

Moris No

Carmen Why?

Moris No we're not doing that, that's not even the truth

Carmen You said get it off your chest, he should know

Moris That's not why Dad – Mum, can we please stop talking about this

Silence.

It's so humid

Carmen You're doing it again.

Moris What?

Carmen You're here but you're not here.

Moris I'm just sweating, that's what I'm saying

Carmen *takes out a handkerchief and dabs* **Moris***'s forehead and neck.*

After a while, **Moris** *gets up and walks around the room, looking at things almost as if for the first time in a long time.*

Moris Maybe it's this flat. With everything that's in it. The paintings, the photos, the furniture, the view, the memories . . . maybe we need to let it go.

Carmen This is all I have

Moris I can't work anymore, Mum. I've been going and going and I'm exhausted. You know how it is. There's barely any business, we're just keeping the shop open for scraps. We had a good business but textile is dead. We can't compete with the Chinese. I could retire. I could look after the garden

Carmen What garden?

Moris Well, there's this place I saw

Carmen Oh!

Moris Bit outside town but it's brand new.

Carmen I hate 'brand new'

Moris It'll get old quick

Carmen I'll die quick

Moris There's large windows all around, it's open plan, shiny new kitchen and opens onto . . . a garden!

Carmen A garden!? In Istanbul?

Moris Yes. We could all be together, away from this . . .

Carmen What are you going to do with a garden?

Moris I will garden and you can sit in it.

Carmen You've never *gardened* in your life

Moris Well . . .

Carmen I like my park. My bench in the park.

Moris Soon there might not be a park. Shall we consider it, have a look?

Carmen I don't think I can do that. I'd be abandoning Elza and Shmuel. I have to stay here for their sake.

Moris Just a look, do me a favour.

Carmen Waste of time

Moris Early morning traffic will be calm, let's go and come back

Carmen Now? I'm not even dressed, Moshe. And not today, I told you I can't and you're insisting. Why are you insisting?

Moris Let's seize the opportunity.

Carmen You're fidgeting

Moris I'm not. I'm very calm. I'm excited. I told you I want us to move on from this flat, it's . . . it's full of . . .

Carmen What?

Moris Stuff

Carmen Stuff?! Life is made of stuff. We can't just up and go because there's a nicer house. I've been here sixty years. You want to throw all that in the bin. I gave birth to you here. And with everything that happened after. And Elza! You have no consideration for what I'm going through, just like your dad.

Moris That's not true.

Carmen I'm going to die in this house surrounded by . . . stuff. Do you hear me now?!

Moris All right.

Silence.

Carmen I'm exhausted already and I still have to prepare lunch. You haven't even asked me what I needed from you?

Moris What did you need me for?

Carmen The rolling pin! I need the thin long rolling pin. I'm going to make Borekitas.

He leaves.

Scene Seven

Kadir *and* **Moris** *sitting around the table.*

Piece of paper in the middle. **Moris** *takes it, looks at it, gestures 'no' with his head. Crosses what's written there and gives it back to* **Kadir**.

Kadir *looks at it, does the same, gives it back to* **Moris**.

The paper goes back and forth several times, with reactions varying and growing.

Until eventually **Kadir** *is happy with what he sees on the paper, takes it and leaves the room.*

Scene Eight

Spotlight on **Yusuf** *centre stage. He's looking out again.*

Yusuf I . . .

I . . .

I am . . .

He starts shaking.

Moris Yusuuuf!!!

Lights up on the whole stage. Now we see **Moris** *and* **Carmen**, *dressed for the Birthday Lunch.*

Through the following scene they're laying the table, they go in and out of the kitchen.

Moris Yusuf. Wake up, for God's sake.

Yusuf I heard you. Don't shout please.

Moris Stop doing whatever it is you're doing and sit down.

Yusuf Are you sure?

Moris What?

Yusuf Why?

Moris He doesn't hear me. It's impossible to get through to him.

Carmen Like father, like son.

Moris Are you drunk?

Carmen *I* am

Yusuf I said why?

Moris Why what?

Yusuf Why do you want to sell the house! It's . . . so abrupt. Why did you not tell us about this before?

Moris You've been asleep all day! We're telling you now, it was a spur of the moment decision

Yusuf Spur of the moment?

Moris Yes . . . make the most of this opportunity.

Yusuf What opportunity?

Moris A special offer. Kadir downstairs

Yusuf That pro-government sleaze? I hate that man

Carmen That's what I said.

Beat.

Moris What are you doing?

Yusuf What?

Moris Standing there like that.

Yusuf What do *you* think, Grandma?

Carmen I've no fucking idea, my darling, I just want to have a good day. Food's nearly ready.

Moris Mum, please don't swear

Yusuf Precisely. Grandma is eighty today. Happy birthday, Grandma

Carmen Thank you, my sweetie, come here and give me a kiss, give me eighty!

Yusuf You've lived in this flat for . . . how long? Sixty years? Dad, you were born here. We've lived here on and off since Mum died. Granddad died here. All those times –

Carmen I'm not going anywhere

Moris A change is long overdue

Carmen Your dad needs to talk it out of his system

Moris It's been brewing for ages.

Yusuf You said it was a spur of the moment thing

Moris Yes, it's been brewing for a long time and then . . . it culminates in a spur of the moment

Yusuf That makes no sense

Moris When I'm in the shop and no customers turn up, this is what I think about

Yusuf Is it?

Moris If you came to help out sometimes you'd have had a chance to give it some thought as well. But you're not interested in work, are you?

Carmen And dressed like that, you'll never get a job

Yusuf I just woke up

Moris You slept in jeans!

Carmen He slept in jeans?

Yusuf Yes, so what?

Carmen Like a homeless refugee?

Moris No job! No girlfriend!

Carmen Nice Jewish girl yes! Yes please, Yusuf. When? It'll be too late soon and you will regret it

Yusuf Grandma, how many times do I have to tell you I'm only 22!!!

Carmen Lame excuses.

Yusuf I don't know what to say

Carmen I won't accept it, not for my birthday. Not dressed like this. Take them off.

Yusuf Grandma please

Carmen I want you in a suit

Yusuf I don't have a suit

Moris The one from your Bar Mitzva?

Yusuf That'll be too small

Carmen One from your granddad!

Yusuf From the last century?

Carmen A good suit doesn't age! And he had the best. I used to wash his clothes and iron them one by one, so he could have them hanging in his cell. When those antisemites threw your granddad in prison, not being able to dress properly was the worst thing for him. He had his first heart attack soon after. Why was he in prison?

Moris Mum

Carmen He was a well-dressed Jew, that's why. And now, look at you! What have I done to deserve this?

Moris That's right, he would place a special order for silk socks from Geneva and he only ever wore Borsalino hats. You know what a Borsalino is?

Carmen Your great-granddad was a tailor from Aydin, your granddad dressed immaculately even in prison, your dad works in textile and you . . . you wear jeans?!

Yusuf It's not the 1920s anymore, people don't wear a three-piece suit to go buy milk

Carmen You're young and you're wrong. Get undressed, I'll bring the black suit

Goes out.

Yusuf All right . . . but, sorry, how is this about me now? I'm sorry but you decided, without asking any of us, to sell this house and move . . . where?

Moris Out of town.

Yusuf Out of town?

Moris Yes your grandma needs some peace and quiet. Maybe a garden

Yusuf A garden!?

Moris Yes, I will garden.

Yusuf You've never gardened in your life.

Carmen *comes back with the suit.*

Carmen That's what I said. Here it is.

Moris New beginnings.

Yusuf Grandma, please

Carmen It's my birthday present, you in a suit.

Moris Do what your grandma says?

Yusuf Fine.

He puts the suit on.

Yusuf I look ridiculous

Carmen You're a beauty

Yusuf Anyway I don't think this is a good time to think about selling the house

Moris Why not?

Yusuf Well . . . It's . . . you know . . . the protests!

Carmen You didn't get involved?

Yusuf No of course not

Moris No Jews are involved, Mum, I told you.

Yusuf What do you mean?

Moris Nothing.

Carmen What is it about then?

Moris Delinquents and looters/

Yusuf What? They're not looters

Moris They're violent

Yusuf It's mainly peaceful . . . I think

Moris The streets are never peaceful. I don't see what the problem with a new shopping centre is. All the top brands will be a short walk away from here

Yusuf Yes but the park will be gone . . . that's what people are saying.

Carmen My park?!

Yusuf Yes they're uprooting the trees.

Carmen Who?

Yusuf The municipality, but the government's behind it. The Prime Minister

Carmen I don't like him, but people shouldn't be making trouble.

Yusuf Did you know that park is an earthquake safety zone? They have no consideration for people. They're squeezing every bit of green in town and making this place totally unliveable and unsafe and what for? Profit?

Moris So, let's move out

Yusuf That would be giving up though

Beat.

Moris What did you say?

Yusuf Well maybe we have a role to play.

Carmen Just like his granddad

Moris Mum

Yusuf What do you mean?

Moris Nothing! You're not going to join the protests, I hope!

Yusuf Not like that

Carmen You dad gets anxious

Yusuf I know. I'm not, don't worry. I'm just saying.

Moris What are you saying for God's sake?

Yusuf Something is happening . . . there's a change, people are talking to each other, I think in a different way and realising that maybe we've been alone or separated. It's like the squares in Ancient Greece . . . this space for communion, for communication, for exchange. And it started online with Twitter and everything and now it's infecting real life and, I don't know, I just feel . . . there's a kind of . . . an interesting shift.

Moris How come you know so much about it?

Yusuf I read it online.

Moris An interesting shift?! What are you, a professor? You're making a fool of yourself. Dangerous, that's what it is. I understand people are fed up, tired of the government. Sure we're exhausted! But you don't go out protesting in crowds. They should be productive, not destroying things. They're good for saying no, no, no. Let's all go out in the streets and say no, no, no. What next? Things are better for the first time in decades. Reforms and stability. Of course, you don't remember the 90s. Inflation, corruption, gangs. Now business is doing well/

Yusuf Is it?

Moris Most people are doing very well. Europe is back on the cards, they're even embracing minorities. Peace with terrorists, for God's sake! Why are people so interested in being negative? I'll tell you who's making a change: scientists, engineers, they're working away, quietly doing their thing and making a difference. The laboratory is where it's happening, not out in the streets! Either way we have nothing to complain about

Yusuf Don't we?

Carmen The Turk has always been good to us.

Yusuf Really?

Moris Of course

Yusuf How?

Carmen We know our place. The others always make trouble. Look at the Armenians.

Moris Now they had it tough.

Yusuf Tough? It was a genocide, at least a million massacred

Carmen They weren't blameless

Yusuf Nobody deserves that! You can't say that

Moris Easy.

Carmen No it's fine, I can defend myself perfectly well. (*To* **Yusuf**.) Yes, darling, what can I do for you?

Yusuf All right. How has he been good to us, 'the Turk'?

Carmen Look out the window. Go on. What do you see?

Yusuf I don't know. A street in Istanbul.

Carmen A posh street in Istanbul. I'm living in the nicest part of town. How is that? I was born in a village, grew up in a ghetto and now I'm 'in'. I haven't been cut into pieces, smoked in an oven before being forced to convert. Seems like someone's watching over me.

Yusuf Is this it? We should be grateful for that?

Moris Well, of course it's not ideal.

Yusuf Not ideal?

Moris You have to face reality. Overall it's fine.

Yusuf I see

Moris It's all relative. There's barely a Greek left in the country, they've all had to leave under dismal conditions. Armenians, wiped out. Or compare it to Jews in other Muslim countries. Not a single Jew is left in Algeria, Tunisia, Syria, Lebanon, Iraq, Egypt . . . you name it, these were all thriving communities and now

Yusuf There's Jews in Iran

Moris There's also Mullahs in Iran! You know what, I've had enough. Why don't you go and live with Mullahs, see what that does to you.

Carmen No talk of Mullahs on my birthday please. It's ready.

Moris Get a taste of what they're getting. See how your liberal values stand up to the Mullahs. Forget about it. You should be grateful for what you have, get a good job, marry and –

Carmen Nice Jewish girl please, my darling, for your grandma

Moris Settle down and think about your future in a serious, grown-up way!

Carmen Here's some Lobyani to start with bean pastry but careful, peppery Georgian style with millefeuille. I made the regular borekitas with minced meat here, and with courgette over there. Here's some Bulekas de Espinaka. And finally, here is your favourite, Hamim de Kastanya, meat with chestnut. Bon appétit. I've got a surprise for dessert so you wolves better leave some space for that.

Yusuf I think those are my favourite words.

Carmen Tuck in

Moris Hold on. Today is a special day for more than one reason. We are starting anew today. So just a moment of reflection. Get the Kippas.

Carmen A moment of reflection with a piece of cloth on our heads.

Moris Mum, please.

Carmen Just saying

They get the kippas.

Moris We are blessed to have you as our mother and grandmother. Despite everything that life threw at you, you never stopped, you never gave up.

Carmen There's still time

Moris Your quiet resilience has been a source of inspiration for your family and your community. At eighty you continue to open new chapters and we are excited to be with you. Dear Lord, on this Shabbat day, we thank you for what you give us and we accept. We thank you for our grandmother. May she live many years to come.

Carmen Not so many, please!

Moris Happy birthday, Mum

Yusuf Happy birthday, Grandma.

Moris Pass me the candles.

Yusuf It's not even sunset

Moris It's the thought that counts, come on.

Yusuf *picks the candles from the side furniture.*

Moris *lights the Shabbat candles and speaks the Shabbat prayer.*

Moris BARUH ATA ADONAY ELO-ENU MELEH AOLAM ASHER KİDESHANU BEMİTZVOTAV VETSİVANU LEADLIK NER SHEL SHABBAT

Shabbat Shalom

Yusuf and Carmen Shabbat Shalom

Carmen All right. If you're done, are you done?

Moris Yes

Carmen Can I say something to God?

Moris That would be nice.

Carmen Baruch ata adonay . . . let me have my bloody drink!

All Lehayim!

They eat.

Yusuf Mmm

Moris Mum, it's delicious. Thank you.

Carmen Pepitada?

Yusuf Thank you. You're not eating?

Carmen I'll have a drink first, I think I've deserved it

Yusuf You have. Health to your hands, Grandma.

They eat in silence.

Carmen *prepares her drink and sips it gently.*

Yusuf What did you mean when you said others always make trouble?

Moris Leave your grandma alone, she's exhausted.

Silence.

Carmen It's Kayades.

Yusuf Kayades?

Moris It's Ladino

Yusuf I know

Carmen The language of Spanish Jews

Yusuf I know that

Carmen We're still speaking the same language we did 500 years ago

Yusuf You don't have to tell me that, of course I know

Carmen That's your heritage, that's your history

Yusuf What does it mean?

Carmen Keep your head down and carry on.

Moris Like the English

Yusuf No that's keep calm and carry on

Moris Anyway that's what got us here safe and sound.

Yusuf And?

Moris And eat your dinner! It means we're focused on *survival,* not on making noise for no reason. It means we accept the conditions and we work with them. We're practical and we are effective. We weather the storm. We are flexible and adapt to what they throw at us. That's what we're good at and that's what's good for us. We've learnt the hard way. Going out and making trouble doesn't get us anywhere.

Yusuf I see, you mean we just shut up basically

Moris Excuse me?

Yusuf Like we don't make a big deal out of things

Moris There's many ways to make a difference, not all of them put your life at risk. There's no need to be extreme

Yusuf 'Life at risk' isn't that extreme?

Moris Protesting is not safe

Yusuf Oh teenagers checking for bombs under synagogue pews before Saturday morning prayers, is that safe? I mean what does that even mean? Safe!

Moris We still have power.

Yusuf What power? Look at the history of antisemitism, countless pogroms, ongoing death threats

Moris And more

Yusuf Is that power? Shouldn't we speak up about all this? Don't you feel sorry Grandma is happy she hasn't been burnt alive in an oven?

Moris There's a reality you have to face. A reality! There's no HR department listening to our issues and helping us out. Punishing someone else and making it all right. Nobody owes us anything. Put that firmly in your mind. Anything we ask for, we give something in return. It's all transactional.

Yusuf What about wanting to become a 'better' country? You said they wanted that.

Moris Of course they do only as much as it suits them.

Yusuf So what do we do?

Moris We do what we've always done. We work behind the scenes. It works for us. The community leaders have direct access to the prime minister! We control the temperature of their relations with Israel and with the US, that's where we get our power from, not from shouting in the streets.

Yusuf You're deluding yourself.

Moris Watch your mouth!

Yusuf The reality is that we are second-class citizens.

Moris At least we're citizens

Yusuf I guess you think we should be overjoyed at that prospect.

Moris Yes. We're still here, don't you understand? We are still here!

Yusuf But nobody sees us! Are we still here if we're hiding all the time? After any ceremony at the Synagogue there's security guards encouraging us to move quickly through the streets and not stay in groups for too long. Doesn't feel like we're here. Feels like we're extinct.

Yusuf *goes back to centre stage and looks out.*

Moris Yusuf, what are you doing?

Yusuf I am here.

Moris Come and sit at the table.

Yusuf I was at the protests last night.

Moris What?

Carmen Oh dear

Moris No he wasn't, he's lying, tell your grandma you're lying

Yusuf I'm not.

Moris You made a mistake, he made a mistake.

Yusuf I was there and it was . . .

Moris It was a mistake.

Carmen It's the same all over again

Yusuf What is?

Moris You don't understand anything . . .

Yusuf What's the same?

Moris Nothing is.

Yusuf Tell me what I do not understand, Dad, because it feels like you really want me not to understand.

Carmen She was in my dream for a good reason

Yusuf Who was?

Moris Nobody

Carmen Elza was

Moris We don't need to talk about that now

Yusuf About what?

Carmen My dear friend Elza Niyego

Moris Mum please

Yusuf I've heard about Elza Niyego

Moris It's in the past

Yusuf The Jewish woman who was stabbed on the square by the son of a Pasha

Carmen Because she refused him

Yusuf Her body was left to rot in the street

Carmen Because she was Jewish

Moris Why did you not tell me you went to the protest?

Yusuf Did you know her?

Carmen I knew her and so did your granddad

Moris That's enough

Yusuf Why can't we talk about this?

Moris All right, you want to talk about things. Let's talk! Why did you hide it from me?

Yusuf I didn't want to worry you.

Moris You still went there

Yusuf I was passing by and, yes, I did go there

Moris And?

Yusuf There's so many people there anyway it doesn't matter

Carmen Jews?

Yusuf Maybe some yes

Moris No! No Jew in their right might would be there. You went out and what?

Yusuf I . . .

Moris Has the devil eaten your tongue? Tell us

Yusuf I went out and I was out.

Moris And what happened?

Yusuf I don't remember . . .

Moris You got dementia now?

Yusuf Something happened and I just cannot remember. I've been trying. There was riot police and they were telling us to move/ and

Moris Listen to yourself: riot police! What have you got to do with riot police? You are endangering yourself, your family and your community

Yusuf Why the community?

Carmen You should tell him!

Yusuf Tell me what?

Carmen The truth

Yusuf What truth?

Moris I'm not going to let you destroy everything we've built

Yusuf What are we talking about?

Moris Whatever is going on outside, it's none of our business. There's police, the state and it's far too big for us. You and that silly girl

Carmen What girl?

Moris He was with a girl

Yusuf How do you know that?

Carmen Is she Jewish?

Yusuf No

Moris You were in a mess this morning. You gave me the fright of my life

Carmen Turkish?

Yusuf Kurdish

Carmen A day of disasters!

Yusuf I'm not marrying her, OK, she's just a girl I met.

Moris You're never seeing that girl again

Yusuf You can't tell me what to do.

Moris Says who?

Yusuf What truth are you talking about?

Carmen The history

Moris It's not the truth, and it's not the history, SHUT UP, Mum

Yusuf Dad!

Moris You shut up as well. I've had it up to here with both of you. One worse than the other. Stop it now with your spoiled liberal . . . protests. I didn't raise you on my own to lose you in the street to some hot-blooded police officer. I've had enough trouble in my life, we all have. There has to be an end to it. There has to be an end to the nightmares, Mum. An end to the memories. And end to being worried day in day out. We have to escape, get away from it all, otherwise it's going to consume us. Look at us! We've been arguing, fighting for I don't know how long and –

I've sold the house!

Silence.

I said I've sold the house

Carmen You . . . You . . .

Moris We're leaving as soon as possible

Yusuf What?

Moris That's the best for all of us

Carmen *feels faint.*

Moris Mum! Mum, are you all right?

He goes to her.

Blackout.

It's a power cut, followed by a flash of light and we momentarily see two Penguins in the house almost simultaneously as **Moris** *hits a chair and falls over.*

Moris Argh!

Yusuf Dad

Moris Mum! Argh

Yusuf Are you all right, Dad?

Moris Go to your grandma

Carmen I'm fine

Moris Bloody chair!

Yusuf *turns on his mobile phone torch.*

Yusuf Stay where you are, Dad. Let me help you

Moris Leave me alone

Moris *leaves the room.*

Yusuf Grandma?

Carmen Yes, darling

Yusuf Happy birthday

Scene Nine

Kadir Don't think about a Pink Penguin!

Beat.

DON'T!

Yusuf Should I call for my dad?

Kadir Are you thinking about it? About the Pink Penguin.

Yusuf I am now

Kadir The more you try to suppress it the more it comes up. The ironic process theory! She's nine and she's taught me that. She's a monster I tell you and she scares me. That's the best way I can put it for you. I love her but she makes me shit myself! Do I look like the kind of guy who gets scared easily?

. . .

Hey, do I look like the kind of guy who gets scared easily?

Yusuf No, no, you don't

Kadir I tell her I'm thinking about a pink penguin. And she starts laughing her head off, her laugh grates on my ears so hard and after a long stressful day at work, it's not easy, I'm confessing something to you here, you know what I mean? I've no idea what's going on. That's how I feel half the time. And you know what? I'll be honest with you, cause you're a nice guy, normally, and we're having a nice chat, I've always thought highly of you, well behaved, normally, you know your place and you don't make no trouble . . . normally!

Beat.

What was I saying? She knows things, from watching TV, on the internet all day long, there isn't a piece of information that's beyond her. I'll be honest with you, I'm worried, she gets something into her head and then it's impossible to get it out. Whatever you do you cannot extract it. Like a stubborn molar. No torture, psychological or physical, would be of any use. Like that pink penguin, get it out of your head now if you can, the harder you try, I'm not going to think of it, I'm not going to think of it, the worse it gets.

Beat.

She's eating me alive, you know what I mean? It's like she's strung me on a stick and I'm being barbequed. Sometimes – one of those dark thoughts that come into my – you don't mind me telling you?

Yusuf Why are you/ here?

Kadir This is between you, me and Allah. You repeat it anywhere, I'll skin you alive.

Yusuf Maybe you shouldn't/ tell me

Kadir Sometimes, I have this thought that suddenly comes into my mind, maybe I first saw it in a dream or something, listen to me: I think about being barbequed! I mean literally, as if I was a piece of meat and I'm being barbequed on a charcoal barbeque.

. . . .

Are you thinking about that now?

Yusuf About what?

Kadir About me being barbequed on a charcoal barbeque?

Yusuf No.

Kadir You're not thinking about that?

Yusuf I'm not

Kadir What's going through your mind just now?

Yusuf Nothing

Kadir What's the image that comes into your mind if you close your eyes now?

Beat.

Close your eyes.

Yusuf Nothing . . . it's empty.

Kadir That's strange. And you don't suffer from memory issues, do you?

Yusuf No

Kadir I'd get that checked out if I were you.

Yusuf Are you here to see Dad?

Kadir Don't disturb your dad now, he's got things on his mind and we're having a nice chat. Where was I? So yes, how long would it take for my meat to soften on a good barbeque? That's the kind of question that keeps me awake at night. Do you think it's closer to bird meat, the kind you might have to burn slightly around the side to seal it or is it more like a meaty fish like monkfish? To make sure it's nice and soft. Because that's how I like my meat. Everybody is different. In the east of the country they like it well cooked, even a little burnt. In the west on the Aegean coast they cook little goats all day long and it comes apart like cotton, it's like fresh bread straight out the oven. I'm definitely not a vegetarian. You know, vegetarians don't even touch meat! Not if it's well-cooked, not even a small piece. That's what they got into their heads and you can't get it out. What do you say to someone like that?

Yusuf Well . . . maybe they have a point

Kadir Like what?

Yusuf You should probably ask them.

Kadir What if they don't tell you anything? You ask, you ask but they don't tell you anything. What do you say then? Cause you need meat to help develop their brain right? Particularly the little ones.

Yusuf Maybe other proteins could

Kadir They're influenced by TV and all the stuff they see on the internet. This animal is going extinct, that island will disappear. Brainwashed they are.

Yusuf That's possible I guess

Kadir All those nature documentaries about the world ending.

Yusuf You mean climate change?

Kadir That's bullshit, isn't it?

Yusuf Well/

Kadir All right all right, say it is true, say the world is going to end. Why is it our fault? They want to punish us. Those in the West, they've had their bellies full to bursting for centuries and just now as it's our turn to get going, just now that's we've starting to be productive and export, it's a red card on us, using climate change as a threat. When are we ever going to be allowed to thrive?

Yusuf I'll call my dad/

Kadir Leave him, I said. We never get to chat like this

Yusuf I've only just woken up so I better/

Kadir You slept in your jeans?

Yusuf Yeah . . . maybe.

Kadir You don't remember?

Yusuf I just fell asleep

Kadir And you hadn't noticed until I told you just now

Yusuf No I don't think so

Kadir That's strange.

Yusuf Are you here to see Dad?

Kadir I'm here to chat with you

Yusuf With me? What about?

Kadir I've already told you, you don't remember?

Yusuf No, when

Kadir It's about what you've been up to

Yusuf Do you mean . . . What do you mean?

Kadir You tell me.

Yusuf I haven't been up to anything

Kadir That's not what I'm told

Yusuf Not sure I'm following

Kadir *starts laughing.*

Kadir I'm joking. God, you need to lighten up a little.

Yusuf Very funny

Kadir You dad called me up. I'm waiting for him.

Yusuf I'll call him

Kadir Hey, you need to eat more fish!

Yusuf *exits.*

Kadir *looking around at the furniture and the photos.*

Moris *comes in.*

Moris What's wrong?

Kadir Let's talk downstairs.

They leave.

Scene Ten

Large bag with lots of penguin costumes in it. **Yusuf** *standing centre stage,* **Devrim** *is trying out the costumes on him. They're all different sizes and styles. Eventually she settles on one. She puts it in his rucksack, kisses him and leaves with the rest.*

He hides the bag under the armchair.

Scene Eleven

Living room lit by candlelight. **Carmen** *and* **Yusuf** *sitting.*

Carmen Am I dead?

Yusuf No

Carmen Are you here to take me home?

Yusuf You are home

Carmen Are you Azrael the grim reaper?

Yusuf I'm your grandson

Carmen Then go and make me drink.

Yusuf Will you tell me the story?

Carmen Which story do you want to hear?

Yusuf Any

Carmen Are you married yet?

Yusuf No

Carmen I can tell you that story

Yusuf Not that one . . . please

Carmen It begins with you falling in love with this girl and she falls in love with you. Do you know where you meet?

Yusuf In a park?

Carmen By the seafront. Walking on a Saturday afternoon. In the hot June air. You see her, she's young and beautiful.

Yusuf Sounds fake

Carmen All right, she's old and ugly, just like me. But it's dark now so you can't tell. Her voice fills the air, her laughter tickles, her manners take you away. Your smooth young skin hasn't met a scar, your legs agile still, your back 'brand new' and strong. You dance. Your bodies pull at each other, doing whatever it is young people do.

He gives her the drink.

What do young people do, Yusuf?

Yusuf I don't know.

Carmen Exactly. Not knowing is what they do. They do it most exquisitely. This drink is good, you have talent. You should get married, have I ever told you that?

Yusuf Just once or twice

Carmen When will you do it?

Yusuf I love you, Grandma.

Carmen Give me a time

Yusuf As soon as you finish the story.

Carmen We have a deal?

Yusuf Solid

Carmen Cross my heart and hope to die. You marry, get a job, have a kid and raise him to do the same. End of story! Maybe there's a tragedy somewhere in there. End of story! Now go and find a nice Jewish girl, quick. What are you waiting for? We have a deal!

Yusuf You're cheating

Carmen All right, you're dancing by the waterfront. Brown eyes locked in desire. Hands touching each other. Hot bodies mixing in love, hot heart, hot head and hot words flying. She's blissfully ignorant, you are an ignorant talker. You talk of life and the world and how things are and should be. You've got papers and magazines and books coming out of your ears. And coming out of your pocket: A ring! You get married to her. You hot-headed, handsome devil. Then . . .

Yusuf Then what?

Carmen Then there's more dancing. Right here in this flat.

She stands up and invites him up to dance.

Carmen Come on.

He joins her. They dance silently for a while.

Carmen Wildflower, that's what your granddad called me. I was free inside. I wanted so many things but I knew nothing. When life is ahead of you, so is knowledge, when you're in the middle you're just too busy to know, when it's all behind, all in your memory . . . you know it all but what's the point!? I beg of you, don't waste time.

Yusuf Are you angry?

Carmen I don't like anger

They stop dancing.

Yusuf I wanted to be there. I wanted to try it out. I can't remember much, it was hot and there were people everywhere and I felt happy . . . I think. I felt safe . . . but then my body did something, it was shaking. I can't stop thinking about it, something took over inside me and I lost sense of myself. I don't really know what I'm talking about. I'm talking about being there and being scared. I kept having this thought that I would be the one bringing trouble to the protests. That's absurd, I'm no one and I've never had a political thought in my life, let alone protested, but I thought I would destroy something, I would endanger someone. Then I crossed eyes with this girl. Like in the story.

Carmen She's not Jewish?

Yusuf No

Carmen But you love her?

Yusuf She's beautiful, curly black hair and I know her. She gestures to follow. That's what gives me the courage to go into the park and there is more joy there than I have ever experienced in my life. More joy than this land has ever seen all in one place, infecting and spreading and mesmerising joy.

Carmen You sound just like your granddad.

Yusuf What is it that you're not telling me, Grandma?

Carmen All the pain.

Yusuf But I know it, I feel it. For years I've felt it.

Carmen What happened to Elza was so unfair and inhuman. It was the beginning of it all, of all our troubles, you dad is blind to that.

Beat.

The cruel, spoiled son of a Pasha made several advances on Elza. She wasn't interested in him, he was creepy and weird. But that wasn't the correct answer for him and even though her family hastily married her off to a Jewish man, that did not stop her being stabbed by her stalker in broad daylight, metres from here. And that wasn't the end. Her slender, bloody, lifeless body was exposed to the world for hours. They wouldn't let us cover her body. It was a punishment, a humiliation for daring to say no. That was the level of their cruelty. That was what a woman, a Jewish woman who refuses a powerful Turkish man, deserves. That's what Jews deserve if they dare say no. We were angry, me most of all. I'd lost a friend, seen her humiliated in front of my very eyes. That's not what I imagined of the world and I wanted to change it. We organised the community to turn the following day's funeral into a march. That was the least we could do for Elza. Didn't she deserve our voice, our chants, our presence? Anger had been building and it burst into the streets during the funeral. Before long, our men clashed with officials and many were arrested. Your granddad was one of them. That was the beginning of the end. They let him go but he was blacklisted for good. At the first opportunity he was in prison, and this time for years. He never recovered, we never recovered. It was my anger that cursed this family. Seeking justice brought us nothing but suffering.

Yusuf It was Elza

Carmen What was Elza?

Yusuf I saw her last night, on the square.

We hear neighbours at their windows making noise with their pots and pans.

Carmen What's going on?

Yusuf What?

Carmen Can you not hear that?

Yusuf Pots and pans! People making noise at their windows.

Carmen What's got into them?

Moris *comes in.*

Moris What's this racket?

Yusuf People at their windows with pots and pans

Moris Pots and pans!?

Yusuf Yes, they're showing solidarity with the protests!

Moris Have they lost their minds? Mum, are you all right? Don't trouble yourself, it's nothing

Carmen It's fine, Moshe, I'm fine.

Yusuf I'm sorry, I'm going

Moris What?

Yusuf *goes up the corridor and comes back with a load of stuff he starts putting into his rucksack. Water bottle, lemon, milk, goggles, empty spray bottle, wipes . . .*

Moris What are you doing?

Yusuf I'm going out, I'm going to try again

Moris What for? For trees?

Yusuf Yeah.

Moris What kind?

Yusuf What?

Moris You don't even know what kind of trees you're going out there for.

Yusuf And?

Moris Shouldn't you know?

Yusuf You care now?

Moris They're your 'comrades' aren't they?

Yusuf Normal trees.

Moris That's all you can say!

Yusuf Marginalised trees. Trees that don't fit. Trees that are under threat.

Moris I bet you they know their shopping malls.

Yusuf I bet you they have no fucking idea.

He goes back up and comes with a penguin costume.

Moris Where on earth did you find that?

Yusuf It was my Purim costume.

He starts putting it on.

Moris All right, stop it now! What is this? A penguin costume? It's silly

Yusuf It's humour

Moris Humour?

Yusuf You don't get it.

Moris No I don't. No one does.

Yusuf People out there get it. Thousands of marginalised, multi-coloured, heterogenous young people get it.

Moris What's with the word 'marginalised'?

Yusuf You're old.

Moris Is that a crime

Yusuf You never dared

Moris How dare you? Since your mum I've . . . I did everything I could. I got you through good schools, I did it all for you

Yusuf You submit. I'm through with that

Moris It's business.

Yusuf It's spineless. But I understand it. You didn't have others. Nothing will change in this country unless we get together and shout stop.

Moris All right, you shout stop, then what?

Yusuf Keep going with the occupation, resist becoming all the same: one religion, one race, one colour, all shopping. We're resisting that.

Moris How long for?

Yusuf I don't know. We're something now.

Moris You're penguins, without a plan, without a leader.

Yusuf Penguins don't have leaders.

Moris And they're all the same. One religion, one race and one colour.

Yusuf We're not literally . . . You don't get it.

Moris You're dressed as a penguin about to take on the state police and you're telling me I don't get it.

Yusuf You're scared.

Moris Of course I'm fucking scared. I've worked hard. For you. You're all I've got.

Yusuf So am I, but there's all sorts of people out there. Normal people.

Moris Why do you need a helmet?

Yusuf They're getting aggressive.

Moris This is not for you

Yusuf What's that supposed to mean?

Moris You know what I mean.

Yusuf You really have to stop thinking of me like yourself.

Moris It's not about me. It's about what we are. Ultimately we're to blame for this, you know that, don't you? When things go to shit in this country somebody has to pay. Somebody always pays. And when it comes to paying, it comes to us. It comes knocking on our doors, it comes smashing our windows. That's why you have to be careful.

Beat.

That bright summer morning when I got on the boat with your granddad to accompany him into town for work, there were dozens of other men there doing that daily journey. Big textile lords. Well-dressed, silent, smoking, reading their newspaper. I felt so proud to be with them. But on the pier it was your granddad they arrested. Currency fraud? Half the men on that boat lived on buying and selling currency. Some of them much worse. But that didn't matter. He was a Jew and that's all they needed to know. You're a Jew and that's all you need to know.

Yusuf *finishes dressing and packing. Full penguin costume with helmet and facemask around his neck. He's about to leave.*

Yusuf London plane, Japanese pagoda, European oak, silver linden, tree of heaven. They've put stickers on the trees with their history and poems dedicated to them. There's dance pieces about the trees and prayers for those who want them.

Beat.

We know what we're standing for. If you look from afar we might all seem the same, but when you come close we're all different. Just like a forest. And if you look close enough at a colony of penguins, I'm sure they've all got their different stories of pain, joy and vulnerability. But for now we're united. And for the first time ever, I feel strong.

Beat.

A strong penguin.

He leaves.

Scene Twelve

The next section can be performed by a chorus of Protesters and Penguins, including **Yusuf** *and* **Devrim**.

I'm climbing a steep hill.
Hot air scratching at my lungs,
Hot lungs knotting in my heart.
Leaving a trace, On my mind.
Tracing my phone, Check

Tweet *Everyone is up here. Fuck you Erdogan. This isn't just about trees.*

You're pulling me up. Up the hill.
familiar, strange.
hundreds, thousands.
Walking, milling, waiting, pulling, running
Shut roads. Dead air waiting fast.
Running from who? Me? Police? The state?
Run my phone.
Check.

Tweet *Music, songs, poetry and dance. This is the real us, this is the real Turkey.*

Scroll down.
Turn right
Right again.
Sweat
Climbing up my back.
Concrete
Heating in my gut.
Gas
Lingering.
Clutching at my throat.
Eating the air
Clutching at my heart.
Fear making me sweat
What am I doing here?
I'm following you
Following my phone.
Check

Tweet *SHIT riot police moving in to clear the square.*

Scroll down.
Turn left.
Go straight.
I'M AT THE TOP
Glass, rubbish, dust,
debris in the air.
A war zone. No zone. A music festival, overturned cars, buses and lives.
milling, people changing, mixing.
Like me,
Like you.
We are like each other and we are here
AT
THE
TOP
Like my phone
Check

Tweet *1.13am they're coming up the boulevard, water cannons, hundreds of them.*

FUCK!

First they're crouching and bouncing together, chanting the below. Initially it's quiet and after a few rounds it builds up until they're jumping.

JUMP!
JUMP!
IF YOU DON'T YOU'RE ERDOGAN!

ZIPLA!
ZIPLA!
ZIPLAMAYAN TAYYIP'TIR!

JUMP!
JUMP!
IF YOU DON'T YOU'RE ERDOGAN!

ZIPLA!
ZIPLA!
ZIPLAMAYAN TAYYIP'TIR!

JUMP!
JUMP!
IF YOU DON'T YOU'RE ERDOGAN!

ZIPLA!
ZIPLA!
ZIPLAMAYAN TAYYIP'TIR!

All waiting. Waiting. Waiting.
Friends. Waiting. For what?
Waiting on my phone.

Check

Tweet *1.13am they're coming up the boulevard, water cannons, hundreds of them.*

To be hunted, to be eaten alive. Fuck!

Move away! Let's run away. Have you not seen the tweets?
We have, it's fake
We must prepare. How do we prepare?
Prepare for what?
An attack
Don't spread panic. We're not soldiers.
More barricades, stones, get tables and chairs, couches, and TVs. They're preparing their guns.
STOP IT! We are not fighters! This is not a war
It looks like a war.
Then are you ready to die?
WHAT?
Are you ready to die?
No!
Then STOP! Look around. See the crowd? Look at them. What do you see?
I see people in the dark. I see people, dead.
I look at you and I see fear in you. So strong I can smell it, touch it, scrape it off your clothes

What then? What now?
We wait. All together, we are still. Like the summer city air, we do not move.
I can't.
Then go, this is not for you. Go and be scared alone.

Yusuf I'm walking, I'm not walking, I am walking away.

Sorry, excuse me, I have to go. Can I please go through? Thank you. Sorry. Good luck. It's just that I've got to . . . I'm sorry to leave you.

Something is moving, I am moving. No. The air, the breeze. Ripples through the crowds. They. The police! They're coming. Fuck! Run!

He starts running on the spot.
Left, now right, Sorry, scroll down, excuse me, not that way. Scroll UP. Watch out!
Bang bang, clouds of gas filling the air. HELP!
Help, my phone
Check

Tweet *Riot police walking in a line clearing the square, beating, burning. SHIT! Is this what you do to your citizens?*

Lost now, Scroll left, lost signal, scroll right, lost my way.
Left and no right. And down and no up, and straight.
And more of them moving in all directions.
Police. I knew it. Police. I'm scared and I'm shaking.
More police. Looking at me and I've got to do something. I'm stuck left, right, up, down I'm stuck. I've got to

Police (*on a megaphone*) *MOVE OVER! Move over.*

Yusuf I am. . . .

Police Move away! Now!

Yusuf I am . . .

OK. OK I will. I want to.

I am . . . moving.

2.18am, 1st June 2013 – Gezi Park, Taksim Square, Istanbul, Turkey, Planet Earth

2.19 am, 1st June 2013 – Gezi Park, Taksim Square, Istanbul, Turkey, Planet Earth

I've got to . . . move.

Do. . . .

I. . . .

I am. . . .

He starts shaking.

2.20am, 1st June 2013. . . .
I am . . .

2.20am . . .
I am . . .

His body going into shock. He screams, a silent scream.

Yusuf 2.19 am, 1st June 2013 – Gezi Park, Taksim Square, Istanbul, Turkey, Planet Earth

I
AM
HERE
I AM HERE

Yusuf *relaxes in his position and is now standing simply in protest. They all are.*

Police Move away!

Protesters
WE
ARE
HERE

Others join the stage to simply STAND.

Heartlines: A Love Story

Sarah Gabriella Waisvisz

Acknowledgements

The writing, development and production of this play would not have been possible without the support of the Canada Council for the Arts; City of Ottawa; Ontario Arts Council; Great Canadian Theatre Company (GCTC); National Arts Centre (NAC); TACTICS; and undercurrents festival / Ottawa Fringe. The playwright would also like to acknowledge the writing, development, or professional support of Lawrence Aronovitch; Rebecca Benson; Liz Bolton; Rebecca Eamon Campbell; Eric Coates; Eleanor Crowder; Maryse Fernandes, and Dominique Gais; Patrick Gauthier; Dr. Michelle Gewurtz; Scottie Irving; Brittney Johnston; Jillian Keiley; Sarah Kitz; Nathan Medd; Margo MacDonald; Hugh Nielson; Emily Pearlman; Ludmylla Reis; Laurie Shannon; Andrea Steinwand; Bronwyn Steinberg; and Kat Wong.

Production history

Heartlines underwent two development workshops supported by TACTICS and the undercurrents festival. During its writing, the playwright was in residence at GCTC and then the NAC. The play had its festival premiere at the undercurrents festival in 2020 and its professional mainstage premiere at Great Canadian Theatre Company (GCTC) in 2022.

Heartlines was produced at GCTC in Ottawa, Canada, from 22 March – 3 April, 2022 in a production by Calalou/RAFT Theatre Projects in collaboration with GCTC / TACTICS.

The playwright would like to acknowledge the extraordinary insights offered by performers Maryse Fernandes and Margo MacDonald who developed the characters of Suzanne and Claude and brought them to life.

Cast

Claude	Margo MacDonald
Suzanne	Maryse Fernandes
Bandleader	Scottie Irving

Creative team

Director	Rebecca Benson
Dramaturge	Rebecca Benson
Playwright	Sarah Waisvisz
Sound Design/Music	Scottie Irving
Video Design	Kim Kielhofner
Lighting Design	Tristan-Olivier Breiding
Costume Design	Vanessa Imeson
Set/Props Design	Andrea Steinwand
Intimacy Coaching	Megan Piercey Monafu
Mapping Technician	Andrew Galligan
*Production Man*ager	Christine Hecker
Stage Management	Rebecca Eamon Campbell
Assistant Stage Management	Arielle Voght and Yutong Ng

The Playwright

Sarah Waisvisz is a playwright, director and performer. Her multidisciplinary solo show *Monstrous*, about being of mixed Afro-Caribbean and Jewish roots, was published in *Alt.theatre* 13.3 and was performed in Canada and the United States. *Heartlines* was produced at Great Canadian Theatre Company in 2022 and at the undercurrents festival in 2020 (Ottawa, Canada). Sarah directed Donna-Michelle St. Bernard's film *Witness Shift* for Obsidian Theatre/CBC Arts' *21 Black Futures* anthology as well as the local chorus for the Ottawa production of *The First Stone*. She is Assistant Professor at the Dan School of Drama and Music at Queen's University.

Playwright's Note

The play is written in English but the characters also speak French, German, Hebrew and Yiddish, and those languages are indicated by italics. In the world of the play, however, the characters are speaking French, not English, although in Act Two I have tried to reflect the bilingual linguistic environment of the Isle of Jersey. The stage directions, titles, and descriptions of music, image and video in the script are merely suggestions. For both our first festival production at undercurrents (2020) and our premiere at Great Canadian Theatre Company (2022), these choices were made by the artistic team and reflected many years of collaborating on the world of the play. In the production at GCTC, we also included original video design created by Kim Kielhofner that enhanced the stage presence of Claude and Suzanne's artistry while also responding to it in a wholly original way. The play's music and soundscape were composed and created by Scottie Irving who, in the role of the Bandleader, played the music live onstage with seven instruments and interacted with the other two performers. In production, instruments included piano, snare drum, harp, synthesizer and accordion. I hope that future directors will use my stage directions as suggestions to create new surrealistic and imagistic playgrounds for the characters. Lastly, although the play is based on historical characters and historical events, *Heartlines* is a work of fiction, and any inaccuracies are either my intention or my fault.

Synopsis
by Malia Rogers for TACTICS

A pair of queer Jewish lovers flee the fascism of the Second World War and find resistance buried deep in their respective artforms. Using play-within-a-play and epic storytelling, real-life artists and life partners Claude Cahun (born Lucy Schwob) and Marcel Moore (born Suzanne Malherbe) take the audience through the dizzying romance of their early life together in Paris and then the fracturing of that life with the rise of Hitler and antisemitism during the Second World War. Identities of all kinds – gender, sexual, religious, national, creative – are explored, negotiated, suppressed, and liberated as Claude and Suzanne invoke their surrealist art through dangerous acts of resistance to the Nazi regime. In *Heartlines*, love perseveres across the perversions of oppression, violence and time itself – perhaps as an ultimate act of resistance to all three.

Heartlines: A Love Story

Dedication

This play is dedicated to the heroes in my own family – Madeleine Desché, Bernard Huët, David Shentow, Jacques Maurits Waisvisz, Pierre Hardy Zizine – as well as to those fighting tyranny everywhere.

For Camille, who led me to these artists.

And for Kate, with all my love.

Dramatis Personae

Claude, *Lucy Schwob, a.k.a. Claude Cahun, an artist*
Suzanne, *Suzanne Malherbe, a.k.a. Marcel Moore, an artist*
The Bandleader

Setting

The realm of memory.

Act One

Prologue

Music: Seascape.

Image/Video: The sea.

Memory: Claude in the sea.

Present: **Suzanne** *unpacks an old trunk and finds a notebook, which she opens to read.*

Suzanne 'Is there anything more powerful than first love? Anything so potent as that first kiss?' Remember? How all the blood from your body rushed into your mouth, your ears, your groin, your cheeks . . . until then I had never felt that tingling in my fingers and the lightness in my head . . . it's miserable but pleasurable and weird . . . Remember? The softness of your lips. The saltiness. And then your tongue – in my mouth – yes, stay there – don't stop doing that – keep doing that – what are you doing to me? That feels so . . . that feels so . . . That first kiss taunted me until finally, I felt your whole body at once under my body, under my hands, under my mouth, under my tongue . . . I never forgot that first kiss.

Claude *is in the water and beckons to* **Suzanne**.

Claude The water's wonderful. Why don't you come in?

Suzanne You always say that. And it's always freezing!

Claude I'm going to drag you in if you don't come in yourself.

Suzanne Don't you dare.

Claude, *playful, emerges from the water and strikes a pose reminiscent of one of the photos from the 'I'm in Training: Don't Kiss Me!' series (*Autoportrait, c. *1927).*

Scene One

Title: 'A Youthful Passion'.

Music: Piano: adaptation of À la claire fontaine *theme; innocent, gentle, pulsing.*

Suzanne I was the older girl. But she seduced me. We were at the Lycée together in Nantes. She was two years younger. I knew she was Jewish, and that her family owned the local newspaper. She claimed she had been paying attention to me. Watching me. She always said she pursued me in such a way that I couldn't refuse. Typical Claude.

Claude I always knew. Most people know from a young age, not necessarily that they love women, or men if they're men, but they know they're different. For me it was like a thirst I couldn't quench. My earliest happy memory is of holding my cousin Marie's hand and walking with her in a field. I never forgot that warmth, that softness. When I met Suzanne I already knew what I wanted from her because I had felt it with Marie when we held hands, and I had felt it again a few years later when Marie and I moved on to exploring each other's bodies. She wanted to practice making babies, and so we did the best we could with what we had . . . so I knew what orgasm felt like even though my technique had been, up until then, largely accidental, and my liaisons had been limited to my cousin. Of course it was forbidden. It was a sin for the Catholics. But for the Jews? I always found their opinion about gay women much less clear. Not that I was religious. Unless it suited me. Which is, some would say, very Jewish.

Suzanne Suddenly there she was one afternoon in the school's art studio: Mademoiselle Lucy Schwob. I asked her if she painted. She said no.

'Why are you here, then?' I asked.

'To meet you. Will you teach me to paint?'

And so I taught her all I knew.

Claude I wanted her to know my name. And then I wanted to steal a kiss. A quick *bisou*. On the mouth.

Suzanne We quickly became inseparable. I was asked to tutor her in painting as well as in German because I was fluent – my family always spoke German at home – but Lucy was not all that interested in the finer points of technique in either art or grammar . . . Eventually, when my widowed mother announced she would marry her widowed father, we became step-sisters, and we laughed and laughed . . .

Scene Two

Title: 'Drawing Lessons'.

No music in this scene.

Image/Video: (this scene references the sketch 'Elles s'aiment', c. *1929).*

The two are adolescents. They both have sketching paper and pencils all around them. They are sketching the landscape before them; it is an outdoor drawing lesson.

Suzanne How is it going? Don't forget to use more contrast this time for the shadows.

Claude Shhh . . . . You're distracting me.

Suzanne Are you ready to show me what you have?

Claude *Pas encore*. Not yet.

Claude *is not sketching the landscape.*

Suzanne Lucy, half the work of drawing is looking . . . You need to look carefully at what you are drawing (**Claude** *looks at* **Suzanne**) . . . What on earth are you up to? (**Suzanne** *snatches* **Claude***'s notebook to look at it.*)

Claude *Merde*! It was going to be a surprise – this meadow is boring. I thought I would draw us instead.

Suzanne I don't see any figures in that sketch.

Claude Look closer, *ma chère*. We are both there. In the lips – I've written my name: Lucy Schwob. In the eye, your name: Suzanne Malherbe. And our initials spell out '*elles s'aiment*.' *Tu vois*? L . . . S . . . M . . . Lucy Schwob Suzanne Malherbe. L.S.M. *Elles – s'aiment –*

Suzanne I see . . . But why did you draw a hand? What does the shoe mean?

Claude You keep me grounded – or else I would fly away. And yet the hand is reaching high above.

Suzanne I like the detail in the hand. Hands are difficult to draw.

Claude I wanted to show how we're *beshert*. Fated. I feel like you're part of me, like the lines in my hand, like the lines of fate in my hand.

Suzanne Like lifelines.

Claude Like lifelines.

Suzanne L. S. M. *Elles s'aiment* . . . (*confession:*) I love you, Lucy.

Claude I hope you do. Because I love you. L.S.M. *Elles s'aiment*. It's a code – our secret code. I'm going to write those letters all over town and you'll know it's for you.

Suzanne Oh yeah? Where exactly?

Claude I was thinking I would start with the synagogue, then the school, then all the churches, then your mother's house, *et cetera*. This way you will be blushing terribly in public all the time, each time you see it, because it will remind you that I love you, and also that I want to kiss you, and fuck you . . .

Suzanne You're terrible! People will talk!

Claude So what if they talk. I love you and I want everyone to know.

Suzanne Lucy, you know that's not possible. But I love you too. Just . . . more quietly . . . In any case, draw me that meadow like you were supposed to!

Suzanne *returns the notebook, but* **Claude** *drops it to the ground and approaches* **Suzanne**. *They slowly move closer until they are almost kissing. This is* **Suzanne***'s first kiss.*

Scene Three

Title: 'Outsider'.

Music: Rhodes synthesizer path with accordion drone. Uncanny, slightly dissonant, in ¾.

In this scene **Claude** *changes clothes from a girl's skirt to pants, shirt, men's shoes, and coat; these have been on the dressmaker's mannequin onstage since the top of show.*

Claude If you've always felt *normal* then you can't begin to understand what it feels like to know you are Other. Different. Eventually in Paris I met other women and men who never felt like they belonged: they were Jews, or Blacks, *métisses*, or queers; often they were artists. They kept traveling, kept running, kept performing, kept writing – always on the fringes no matter where they landed. But there will always be someone who refuses to hide, who refuses to wear a skirt or be married off. For me, it's like my body never matched me. As a girl I tried to match me to my body, but it felt like the inside of my head was on fire every time I acted like a good little girl. So to stop the feeling of the fire in my head I stopped trying to match me to my body: I wore a girl's school uniform but I wore *tzizit* under my blouse, put a *kippah* on my head . . . I wanted to be like the Jewish boys at religious school, learn what they were learning . . . But it got me in trouble; first it was just teasing from those boys, and then one day some *goyish* kids tied me to a tree and pelted me with rocks. After that my father sent me to boarding school in England. But I got into a different kind of trouble there, and I was dragged home to go to the local *lycée.* That's when I met Suzanne.

The ultimate betrayal was my own body. How would I stop that bleeding every month? I couldn't believe how wasteful it was: all that blood and pain and I knew even then that I never wanted to be a mother, never wanted a man near me. But my breasts, my hips, my belly, my thighs . . . so soft and rounded – as if to spite me. I wondered how thin I would have to get until my woman's body disappeared. I knew I could make my breasts disappear under tight bandages or cloth, but how could I get rid of them forever? Don't get me wrong: I didn't want to be a man. I just didn't want to be a woman. Could I be neither? I didn't want a prick, I just didn't want to live in this soft body – I never did – Was there another option? A third option? The space and possibility of a third sex excited me. An in-between space between man and woman. A third sex. Neuter. Not feminine or masculine. Not *femme* or *homme* but *neutre.* That's what I knew I was. And I was certain there were others like me. But in Nantes? I felt utterly alone. Even after I met Suzanne.

Music: Transition to piano with accordion drone for Suzanne's sea music; airy, sublime.

Suzanne The smell of the salt on the air. The cry of the seagulls. That was Brittany. But actually in Nantes we were inland, locked in the city, and I had to wait for holidays to go to the water. When I was young I always dreamed of sailing into sunsets saturated with colour: orange, vivid purples, rose, reds that met the sea. I painted these sea-sunsets in my mind and on paper before I ever saw them. I yearned for them, for that taste of salt. Later, I realized that it was those sea-sunsets that made me yearn for God – but not the Catholic God I was raised to fear. It was Claude's God I wanted to know.

Scene Four

Title: 'A New Beginning'.

Video: Paris with cat.

Music: Travelling music on accordion. Allegretto, tonal, symmetrical.

In this scene, props, clothing, art and writing supplies, and camera emerge from the trunk to become the Parisian apartment of **Claude** *and* **Suzanne**.

Suzanne Inevitably, we left Nantes.

Claude It was only a matter of time.

Suzanne We moved to Paris. We lived there for seventeen years.

Claude I had to leave Nantes. I would have died otherwise.

Suzanne It was so we could study art properly.

Claude And be together properly.

Suzanne And study philosophy and literature. I threw myself into design and drawing, while you took up writing and theatre. And we both began to explore photography. I hoped Paris would be an ideal place for us to –

Claude – love each other properly.

Suzanne *And* grow into ourselves as artists and as intellectuals –

Claude – and as lovers.

Suzanne But also as artists. *Silly.* It was then that we decided to choose pen names.

Claude You picked Marcel Moore and I chose Claude Cahun – androgynous names –

Suzanne – or else no one would have ever looked at our work: my drawings, your writing, our photographs. I picked Marcel for your uncle: everyone needs a Gay Jewish Uncle.

Claude Just so. And I picked Cahun for my more obscure Jewish relatives – all those rabbis. Cahun. Like Cohen.

Suzanne Cohen means your family were priests in ancient times. See: you *are* neglecting your responsibilities by choosing art.

Claude Making sacrifices and running the temple? Only if you were a man.

Suzanne Right. As usual. (*Music finishes.*)

Claude Is it time?

Suzanne It's time.

Music: Introductory flourish.

Title: 'An Ode to Paris'.

Image/Video: montage of images from c. *1926, 1927.*

Claude Welcome to our home!

Suzanne *Bienvenue chez nous*!

Claude Welcome to our bedroom carnival! We have a special presentation for you tonight, and then we promise, there will be more dancing! And more drinking! (**Suzanne** *opens the champagne and pours glasses, perhaps even to the first row of the audience.*) We want to share a new piece of writing that we wrote together and therefore it's a little different from my usual work, which you've been kind enough to suffer through before. This piece is a duet! A two-hander. It might be terrible but we're going to try it out on you now, providing you've had enough champagne.

A toast:

Claude May we present:

Together 'An Ode to Paris.'

Suzanne By Marcel and Claude. **Claude** By Claude and Marcel.

Claude Maestro? Some music if you please . . .

Music: Cinematic scoring, with annunciatory musical flourishes, fanfares, and ironic musical jokes accompany this bit of clowning.

NB: Each 'Ode' in the play is a clown scene (interlude / lazzi): highly theatrical, ironic, absurd and is different from what comes before and after.

An Ode to Paris

Claude Our days in Paris were magnificent. Paris was impossible not to love in those days. Everyone was there:

Music: 'The Star Spangled Banner.'

Suzanne American writers and American queers:

Claude Bonjour. Je suis an American in Paris. Je m'appelle Gertrude Stein. No, Stein, not SHTEEN, Stein. I am **very famous** in America! That's Alice.

Music: 'Rule Britannia' or 'God Save the Queen.'

Claude British writers – mostly queers:

Suzanne Cheerio, Marguerite Radcliffe Hall here, pleasure to meet you. John to my friends. But *we* aren't friends yet. Question: does everyone always greet each other so . . . *intimately* here *all the time* . . . No no no I didn't order wine I ordered tea. TEA! Harumph. France!

Music: Tchaikovsky's theme to Swan Lake.

Suzanne Russian princesses – often queers:

Claude *Speziba*: your most expensive vodka and caviar *s'il vous plaît, garçon.* Now. Now. Here now. Now. Here now. Here. Now . . . *Oh la la*, you *are* cute. We fuck now, yes?

Music: Lively 'Hava Negila' or other Yiddish tune.

Suzanne Russian Jews – mostly penniless painters . . .

Claude *groans miserably, head in hands.*

Suzanne Soutine! Are you ever going to pay your tab? You owe me 200 francs! Who do you think you are, the next Chagall?!

Claude Would you take a painting of a rotting beef carcass? It's all I have . . .

Suzanne Ah! *Les artistes*!

Claude *groans.*

Music: Concluding flourish!

End of Ode to Paris

Music: Accordion music continues: 'Parisian cliché style', in ¾.

Claude Paris – *la ville lumière*. Everybody wanted to be there. The foreigners came all at once, for the season, and acted as if the cafés belonged to *them.* They didn't notice that while yes, this is where we drank and flirted with them and watched life go by, this was also where we planned and plotted against capitalism, slavery, the government increasingly turning fascist! Paris was our lover and our war room. The city vibrated with energy. It was . . . sexy.

Suzanne Each morning felt like a new world. When I couldn't sleep I got up early and went out into the city. Claude liked to sleep in and wake up only in time for lunch, but I loved the mornings. I knew the bakers and the whores and those who opened their bistros early . . . I walked for hours. Sometimes I followed the Seine as far as I could – I knew it would eventually lead me to the sea, if only I could walk that far – I loved the stillness and the calm of Paris just waking up. I loved our nights too, but somehow the days were hard work.

Claude Nice to hear you say you loved our nights. Paris at night: nothing better.

Suzanne – but the mornings for stillness. If I could have had it my way, I would have skipped over the days entirely and moved from the half-light of dawn to the half-light of dusk, ignoring the rest.

To each other and at once.

Suzanne It was the mornings I loved. **Claude** I loved Paris at night . . .

Claude Maybe for you, Suzanne, but not for me. *Non*, it was the **night**! Paris was at her best at night! (*To the* **Bandleader**.) You remember, *mon ami*! You were there too! The scandals, the champagne, the dancing—

Bandleader *and* **Claude** *sing this (anachronistic) song together.*

Music: 'Sous le ciel de Paris / s'envole une chanson, mmm mmm'

Claude How many times did we fall asleep in each other's arms on a park bench or on the cobblestone streets? 'America is my country but Paris is my hometown,' said Gertrude, and on this point we agreed. We all loved Paris fiercely – and we would have killed to defend it even as it drove us mad.

Suzanne People came from everywhere to live here. Remember Eli? He was a lover of Nadja's at first. He was here without any money, a Jew from Seville. He was the most beautiful man and Claude and I . . . well, even we danced with him a few times and somehow he managed to get Claude quite flustered –

Claude – a Spanish *Adonis* –

Suzanne – he lived at *La Ruche* with the other poor foreign artists. Then suddenly he was gone and Nadja came crying to us and said he had left her for a German actor who had just played in the cabaret we had seen the week before. They went to Berlin. *I* wouldn't want to go there – this Hitler sounds like a real fanatic, wouldn't you agree? (*Music stops abruptly.*) And he certainly doesn't like queers. Or Jews. Or queer Jews!

Music: Music only resumes when **Claude** *continues the narrative.*

Claude Everyone wants to live in Montparnasse with its *ateliers* and cafés. If you are bored or frustrated with your own work, all you need to do is walk to La Dome and order a coffee or some wine and next to you will be an actress you admire who you can fawn over until you forget your own troubles: *Bonjour, Mademoiselle*. I know you. You played last week at *La Comédie*. My name is Cahun. Claude. I'd like to photograph you. May I sit? . . . Montparnasse! Forget Montmartre! Only Picasso is still there, and for how long? It is from here in Montparnasse that Paris will delight and shock the world, especially America. It is from here that true liberty will be fought for and come to be – *Vive Contre Attaque*! *Vive la liberté*!

Music: Musical flourish begins: **Claude** *begins to bow, but* **Suzanne** *interrupts – she has perhaps had too much champagne . . .*

Suzanne But life in Paris can be hard. When the sky is as grey as the Seine, sometimes I think about throwing myself into the water, floating my way to the sea. And then the only question is: from which bridge? There are so many to choose from.

Music: Music out.

Claude *and* **Suzanne** *recover and smile for the audience. They take their bows.*

Now they are alone in their apartment after everyone has gone home after the party. **Suzanne** *is still drinking champagne.*

Claude (*aside*) I hate it when you talk like that. You can be so . . . morbid.

Suzanne Give me a break . . . It's just a play.

Claude I swear, Suzanne, this is the last time we perform together. You can't just go off-book like that.

Suzanne This was supposed to be a collaboration, NOT one of your solos. I was collaborating.

Claude You were going rogue. If there is a next time, we will do one of my scripts. No more co-writing.

Suzanne You need to be in control all the time, don't you? *You're* not famous yet for all your ego. You haven't exhibited or published a thing!

Claude But I will. And when I do, it will be a sensation.

Suzanne Well when you do, I demand co-credit.

Claude You know the portraits are more impressive if it seems like I did them alone.

Suzanne They are already impressive!

Claude Yes, but as auto-portraiture . . . as the work of a single *auteur* . . .

Suzanne If the design is mine or the shot or the composition is mine, then it's not an auto-portrait, it's a collaboration, and you know it.

Claude I thought you didn't want to be in the spotlight! Come on, Suzanne! Think about it – think about how astounding the portraits are as the work of a **solo** artist – you can still help me to make them – but if they are exhibited it will be as by Cahun . . . as done by Claude Cahun, *alone* . . .

Suzanne You're impossible. Do what you want. But don't come crying to me if someone accuses you of being a fraud.

Scene Five

Title: 'Auto-portraiture'.

Image 1: Self portrait of **Claude** *with aviator glasses and scarf,* c. *1927 or other self-portrait.*

Music: Harp. Intense, minor key, precise.

Claude (*setting up the camera*) Auto-portraiture is not a selfish, egotistical whimsy. It is practical. It is simpler to use myself rather than someone else; *c'est tout*. I think Suzanne is jealous that she is not my muse. But she is my everything else. Isn't that enough? I do not have a muse because I do not need one. Why is she jealous of that?

Auto-portraiture is very technical. I said it was simpler and it is, emotionally, because you don't have to consider the needs of the model, but it does require the precision of the instruments, the lighting, and above all the timing. So in those respects it can be difficult to do well. But the liberty is unparalleled. There is no one to get in the way of the shot I want to get.

I had a muse once. Vanessa. Her given name was Esther but she took on Vanessa to make herself sound **exotic**. I thought she was gorgeous, *ravissante*. Such long limbs

– always entwined around some piece of furniture, or around themselves. You couldn't help but imagine her legs wrapped around your own body. And when we made love it was like that: all legs, all arms, all writhing and tangled limbs, sweaty musky athletic sex. Nothing tender about us. Vanessa was as strong as she was long, and she liked to compete with me for power. We fought it out in her bed, in stairwells, in a park once in the dead of night. Vanessa. I painted her. I painted her skin too, once, and arranged her body against a blank canvas. Then I told her to move as if she were making love to me. I stayed back and watched her move alone on the virgin canvas, until it was covered in paint and sweat, and we were both spent. Just watching her brought me to orgasm. I had never felt so done in before, so undone.

Music: Harp ends, piano begins: sparse, tip-toeing, minor key.

Suzanne (*absorbed in her work on the easel*) It was fine with me when Claude went out. I Liked having quiet to draw and to think, to be alone in our tiny apartment with my thoughts and my pencils. I liked to host, but I preferred when others did, like the rich American Natalie Barney with her 'Friday salons' on *rue Jacob*, near our flat. Natalie was known as *L'Amazonne* but I used to call her *La Lesbienne*, because she was **Not Interested in Hiding It**, and she made it clear that Claude and I had an open invitation to her salons. Sometimes I sent Claude to Natalie's for a few days so I could work in peace and quiet. This was my ideal version of a *ménage à trois*: everyone was satisfied.

Scene Six

Title: 'Inaccrochable.' *(Trans.: 'It will never sell.')*

Image: One of the many photomontages from Aveux non avenus, c. *1929*

Music: Stormy piano introduction for **Claude***'s entrance. Then no music until the end of the scene.*

Suzanne *is cutting out images and moving them around on her easel.* **Claude** *storms into the apartment.*

Claude Suzanne! Suzanne! Adrienne Monnier doesn't want it. She said it would never sell. '*Inaccrochable*,' she said, quoting Gertrude! Can you believe it? And they say they can't stand each other! *La vache!*

Suzanne Slow down, please.

Claude I showed Adrienne the manuscript like we talked about and she doesn't want to publish it. She doesn't want to publish *Disavowals*.

Suzanne I'm so sorry, sweetheart. I thought for sure she would want it. Maybe it needs a little more work?

Claude I thought it was ready. I feel so stupid. Adrienne said the writing was strong but that it was too 'opaque' and 'confusing,' that the reader would have to work too hard. But that's the whole point! I *want* them to work! I want the reader to be challenged by the structure, by the ambiguity – otherwise it's just a novel! I argued with Adrienne about that, saying I wasn't interested in tradition, in being the next Balzac, and *THEN* she suggested I try my hand at a *journal intime*! A Tell-All-Memoir?! I couldn't believe it! *Shiksa* cow. She didn't even catch the *Yom Kippur* reference in the title. She's a philistine.

Journal intime?! That's fake writing for and by little old ladies . . . I'm done with her, with Sylvia Beech, with their conjoined-twin bookstores, with everything ... For my revenge I'm going to seduce Gertrude and Alice both and be a social pariah and write opaque novels in invisible ink, since my writing is so unsellable.

Suzanne Makes sense.

Claude Do you think my book is too weird? . . . I'm going to make the book even weirder then. So weird no one will want to read it, let alone buy it.

Suzanne Mmmhhmm. You do that, sweetheart.

Claude You're not even listening to me! What are you working on that is so important?

Suzanne (*finally looks up to* **Claude** *and softens*) I'm sorry. I'm just playing with that technique of Picasso's and Braque's – collage – with some cuttings of our photographs – and seeing what happens if the pieces are assembled randomly, like the images in a kaleidoscope when you turn the barrel. Remember those toys? The shapes in the toy are geometric but what if they weren't? What if they were motifs from our photographs? How can they keep changing and transforming on the page?

Claude You are brilliant, my love. Collage. I love this! The images don't make sense together – but in a way they do? Does each collage have a central theme or is it entirely random? How did you choose what goes together? Tell me everything! Wait! I hereby commission you to illustrate my un-publishable, unsellable, inaccrochable book. I want you to make me the most confusing, unique, mutant illustrations possible. We'll never sell any books but to Hell with it. And then we'll bestow a signed copy to Adrienne with thanks for the inspiration. She can share it with Sylvia. That cow.

Claude *sweeps* **Suzanne** *off her feet, and they dance around the apartment, laughing, mooing, and scattering all the collage material. Music begins again on accordion to accompany their dancing: valse, sweet, jocose.*

Scene Seven

Title: 'Working with Models'.

Image: Options include **Claude** *with shaved head and sleeveless shirt (*Autoportrait, c.*1928) or the double autoportrait* 'Que me veux-tu' c. *1928.*

Music: Pianoforte with snare (or tapping on wood of harp). Understated music with very gradual development; by the middle and end of the scene the music is quite threatening.

Towards the end of a long photography session. **Claude** *is costumed in a shirt with vertical stripes.* **Suzanne** *is in regular house clothes including a skirt, or a kimono.* **Suzanne** *is posing for* **Claude** *who is behind the camera.*

Claude Why won't you keep still?

Suzanne I have been sitting here for a long time, *Monsieur le photographe*, and I have a cramp.

Claude Well, stretch a bit and then be still for God's sake or we'll miss the shot.

Suzanne I've been holding this pose for hours while you find the perfect light. Can I ever be more than simply your object, *monsieur*?

Claude Shut up, Suzanne. You are Marcel Moore, my esteemed collaborator. But for this session, you are merely my placeholder, not my model. Now be still, for God's sake.

Suzanne Or else what?

Claude You are really trying my patience today – why is that? Just one minute and I'll almost have it. Don't move!

They are both still for thirty seconds while **Claude** *finds the light.*

Claude OK! Good. Now let me in there.

They switch places. **Claude** *takes on the pose* **Suzanne** *has just held. There is something luminescent when* **Claude** *models.* **Claude***'s pose echoes the image at the top of the scene.*

Claude Now! Take the photo!

Silence as **Claude** *freezes and* **Suzanne** *takes the photo, expertly.*

Claude Good. Now come here. Please. (*Beat.*) What's the problem? You've had nothing but attitude all afternoon. What's wrong?

Suzanne I don't like your . . . look.

Claude You don't like my 'look'?

Suzanne *Non.*

Claude (*laughs*) It's just a shirt, Suzanne, which YOU made for me. This 'look' is *your* design which you dreamed up in one of your nightmare *visions*.

Suzanne Yes, but you look – more – frightening – that I expected. You look like a prisoner. I don't like it. Why did you have to cut your hair so short?

Claude I thought you liked my hair short.

Suzanne Not that short.

Claude Is that really what's bothering you? What exactly is your problem today? (*Mocking/tongue in cheek.*) Oh I know what's going on. You think I get to have all the fun while you toil away in obscurity with your drawing. But it's not all fun and games, *ma chère*. I am Claude Cahun. I am a visionary. But fine, if you think you want to pose for me, really pose for me, you'll have to wear a costume too.

Claude *takes off* **Suzanne**'*s kimono and gives her a soldier's coat.*

Suzanne Fine. (*Beat.*) Now you put this on. (*Gives* **Claude** *a skirt.*)

Claude *Non.*

Suzanne Do it.

Claude *puts on skirt and curtsies.*

Suzanne Now you photograph me.

Suzanne *mockingly takes up a pose from the 'I am in training' series.*

Claude I would rather fuck you.

Suzanne Too bad. Take my photo. (**Claude** *takes a photo.* **Suzanne** *strikes another pose, playing as* **Claude**.) 'I am in training: don't kiss me.' (**Claude** *approaches* **Suzanne**.) *Arrête!* . . . Don't come any closer . . . I said: take my photo! (**Claude** *returns to the camera and looks through it as* **Suzanne** *takes a pose she knows will arouse* **Claude**. **Claude** *takes another picture but then . . . They can't keep away from each other.*)

NB: Music: by the end of this scene the music has reached a 'local' climax, although the ultimate musical climax must be saved for the end of Act One.

Scene Eight

Title: 'Vive la France'.

Image/Video: Option could include a scene from a Nazi rally from the late 1920s.

Music: The radio in the apartment plays a live broadcast from 5 August, 1929. The broadcast is prerecorded in the voice of the **Bandleader**; *the text is based on actual BBC radio broadcasts of the time. The voice over on the radio should build in intensity from urgent to bellicose. All future radio broadcasts are also pre-recorded by the Bandleader.*

Suzanne *and* **Claude** *are listening to the radio.*

Radio This is the BBC World Service for August 5th, 1929. Herr Hitler and his Nationalist Socialist 'Nazi' Party held their 4th Party Congress in Nuremberg, Germany, from August 1 to 4th –

Suzanne Fucking Nazis.

Claude A *fourth* congress?

Radio **. . . This Fourth Rally was given the name 'The Day of Composure' . . .**

Suzanne How poetic.

Radio **. . . a fireworks show enthralled the crowd of attendees, including Great War hero General Van Opp . . .**

Claude Whoever that is.

Suzanne Are you sure we shouldn't leave? We could go to America.

Claude We don't know anyone there. Besides, they hate queers and Jews and Blacks in America, just like in Germany.

Suzanne Antarctica then. Canada. Palestine. This is ridiculous! He's a madman.

Claude The Germans elected him.

Suzanne Then they're all equally mad.

Radio **. . . French-Jewish communities as well as scholars and intellectuals are pressuring the government to intervene, but sources say *l'Élysée* would rather not have a repeat of the Dreyfus Affair . . .**

Claude Next he will go after the queers and the Blacks and the communists. Like always. Hitler hates all of us – and he's not even hiding it anymore!

Suzanne (*spits*) Don't say his name in this house.

Claude Someone should shoot him. Before he does any more damage.

Suzanne What if they have someone worse than Hitler waiting in the wings?

Claude God forbid. (*Spits.*)

Suzanne Fuck you, Hitler!

Claude (*making a Hitler mustache with finger between nose and lip*) You didn't salute, soldier.

Suzanne (*also making a Hitler mustache*) *Verzeihung, mein Kapitän*. I beg your pardon, *mein Herr.*

Claude (*clicks heels, gives a mockery of the Nazi salute*) *Heil Hitler*! Long live *das Vaterland*!

Suzanne *Nein*! Long live *die Mutterland*: *Vive la France*!

Claude *Heil la France*! *Heil l'*Alsace et la Lorraine!

Suzanne *Heil* Paris! *Heil* Montparnasse!! *Heil les gaies parisiennes*!

Claude *Heil* Claude Cahun! *Heil* Marcel Moore!

The two mock goose-step around the apartment. Each has a hand raised as a mustache, the other arm raised in salute. The radio broadcast gets louder and merges with their salutes.

'*Heil* les Deux Magots!' 'Heil Café Flore!'

'*Heil* James Joyce!' '*Heil* Jean-Paul Sartre!'

'*Heil* André Breton!' '*Heil* Picasso!'

'*Heil* les Folies Bergères!' '*Heil* Josephine Baker!

'*Heil* Gertrude Stein!' '*Heil* la Ville Lumière!'

Music: The sound of metal-tipped boots increases in intensity as the volume of the radio increases.

Image/Video: Image of a Swastika appears, faded at first, and then it flashes to solid and begins to turn, as if in a kaleidoscope.

Claude *and* **Suzanne** *listen to the next broadcast and watch the swastika image turn and grow.*

Radio This is the BBC World Service on the 3rd of September, 1939. This is London. You will now hear a message from the Prime Minister of Great Britain: 'This morning the British Ambassador in Berlin handed the German government a final note stating that unless we heard from them by 11 o'clock that they were prepared at once to withdraw their troops from Poland, a state of war would be declared by us . . . consequently this country is at war with Germany. I repeat: this country is at war with Germany.'

Claude *and* **Suzanne** *kiss each other in deliberate defiance of the rising Nazi tide, and perhaps give the finger to the terrifying and ominous image of the swastika.*

Lights go out suddenly. End of Act One. Brief musical outro: tense, alarming.

Act Two

Prologue

Image/Video: Animated map of Europe and of battle lines/invasions to show incursions.

Music: Snare and accordion intro: alarm, cacophony, spinning. Intro transitions to pulsing accordion and piano music for the scene that is both meandering and threatening.

Radio This is the BBC World Service. In April 1940 Germany invades Denmark and Norway. On the 10 of May 1940 Winston Churchill is appointed Prime Minister of Great Britain. On the same day, as a token of their congratulations, Germany invades north-eastern France, sweeping past the Maginot Line and through the Ardennes Forest to also take Belgium, the Netherlands, and Luxembourg. On the 14th of June 1940 our beautiful Paris falls to the Nazis. Collaboration becomes a dirty word. France is now under occupation by Germany and its ally Italy. On the 28th of June 1940, German squadrons bomb the harbours of the tiny islands of Guernsey and Jersey, in the English Channel; 44 islanders are killed. On the 30th of June 1940, Guernsey and Jersey surrender to the German army. Occupation is declared. In July 1940, relentless bombing begins on London and other cities in Britain in what will become known as the Blitz. In Jersey today it is below seasonal but sunny. Ten years have passed since we last saw our protagonists. They are no longer quite so young but are just as, ahem, queer as ever . . .

Scene One

Title: 'Away to Jersey.'

Music: Seascape. Piano. Ambiguous, undulating, uneasy music.

Image/Video: Photographs of Jersey from c. *1938, 1939.*

Suzanne *and* **Claude** *have left the freedom of Paris behind and they are now both dressed in 1940s skirts, sweaters, and headscarves.*

Claude It was Suzanne's idea to go to Jersey. I didn't want to leave Paris. But in 1937, we did.

Suzanne That's a lie. It was YOUR idea to go to Jersey. Everyone we knew was trying to leave Paris. We could have gone to Italy with Natalie or gone to America with her sister – but you wanted to not be too far from Paris – and Jersey seemed far enough away from Berlin and that madman.

Claude I thought we would be safe here. No one knew us on Jersey as Jews or as lovers – we were just eccentric middle-aged artists.

Suzanne And it was fine at first for Claude to wear trousers. Before the war our friends visited us regularly – just a train ride and ferry from Paris . . . And we got a cat!

Claude That's true. We got the first of our several cats. Each of them was called Kid. And each of them learned to walk on a leash.

Suzanne And Jersey was beautiful. You loved our house. We named it '*La ferme inconnue*.' It had a terrace, and a garden, and we could walk to the sea. Remember? We would take the cat with us and go to the beach every day to see the sunset. The water and the sky was all around us.

Claude We took marvelous photographs on Jersey. Suzanne had to make weekly visits to the druggist to develop the negatives. He blushed every time she came to pick them up!

Suzanne I went to sleep each night and woke up each morning with the sound of the crashing waves, with the smell of salt, with the wide-open sky above us, with Claude next to me in bed. We were safe.

Claude We were safe. For three years. And then Nazi Germany came to us.

Suzanne I wanted to keep you safe.

Claude And I you.

Suzanne How could we know that *les boschs* would take Paris, make it all the way across France to Normandy and Brittany and then across the Channel to Jersey, to this tiny speck of grass?

Scene Two

Title: 'An Ode to the Occupation.'

Music: Piano.

Suzanne May we present . . .

Together An Ode to the Occupation! (*Pause. They look at each other.*)

Claude By Adolf Hitler (*mustache gesture*).

Suzanne Maestro? Some music if you please?

Music: Musical flourish: lively oom-pah, darkly absurd, each vignette concluding with a musical flourish as in all the odes.

Scene Two A: On Patrol

Claude *takes up the ridiculous goose-stepping again from the end of Act One, and* **Suzanne** *clomps boots or a prop to make the sound of boots on the cobblestone street. They pretend to be German soldiers in the following clown scene.*

Suzanne *Guten tag*, Hans. *Heil Hitler*!

Claude *Guten tag*, Franz. *Heil Hitler*!

Suzanne What shall we do today, Hans?

Claude I don't know, Franz. So many choices. Well, first we could arrest some people for no reason, then we could march around the village with our chests out really big and our legs very stiff – like so – and look very constipated.

Suzanne *Yah*, Hans, that is an idea most *wunderbar*.

Claude *Prima*! And then, what shall we do after that, Franz?

Suzanne Then it will be time for a big sausage!

Music: Musical flourish.

Scene Two B: Two Villagers from Jersey Meet on the Road

Suzanne *Bonjour*, Pierre.

Claude *Bonjour*, Jean.

Suzanne (*whispers*) Did you hear what happened to M. LeClaire? He tried to hide his pig Jojo so the officers wouldn't confiscate him, but then his neighbour – that busybody *anglaise* Mrs Ross – denounced him! He hasn't been seen since!

Claude Jojo?

Suzanne No, *imbecile*, M. LeClaire! Jojo has been promoted to *Kommandant*. (*Snort.*)

Music: Musical flourish.

Scene Two C: A Soldier Visits a Villager's House

Claude (*playing a soldier*) Knock knock. *Heil Hitler*! On orders from Berlin, from the *Führer* himself, *Heil Hitler*, you must turn in your radio, *Heil Hitler Heil Hitler*!

Suzanne (*playing a middle-aged English woman*) Yes, yes, what you said. Here is my only Radio, soldier.

Claude *Gut.* (*The soldier takes the radio brusquely.*) *Heil Hitler*!

Suzanne *Auf Wiedersehen*! (*As he marches away, she gives him the finger, then she pulls out a second radio, along with both a French flag and a Union Jack.*)

Music: Musical flourish.

Claude *and* **Suzanne** *bow.*

Scene Three

Title: 'Away to Jersey, bis.'

Music: Transition. Pianoforte. Music is drab; ¾; dissonant; smeared tonality.

Image: No image, or perhaps a landscape photo of Jersey without a figure.

Suzanne Some of the officers are charming to us, even friendly. It makes me nervous. I keep thinking it's a trick to pull information out of us like about who is secretly a Jew. (*Camping / mocking.*): 'My Catholic step-sister and I are being good little old ladies.' I have no idea how long we can keep this up.

Claude So far, here on Jersey, 'Occupation' means rigid politeness, a few shows of might, constantly changing curfews, the threat of random arrest, starvation and illness, repossession and seizure of goods. No big deal.

Suzanne There are terrible rumours. People are disappearing in France now too.

Claude Nobody can tell me where Gertrude and Alice are, and I haven't heard from Vanessa since . . . I don't know what's happened to Vanessa. Or to Eli and his boyfriend in Berlin.

Suzanne Resistance groups are forming. People are rising up, taking action.

Claude Not Jews. I'm sure it's not other Jews. Everyone's in hiding.

Suzanne We have to do something.

Claude We are artists. Our job is to make art.

Suzanne (*aside*) When the soldiers landed I lost all my colours, all my senses. Just like that: I couldn't even smell the salt of the sea.

Scene Four

Title: 'Oneg shabbat/*Who's Afraid of Virginia Woolf?'*

Music: Subliminal electric background hum; foreboding.

Claude *is fussing with some writing.* **Suzanne** *is doing some mending. The lights flicker, then go out, as they do sometimes now. Music: hum out abruptly.*

Claude *Merde. Merde . . .*

Suzanne *strikes a match, which illuminates her lighting first one candle, then another candle in a second candlestick. It is very quiet.*

Suzanne It's Friday.

Claude Hmm?

Suzanne It's Friday night.

Suzanne *extinguishes the match and sets it down.* **Suzanne** *brings her hands together three times then covers her eyes and sings the blessing quietly, quietly.*

Suzanne *Baruch atah adonai, Eloheinu Melech Ha Olam. Asher kideshanu bemitsvotav vetzi vanu, le hadlik ner, le hadlik ner, shel Shabbat . . .*

Claude *Amen.*

Suzanne *Shabbat shalom.* **Claude** *Shabbat shalom.*

They bless each other. Then **Suzanne** *separates the candlesticks so it's less obvious what they are.*

Claude (*stalling*) Suzanne, sweetie, I have some terrible news. I didn't know how to tell you earlier . . .

Suzanne What happened?

Claude Virginia Woolf died. She took her own life. They say she didn't want to live through another bombing of London. She was afraid of going mad. It was on the news. Michelle told me when I was in the village. She heard it from Pierre who heard it himself on Jean's hidden radio. We can listen for it later tonight . . . I can't believe it. She just gave up.

Suzanne –

Claude She was a coward. That was a cowardly thing to do.

Suzanne No. I don't believe that.

Claude She's just like us, *Suzoleh* – none of us can stand this war. What about Vita? And Leonard? He's *Jewish*! What will happen to him? And what about her writing? This means there won't be any more books – my God-

Suzanne But she was able to choose how and when to die. I envy her.

Claude Don't you dare talk like that. I won't have it. Our job is to live. Hitler wants us dead. Each day that we live is a wound to him.

Suzanne I couldn't live without you.

Claude I'm not going anywhere!

Suzanne Claude. Claude. Look me in the eyes. I couldn't live without you.

Claude Of course you could, *chérie.*

Suzanne Never. It will only ever be you. If you were to die tomorrow I couldn't manage. I would take my life like Virginia did.

Claude You're talking nonsense. I'm going to live until a hundred and twenty. However, if *you* died before me, I would (*lights flicker back on*) . . . take it as a great opportunity to get rid of all your excessive sewing supplies and ridiculous bags of useless cloth, and then I would find a beautiful, fresh young lover to cook and clean for me – it would be just fine.

Suzanne You're impossible! Anyway, you know very well those bags of cloth have been pillaged by everyone up and down the street already. And a lover! Ha. Your fantasy assumes the end of the Occupation . . . Virginia Woolf – how did she die?

Claude . . . She put rocks in her pockets and jumped down into the river. It's terrible. She must have been very afraid. I'm so sorry she's dead.

Scene Five

Title: 'Two Hard Lines'

Image/Video: Photograph of two figures lying in parallel, upside down to the other, Autoportrait c. *1929–1930.*

Music: Pianoforte; cold and staccato, brittle, completely atonal.

A lonely moment in the middle of the night.

Claude We don't make love anymore. Not since the Occupation began. I think I want to, as a distraction or a lark, but I can't summon the energy and neither can she. In bed our bodies are two cold hard lines. If we hold each other it's for warmth and because we are frightened. She's too skinny and she tells me I am too. But actually I like how it's taking away my breasts and belly, little by little, this hunger. I will look more and more manly, less and less like a woman, if this keeps up. Hitler is starving the feminine out of me, it turns out. It makes me laugh to think he is getting the opposite of what he wants. But Suzanne is too thin and too cold. Her body reminds me of her body when we first met, but instead of desire now it just fills me with loss. Maybe this is why we don't make love anymore. Her body looks like the body of a child, barely a teenager. I'm not sure she realizes how much this war has changed her. Now in bed I feel I am protecting a little girl. As if I can save either of us from anything.

Scene Six

Title: 'It's Just a Drawing'

Image/Video: One of Suzanne's propaganda cartoons.

Music: Hum. Snare drum. Sound of drips / leaking. Internal, incremental, quietly oppressive.

Electric lights are working again. **Claude** *is writing in a notebook;* **Suzanne** *is drawing. The following three scenes echo each other; the house should feel more and more claustrophobic.*

Suzanne What are you writing?

Claude Nothing.

Suzanne Well don't waste paper on nothing. It's unseemly.

Claude What are *you* working on?

Suzanne Nothing. (*Beat.*) Just a silly drawing.

Claude You haven't drawn in ages. What is it? Show me.

Suzanne I'm not sure – *Attends*! –

Claude *takes hold of the paper.*

Claude What exactly is this?

Suzanne It's just a *brouillon*. Give it back.

Claude No, not yet. Let me look . . . What does this German phrase mean? Does that say 'pigs?'

Suzanne Translated it means 'Go home to your squealing mommies, little pigs . . .'

Claude (*laughs*) I hope you plan to destroy that.

Suzanne I will. Only I had another of those dreams last night. This time I dreamed that the officers tried to raise up their hideous swastika flag at their HQ and instead what came up was our *Tricolore*. The one we hid in the latrine. In my dream I was the one who had switched the flags.

Claude You wouldn't.

Suzanne I won't actually do that, Claude. But can't we do *something*?

Claude We *are* doing something. Our job is to *not* get arrested.

Suzanne That's not enough. I'm sick of doing nothing. I don't want to ration paper anymore. I don't want to eat soup made from vegetable skins or worry that another of our friends has disappeared. People are being rounded up! Where the fuck are they being taken to?

Claude You need to keep your voice down. Do you think I don't know all that? But someone might hear you. We can't trust anyone anymore.

Suzanne What happened to all your bravado? You're telling me to keep my voice down? You? The one who used to dance all night on the street, drunk, singing with the musicians until you lost your voice? You, who dragged ME into *Contre-Attaque* with all those arrogant men like Breton so you could wage surrealist battle on fascism – you want *me* to be quiet?

Claude You're not the one they're after. You're not the Jew.

Suzanne (*is stung by this*) I am a Jew too, inside, where it counts. And we're *both* disgusting homosexuals to them.

Claude (*beat*) I know.

Suzanne I'm sick of doing nothing, Claude. If I were a man I would sail to London right now and enlist with the Allies.

Claude Or join a band of resistors and blow up some train tracks.

Suzanne Or steal some guns.

Claude Or kill a German. Slit his throat.

Suzanne No.

Claude Just how far would you go, *chérie*?

Scene Seven

Title: Reprise

Image: Another of Suzanne's propaganda cartoons.

Music: Rain falling. Hum. Snare drum. Drip/leaking/ticking hints at upcoming adventure music from 'Paper Route' scene.

Suzanne What are you writing?

Claude Nothing.

Suzanne Well, don't waste paper on nothing. It's unseemly.

Beat. Sound of drip.

Suzanne I had that dream again last night.

Claude The flag?

Suzanne Yeah.

Beat. Sound of drip.

Suzanne I passed a soldier today on the High Street. He looked so young, still a kid. And was he ever cute, with a little smile as he wished me *bonjour* . . . Why is he here? Why did he join the army? He seemed so sweet.

Claude Maybe so, but I wouldn't trust him.

Suzanne Oh I don't trust him either. But it made me think – maybe a few of them just got swept up in the frenzy. Maybe they were poor and had no future. Maybe they love their country and got confused about how to show that love.

Claude But they're here. An occupying force. Looking to arrest or deport us.

Suzanne Could we convince them not to? Could we convince them to quit, leave, even stand up to Hitler?

Claude Impossible.

Suzanne In *Contre Attaque*!? Your pamphlets, your leaflets – we passed those around Paris to convince people to join you. And some of them were funny!

Claude Like that cartoon you showed me with the pigs . . . You think pamphlets could convince them to leave Jersey?

Suzanne Maybe. I bet they only hear Berlin-approved news. I bet they don't even know the truth.

Claude We could distribute bulletins telling them what's really happening: show them the truth.

Suzanne I could translate the news from the BBC into *der Muttersprache*. Type it all in German. Remind them that the Allies haven't given up, that Germany isn't invincible.

Claude Convince them to defect before it's too late . . . It doesn't make sense that they all could be so . . .

Suzanne But it would have to be just the two of us. We can't trust anyone. You said so yourself. It's not safe.

Claude I know. I know.

Scene Eight

Title: 'Resistance Q'

Image: One of Suzanne's propaganda cartoons.

Music: Hum. Drip. Snare drum. Ticking/leaking/dripping of 'Paper Route' as the idea grows.

Suzanne What are you writing?

Claude Nothing.

Suzanne Well don't waste paper on nothing. It's unseemly.

Claude Ok, then, what have you got?

Suzanne I think our best strategy is the angle of dissuasion – instead of persuasion. Not so much *propaganda* as . . . I don't know what to call it. And you'll have to trust me on the German.

Claude Fine. Let's hear it.

Suzanne Ok, three options. First: 'The Fatherland is bereft without us! Defect Defect Defect!'

Claude Too long.

Suzanne Ok . . . Second option: 'Get the fuck off our island.'

Claude Seriously?

Suzanne Of course not! (*Beat.*) But I keep having that dream –

Claude What about: 'We're going down! Abandon ship!' and we sign it: *Le soldat inconnu* . . . I like it. It has a certain . . . flair.

Suzanne *Le soldat inconnu.* '*Der Soldat ohne Namen.*' The Soldier with No Name.

Claude Admittedly I do like your suggestion of 'Get the fuck off our island.'

Suzanne And then tomorrow we'll follow the serving staff into the mess hall and put these tracts under the plates. 'What's for lunch today, Hans? Oh, a note!'

Claude You know how they keep having their funerals in *our* churchyard? I bet when they're not paying attention, we could put these on the windshields of their waiting cars.

Suzanne I like it.

Claude Let's do it.

Scene Nine

Title: 'Paper Route'

Image/Video: Propaganda cartoons / Resist / Witness.

Music: Adventure music begins on heels of 'Let's do it' in previous scene so that the transition is seamless. The music is Morse-coded, furtive, at times humorous and other times tense.

This is a silent Clown Ode/Interlude/Vaudeville bit. **Suzanne** *and* **Claude**, *costumed as elderly women, deliver leaflets around the theatre as if doing so secretly in the village: carefully in the mess hall, under windshield wipers, slipping them into cigarette packages et cetera encouraging people to pass them along through the audience; the lazzis build in intensity and elaborateness. In production the dressmaker's mannequin played a starring role in this scene (dressed in a German Officer's uniform) and a Paper Drop was done from the ceiling so propaganda leaflets rained down on the audience at the scene's climax.*

Scene Ten

Image: Combat de pierres, *1931.*

Music: Electric hum with dark piano rumble and reverse cymbal. Wincing, metallic, awful.

Suzanne *is waiting up for* **Claude**. *The house looks even more shabby than it did. Electricity is off again; just two or three candles light the space.* **Suzanne** *lights a* *candle. It is dark – past curfew, night – and* **Claude** *should be home by now. With each sound Suzanne hears, she startles.* **Claude** *enters.*

Suzanne *Mon amour*! What happened? Oh my God.

Claude I'm fine, help me to sit down.

Suzanne You're not fine. Are you hurt? You're hurt.

Claude Don't shout. Please. I'm fine.

Claude *sits carefully on a chair.* **Suzanne** *begins to undress* **Claude**; **Claude** *is covered in bruises and blood. The undressing happens very slowly, by candlelight.*

Claude Suzanne. *Suzoleh* . . .

Suzanne Shh, sweetie. Please don't say anything. I'm going to bring some hot water and soap to wash you, ok?

Claude I don't want you to see.

Suzanne Let me.

Suzanne *returns with water and begins to bathe a now shivering* **Claude**, *who can't speak yet.*

Suzanne Shhh, shhh, shhh.

Music: 'À la Claire Fontaine' reprise; add drone; add wail. **Suzanne** *hums the song to stay calm.*

Claude There were six of them, on patrol. They stopped me – they said it was past curfew but it wasn't, it was still light out. They pushed me around and called me names. Bitch. Cunt. Dyke. Not Jew – they didn't guess that. Thank God. Then they forced themselves on me. They took turns. And then one beat me up because finally it was dark and it was past curfew, then, and the others watched and laughed. Then they left me on the road.

Suzanne Shhh, shhh, sweetie . . . *Chéri*(*e*), I've got you. Shh, shh, baby, I've got you.

Claude *begins to cry but can't; their silent cry becomes a wail in the music. The sound of boots on cobblestone streets mixes with the lullaby and the wail.*

Scene Eleven

Title: 'Le soldat inconnu. "Der Soldat ohne Namen." *The Soldier with No Name.'*

Image/Video: Revolution certain.

Music: Electric hum (subliminally) rises and falls in intensity.

Six weeks later. The house is more claustrophobic. **Claude** *is sitting still, in a chair, thinking.* **Suzanne** *comes in from outside. Long, uncomfortable pause before* **Suzanne** *speaks.*

Suzanne You won't believe what I heard on the road. Apparently, even though I can barely believe it, *les Boschs* think there is a GANG of resistors at work here on Jersey. Here!

Claude Why? Because of our shitty leaflets?

Suzanne Because of our *relentless* shitty leaflets! Because there has been so much propaganda and so many small acts of insurrection. They are going to search the woods to find the gang of resistors who they think must be hiding there. I was so shocked; it was hard not to react. But then they would have seen I understood their German.

Claude What did they say exactly?

Suzanne They think we're an army. Well, not quite that. But more numerous than two little old ladies.

Claude Speak for yourself, *ma chère*.

Suzanne Well, in any case it's working. They're getting nervous.

Claude They'll be so pissed when they spend hours in the rain looking for us.

Suzanne I hope they don't actually come across any resistors and hurt them. While looking for us.

Claude They might. It's possible.

Suzanne But wouldn't we know of them?

Claude I don't know. Would they know of us? Did anyone see you when you overheard that conversation with the Germans? Did anyone see that you *understood*?

Suzanne I don't think so.

Claude Ok. Good. If they're beginning to get worried –

Suzanne – it means it's working . . .

Claude If only they would just fuck off.

Suzanne . . . This is an opportunity to do something really big.

Claude There are two of us and a whole barracks-full of them!

Suzanne And yet we've managed to get under their skin. They're nervous. And they think we're a whole gang. I bet they also think we're men.

Claude Probably.

Suzanne What if . . . I disguise myself as a soldier and go listen to what they're planning . . . infiltrate their HQ!

Claude Now you're going to become a spy?

Suzanne Observer, Claude. I want to *do* something. Make them pay for what they did to you . . . You used to disguise yourself for years; it can't be that hard.

Claude You know that wasn't a disguise. *THIS* is a disguise!

Suzanne That's not what I mean! I mean you were convincing as a soldier. In your photographs and onstage you played any character – soldier, sailor – I watched you that whole time . . . I could do it too.

Claude Suzanne, that wasn't just theatre for me. That wasn't just make-believe. That was – is who I am – This is not. (*Gutted by this betrayal.*)

Suzanne I didn't mean to . . . suggest it wasn't important for you to wear men's clothes. But couldn't I do that, Claude? Disguise myself as a German soldier and break in and listen to them? Couldn't I pretend to be one of them?

Claude Stop. Just stop . . . Disguise yourself? Five years of me being forced to wear this – this fucking skirt – being trapped like – an animal – Have you forgotten who I am? Have you forgotten, Suzanne? Do you even know me? This has never been me.

Suzanne I didn't mean to – it wasn't about you –

Claude It's different for you. You are yourself either way, in pants or in a skirt. But I need to choose. I need to decide – for me – how I'm seen. Who I am in the world.

Suzanne None of us has that luxury anymore.

Claude You do! I'm the one who has a target on my back. I'm the Jew! And I'm the one who looks like – an invert. They attacked me! You could just – leave – fade into the countryside.

Suzanne Leave? Is that what you really want? You don't mean that. I have never left you and I never will.

Claude Listen to me, Suzanne. You need to leave. I need you to go someplace safe – and forget your bullshit plan –

Suzanne You haven't even heard my plan.

Claude You have no plan! You would be discovered in a second! Suzanne. Look at yourself. The leaflets are one thing. It's been dangerous doing just that. But breaking into the HQ? That's just madness. No one would ever believe you were a German soldier. You'd never pass. I forbid it.

Suzanne Claude – Claude . . .

Beat.

Claude I'm the one who's going to do it.

Suzanne Do what? Be a German soldier?

Claude I'm going to switch the flag.

Suzanne What?

Claude Like in your dream. Don't you still dream of switching the flag, of getting rid of their swastika? I could change it to the Union Jack or the *Tricolore* –

Suzanne *That* is never going to work. Your German isn't good enough! The minute you spoke you would be found out. It would be a suicide mission.

Claude You've been right all along, Suzanne. We do need to do something big. But we need to do it *right*. You keep dreaming of the flag. I keep dreaming of being attacked on the street and the stench of their bodies as they . . . I am NOT going to wait until that happens to me again – or to you – God forbid (*spits*) – and I am not going to die slowly in some labour camp or *disappear* like our friends have. I'm ready to fight. If they want me, they'll have to catch me.

Scene Twelve

Title: 'Kaleidoscope'

Music: Pre-recorded collage soundscape of voices and À la Claire Fontaine *theme, in combination with live piano rumble, snare drum, and harp. Disorienting, spinning, thunderous.*

Claude *begins to transform into the Soldier with No Name.* **Suzanne** *helps with this transformation.*

Voice over.

Claude Auto-portraiture is not a selfish, egotistical whimsy. It is practical. It is simpler to use myself rather than someone else, *c'est tout*.

Suzanne Claude was the only one I ever needed, ever wanted.

Claude I always knew. Most people know from a young age, not necessarily that they love women, or men if they're men, but they know they're different. Something sets them apart.

Suzanne *À la claire fontaine, m'en allant promener*. *J'ai trouvé l'eau si belle* . . .

Claude One day they tied me to a tree and pelted me with rocks.

Suzanne – *Que je m'y suis baigné* . . .

Claude Then they left me on the road.

Suzanne *Heil* Claude Cahun! *Heil* Marcel Moore! *Heil les gaies Parisiennes*!

Claude For me, it's like my body never matched me.

Suzanne I had another of those dreams last night.

Claude The inside of my head was on fire when I acted like a good little girl.

Suzanne It was Claude's God I wanted to know.

Claude It was just us. Suzanne and me. *C'est tout*.

Suzanne . . . *jamais je ne t'oublierai* . . .

Claude It was always just the two of us.

Sound: The soundscape quiets to a sustain before building back up.

Dialogue is now resumed by the actors. **Claude** *now wears a repurposed, German-looking army uniform that* **Suzanne** *has been mending throughout Act Two; it was on the mannequin.*

Claude And once I've switched the flag, what's the plan? What do I need to do?

Suzanne It's simple: end the war, my love.

Claude And if it doesn't work? And I get captured?

Suzanne Then I burn all the evidence.

Claude And if they kill me?

Suzanne Then I take the pills. And we meet each other again on the other side.

Beat.

Suzanne *Bonne chance, mon amour.*

Claude *Je t'aime, ma chère.*

Sound and Music: Building to CHAOS. Boots on the cobblestone; marching; 'Heil Hitlers!' and then CHAOS: running; gunshots; chaos; yelling in German; fire. Simultaneously **Claude** *and* **Suzanne** *are stopped.*

Sound: HALT! Halt gleich da! Sie sind festgenommen!

Claude Took you long enough. **Suzanne** Took you long enough.

Sound FX: Prison doors being slammed shut.

Scene Thirteen

Title: 'The Confession'

Music: Snare drum used to signify punches/hits/slaps.

In a German prison on Jersey. **Suzanne** *and* **Claude** *are held in separate cells.* **Claude** *is being interrogated.* **Suzanne** *strains to hear from her cell.*

Claude What else can I tell you? It's not my problem that you don't believe me. We did it all, *for years*. All by our lonesome. Without any man. And I know Suzanne has been telling you the same thing! It's you and your people who are ignoring the facts! We're not covering for anyone. We didn't have a leader. No man at the helm. No 'Mr. X.' It was just us: the slogans, the leaflets, the propaganda. As for the switched flag at the very heart of your precious HQ – that was me. Alone. That was way too easy, by the way: I had the French flag rolled up in my trousers. No one doubted me for a second. I can't believe how blind you can be. I walked all the way through the town to the barracks, all the way inside your headquarters, and executed each part of the plan: leaflets in your officers' coat pockets: check. Revolver stolen and placed in *my* pocket: check. Mess hall Radio Berlin switched to the BBC: check. Portrait of your *Führer* defaced: check. Requisite '*Heil Hitlers*' and heel-clicking: check. Did you know I made it all the way to your *Kommandant*'s office and tasted some of his whisky? It was lovely. His secretary is pretty good-looking, wouldn't you say? . . . For all your worries about a gang of resistors storming the barracks, your security is shit. The only reason you caught me is because I drank too much of that whiskey and made a pass at your *Kommandant*'s secretary . . . I was out of practice, as was my German . . . *Hélas*. That wasn't part of the plan. But what did I have to lose? I was as good as dead anyway. *Vive la France*! *Vive la France*! (*Sings:*)

'*Allons enfants de la Patrie! / Le jour de gloire est arrivé*!'

Claude *reels back from being slapped.*

Sound/Music: **Suzanne***'s voice takes up the song and bangs on a bucket;* **Bandleader** *defiant voices join from the prison to sing 'La Marseillaise'* (*rough, rowdy, a capella*):

'*Contre nous, de la tyrannie,/*

L'étendard sanglant est levé;/

l'étendard sanglant est levé./'

Claude You hear that?! (*Shouts:*) I hear you, Suzanne! *Vive la France*!

[All together] *Aux armes, citoyens*! / *Formez, vos bataillons*!

Claude *is hit again.*

Sound/Music: (*broken up, and from all around the prison:*)

'*Marchons, marchons*!

Qu'un sang impur,

Abreuve nos sillons!'

Claude *is hit again.* **Suzanne** *is hit. The singing stops abruptly.*

Claude Fuck you. I'm not lying! There is no Mr X! Oh my God what kind of proof do you need? I executed the plan at your HQ – not Suzanne – she had nothing to do with that – but somehow you can't get it through your skulls that anyone other than a man could do anything against you. I'm sorry your little boy soldiers were so scared of . . . two old . . . *spinsters* . . . But I can't confess to something that isn't true. It was just us. Suzanne and me. *C'est tout*. (*To audience.*) It was always just the two of us. But believe what you like. We know what we did.

Scene Fourteen

Title: 'Libération'

Image/Video: Photos of the Liberation of Jersey, including the one with Cahun in crowd.

Music: Music of liberation and triumph. 'La Marseillaise' *reprise. Snare, accordion. Marching, victorious music.*

Claude *and* **Suzanne** *reunite after the Liberation.*

Radio This is the BBC World Service bringing you Prime Minister Winston Churchill: 'Hostilities will end officially at 1 minute to midnight tonight Tuesday the 8th of May 1945. The German war is therefore at an end. Today is Victory in Europe Day.' The war is over! I repeat: the war is over! The Germans are retreating. Paris has been liberated! Belgium is free. The Dutch are still starving. That fucker Hitler is dead. The Americans are taking credit for everything; but they will have the horrific task of liberating the camps and won't ever forget it –

Scene Fifteen

Title: 'An Ode to the Liberation'

Music: Accordion.

Claude May we present:

Together An Ode to the Liberation.

Suzanne By Claude and Marcel // **Claude** By Marcel and Claude//

Claude Maestro, some music if you please . . .

Music: A cheerful and ironic musical response accompanies these clown scenes. Prestissimo oom-pah and irreverent.

Scene Fifteen A: Two Men at the Bistro

Claude Hé ho, *camarade*?

Suzanne *Oui, mon homme*?

Claude Are we still in prison?

Suzanne *Non, mon ami.* We are at the bistro in the *village*. The war is over.

Claude Does this mean we can eat cheese again?

Suzanne *Oui mon ami.*

Claude *Vive la France.*

Suzanne God Save the King!

Claude Hé ho, *camarade*?

Suzanne *Oui, mon gros*?

Claude If the war is over, does that mean we are free?

Music: Musical flourish.

Scene Fifteen B: Two Men on the Road

Suzanne Bonjour Pierre.

Claude Bonjour, Jean.

Suzanne I wonder if you could tell me – has *Madame Lévi* come home?

Claude Yes, she came back just a few days ago . . . But not *Monsieur Lévi* . . .

Suzanne Aaah . . . *quelle dommage.*

Claude *Hélas* . . . And have you seen *Mademoiselle* Schwob and *Mademoiselle* Malherbe since they were freed?

Suzanne *Non*, not yet. How long were they imprisoned for, in the end? A year?

Claude Ah, I don't remember. How long were those fuckers here?

Suzanne I don't remember. Forever? Ten years?

Claude Five years. Five years that felt like ten years.

Suzanne You got old in that time, *mon ami.*

Claude You died in that time, *mon gros.*

Music: Flourish.

Scene Fifteen C: In the Bistro, bis

Claude Hé ho, *camarade*?

Suzanne *Oui, mon homme*?

Claude Are we still in prison?

Suzanne *Non*! We are again at the bistro in the *village*!

Claude Oh. *D'accord*. . . . *Hé ho, camarade*? When we were in prison, did anything funny happen?

Suzanne Funny?! . . . Well there was that one time someone tried to hang himself but he couldn't get his *pyjama* to knot together quite right and it was awkward and eventually he cried out *'au secours!'* until one of the guards came in and untied him. That was pretty funny, because he did not die.

Claude Haha! Oh yeah! And I remember when one of those two old ladies tried to kill herself and couldn't! I can't remember if it was *Mademoiselle* Malherbe or *Mademoiselle* Schwob. But *anyway* she tried to cut up her wrists but the knife she had stolen wasn't sharp enough and she was bleeding and she was crying, and then the other lady, she was in a different cell and she couldn't help her, but she could hear her crying, and then *she* was crying, and it was terrible.

Suzanne *Nom de Dieu*! *Mon homme*! That wasn't funny at all.

Claude *Non*?

Suzanne *Non*! That wasn't funny at all!

Music: Flourish.

Scene Fifteen D: In the Market

Suzanne *Bonjour* Michelle.

Claude Good morning Sylvie. Did you hear what I heard about how our two lady artists survived their captivity?

Suzanne Yes! I did! They had sex with the guards!

Claude My goodness, non! (*Tittering*.) How crude! No, it was because the officers needed permission from Hitler himself to execute female prisoners . . . and somehow their execution kept getting delayed and delayed until finally Jersey was liberated!

Suzanne But they could have been killed!

Claude They *should* have been killed. (*Beat*.) They're Jews! (*Beat*.) But they weren't killed, they survived.

Suzanne Not everyone survived.

Claude No. Not everyone survived.

Music: Final flourish.

Suzanne *and* **Claude** *take their bows.* **Claude** *disappears.* **Suzanne** *is alone.*

Scene Sixteen

Title: '19 February, 1972'

Image/Video: Autoportraits / negatives c. *1948 of Claude in garden and seaside in Jersey.*

Music: Sound of the sea: sea birds, crashing waves, smell of salt, as elsewhere. 'À la claire fontaine' *reprise. Harp. Inexorable, eternal, resolute.*

At top of scene **Suzanne** *is at the trunk, as in Prologue, with notebook.*

Suzanne My love. I've been reading through all our old papers. At least, what remained after *les Boschs* raided the house while we were in prison. I found the manuscript to the 'Tell-All-Memoir' Adrienne had asked you to write all those years ago. You never told me you had taken up her challenge – it's beautiful. I liked reading about us when we were young, and about you, in your voice. I wish I had known you were working on it. I would have encouraged you: it's not *at all* a second rate book written by and for old ladies! I wish you could have finished this memoir ... I've been amusing myself by writing some responses, adding a few confessions of my own to complement yours. I made it a two-hander! A duet. Like our old theatricals (Beat) I'm *tired.* I went to the doctor last week and he says I'm as healthy as a horse – he said I could live for decades. Can you believe it? Decades! I asked if he could prescribe a quick cancer like the one that did in Gertrude but he didn't think that was funny. I still feel guilty that you died when you did; you should have lived until a hundred and twenty. I know it was our time in prison that weakened you, and you never blamed me for what got us there – you just blamed those bastards – but you were never the same again. After you died, my pictures were full of your ghost . . . I'm going to make sure that you're remembered correctly, so I've burned everything I could find that suggests I helped you with the auto-portraits – some of your notes, my memoirs. The auto-portraits are yours now, entirely. I used to care but I don't care now. More than anything, I want you to be remembered for your boldness, your inventiveness, your courage, your brilliance. The auto-portraits can do that. My final work is this: to make sure you're going to be remembered as you wanted to be, and it makes me glad . . . My Claude. L. S. M. *Elles s'aiment*. Now for one last *Kaddish* in your name, my love.

Suzanne *places a stone as if on a gravestone. She lights a candle and whispers 'The Mourner's Kaddish' as she gathers up several stones and puts them into her pockets.*

À bientôt, mon amour.

Epilogue

Image 1: Landscape of Jersey seaside.

Music: Continuous with music of previous scene.

Suzanne *walks towards the shore. There is* **Claude** *in the water, waving like in the Act One Prologue, or simply listening or waiting after the previous monologue:* **Claude** *has heard all of* **Suzanne***'s words. Now* **Claude** *beckons for* **Suzanne** *to join them. This time* **Suzanne** *walks towards* **Claude**. *They take hands and hold on.*

Images 2, 3, 4, 5/Video: Portrait of Suzanne Malherbe 1928 (with striped cap, at mirror) and Autoportrait *of Claude Cahun 1928 (in checked jacket, at mirror) merge with photos of the two actors recreating the same photographs.*

The theatre lights dim with the rush of the seascape until the only light is the flame of the remembrance candle.

The End.

The Kahena: Berber Queen

A versified play in three acts and seven scenes

Berthe Bénichou-Aboulker

Translated by Jessica Benhamou

Synopsis

Written by Berthe Bénichou-Aboulker, the first published female playwright of Algeria, and translated by Jessica Benhamou, *The Kahena: Berber Queen* tells the story of the warrior queen and seer, Kahena, often described as the Jewish Joan of Arc. A feminist tale of love, revenge, political and religious freedom, this legendary figure leads her Berber people in resistance to the Umayyad Caliphate invasion of North Africa in the seventh century CE.

The Playwright

Berthe Bénichou-Aboulker was born in Oran, French Algeria, in 1886. She was a writer, musician, singer, painter and an active member of numerous Jewish intellectual circles in Algiers. Bénichou-Aboulker published a number of collections of poems and plays, becoming the first published female playwright of Algeria. During the Second World War, she and her family had a leading role in the Algerian Resistance. Her husband received the Médaille de la Résistance, her son José was awarded the Croix de la Libération, and her daughter, Colette, the Croix de Guerre.

The Translator

Jessica Benhamou is a writer and filmmaker whose father is a French-Algerian repatriate. Having grown up in three countries, she is committed to shining a light on captivating stories from around the world. Her films have been BIFA-longlisted and screened at BAFTA and Academy Award festivals such as BFI Flare, Edinburgh and the UK Jewish Film Festival. Jessica is excited to be bringing the titular Kahena to a wider readership, particularly as she likes to imagine that this fiercely stubborn, legendary warrior queen could be a distant ancestor.

Translator's Note

I would like to thank my father, Albert Benhamou, who has helped me immensely with this translation and who supports me in all that I do.

Berthe Bénichou-Aboulker's French-language play, *The Kahena: Berber Queen*, was published in 1933 around thirty years before the Algerian War of Independence. It has the unique status of being the first published play by a woman in Algeria, and represents a highly underrepresented community and body of literature: that of the Berber Jews from the Maghreb in North Africa.

Around a century earlier, in 1830, France had invaded Algeria, the first colonisation of an Arab country since the days of the Crusades. The Crémieux Decree was passed in 1870, granting French citizenship to Algerian Jews but not to Muslims. This led to growing tensions between indigenous Algerians and by the turn of the century there was a wave of antisemitic riots. Later in 1962, when Algeria finally became independent, all non-Muslims were denied citizenship, ethnically cleansing the country of its 140,000 Jews. These French-Algerian repatriates fled mainly to France – including my own family – and a tiny few moved to the recently created state of Israel.

While the Berber Jews are often thought of as being Sephardi, arriving from Spain and Portugal during the Spanish Inquisition of 1478 to 1834, there is evidence of Jewish settlements in Algeria from at least the Roman period and the time of Carthage. Many Algerian Jewish immigrants are in fact Mizrahi – the Hebrew word for 'Easterner', denoting Jews in North Africa and the Middle East – even if many are unaware of their true heritage.

This play shines a light on a slice of Mizrahi history that has been all but erased and forgotten: that of the extraordinary Berber warrior queen and seer, Kahena, nicknamed the Jewish Joan of Arc. Bénichou-Aboulker conducted considerable research into Kahena's story, reading a number of books that have never been translated into English. She would also have presumably been familiar with the oral history passed down. This play can therefore be considered an important historical source.

Kahena may mean 'prophetess,' 'witch' or 'priestess' (like the Jewish surname 'Cohen') and much of her story is shrouded in mystery. There is even some debate regarding her Jewish heritage. The warring between Jews and Muslims may seem at times uncomfortable to a contemporary audience, but it is noteworthy that both in the play and in Bénichou-Aboulker's Algeria, it was the arrival of a colonial power – the Roman chief and later the French – that ignited a bloody conflict. I trust that any reader will approach this faithful translation with a critical mind also with regards to some of the more dated or religious positions regarding the virtue of virginity and the transgression of marrying non-Jews.

While Bénichou-Aboulker was born and died in Algeria under colonial rule, the heroine of her story fought to defend her homeland, and the Berber Jewry are now dispersed all around the world. The existential struggle for survival at the heart of this play is not unique to Kahena's people, nor is it unique to the Mizrahi and Sephardi Jews of Algeria. It's because of this shared history and trauma that I remain hopeful Algeria will one day invite its Jews to return.

Characters

Julie Tabet, *Kahena*
Rachel, *her mother*
Sarah, *her nurse*
Little Gazelle
Eight maidens
Maids
Berber warriors
Umayyad Caliphate warriors
Prisoners
Crowd

Khaled, *Umayyad Caliphate Prince*
Sekerdid, *Roman Chief*
Tabet, *Son of Enfak, of the Djerraoua tribe*
King Koceïla
Hassan, *The Rhassinid*
Temsit, *Son of The Kahena*
Nefous, *Son of The Kahena*
Tangar
An old man
Koceïla's shadow
A soldier
A chieftain
The Head of the Roums
The Leader of the Numidians
The Leader of the Aureba
The Leader of the Nefuça
The Leader of the Veiled
A priest

In IFRIKIA in the seventh century.

Roums (Romans)

Aureba (Beranès Tribe)

Numidia (Region of Constantine)

Djerraoua (Zenata Tribe)

The Veiled (Bothr Tribe, descendants of Tiski the Lame)

Aurès

The Aurès Mountains, to the south east of Batna, where the highest summits of Algeria rise (2,327 metres), is a captivating region.

They consist of powerful parallel ridges, oriented north south-west, whose tight folds like fabric pleats outline the narrow ridges separated by deep valleys. The mountain range plunges southward in steep escarpments on the Saharan depression which reaches 150 metres at most.

Between the two rims, where one belongs to the cold temperate zone – (mountains, hills, valleys) – while the other touches the torrid zone – (region of El Kantara – Biskra – Sahara) – there are fewer than 100 kilometres as the crow flies and, over this space, one after another along the valleys, are wildly opposed vegetations. Cedars, meadows, green moors and date palms.

These valleys have wonderful aspects: wild gorges, rocks, greenery and hot desert sand.

Here live the Berbers.

Author's Preface

Many historians have studied with interest the story of Julie Tabet, a woman from the Jewish tribe of Djerraouas who was nicknamed Kahena and named Queen of Ifriqiya by all the Berber chiefs, during the struggle undertaken to repel the Umayyad Caliphate invasion towards the end of the seventh century.

They collected their documents in signed books: IbnKhaldun, the Bayan, Al-Bakri, Abu Zakariya, Arab historians and geographers who studied the Maghreb. Some French scholars have translated and commented on these books.

For this work, we have consulted the translations of Baron de Slane, Émile Masqueray, Edmond Fagnan, Aimable Pelissier and Charles de Rémusat and drawn useful information from *The History of North Africa: The Obscure Centuries* ('Le passé de l'Afrique du Nord: les siècles obscurs') by Emile Félix Gautier.

We have collected some precious details in the beautiful lecture given by Mrs Stora-Sudaka on the 'First Jewish Immigrations in Berberia' ('Premieres Immigrations juives en Berbérie.')

Finally, the legend which, in North Africa, surrounds the name of the beautiful Berber heroine, encouraged us to reconstruct her life.

We have very closely followed the story. We didn't ignore the legend and created some characters that, under other names, must have existed: Sarah the nanny, Little Gazelle the dancer and Tangar the old servant. Having been unable to discover in our research the names of Julie Tabet's mother and sons, we named them Rachel, Nefous, Temsit. All other characters are listed under their real names.

Julie Tabet, the Berber Joan of Arc, made headlines in Africa for eleven centuries. This astonishing woman whose beauty was equal, it is said, to her knowledge and audacity, united all the Berber forces after the Berber king Koceïla was killed in front of Mems, and repelled the attacks of Hassan the Rhassinid. She was victorious and drove back the Umayyad Caliphate troops to Tripolitania borders. She reigned for ten to fifteen years. She lived in Kairouan or in her mountainous castle in the Aurès, which she had inherited from her father, Tabet, son of Enfak, prince of the Tribe of Djerraouas.

Contrary to the Arab legend that she ransacked this splendid country, the former granary of Rome, in order to discourage the Umayyad Caliphate invasion, it has now been proven that it would have been impossible for Julie to accomplish these disasters. Instead, she administered her country, which she regarded with a passionate love, with authority and wisdom. Her dream was to set these people, who were hungering for independence, free again. She was called Kahena (the Priestess).

Kahena died after the last fight. For six months, she had held back the superb battalions of Hassan, freshly harnessed, which arrived from Egypt, in front of the citadel of El Djem (the former coliseum of Thydruss, admirably preserved today). Yet, after a year of battle, Hassan had her head cut off and sent it to the Caliph. Her image remains alive in Berber folklore.

Act One

PART ONE

Scene One

A vast hall with plastered walls; the ground paved with enormous flat stones; on the wall horns of gazelles and rams are hung, as well as skins of lions and panthers. On one of the walls, a large tabernacle is covered with a golden hanging with fringes. In each corner, weapons of all sorts lean against the walls; bows, sabres, large cutlasses, axes, etc. . . . and brightly coloured flags.

Stone or wooden benches are covered with panther or goat skins. **Julie** *is lying on one of them.* **Sarah** *fans her.* **Julie** *is dressed in purple fabrics; her sparkling hair is dishevelled. Her nurse wears a camel hair tunic.* **Rachel** *is imposing, dressed in a white tunic, her head girdled with a wide headband to which jewels are encrusted with emeralds and pearls. Around her neck, multiple necklaces with uncut stones.*

Sarah – Rachel – Julie

Sarah
Rest my grace, I will watch over you,
I'm keeping an irritating fly away from your forehead.

Rachel
Sarah! I am consumed with constant dread!

Sarah
Relax, you need to hide your fear,
Look at that broad forehead and that golden mane,
That childish mouth; she's asleep, my dove!

Rachel
How many months, alas! How many more days
Will I see her before lying in my grave?

Sarah
Mistress! We mustn't always be so morbid.
And think of the great departure! See how beautiful she is,
She lights up your nights, she enriches your days,
Sleep, my love, extend your arm, like a wing.
By the hill or to the mountain
On your sweating horse
Racing like a demon
Making sparks fly!
On the plain, near a large lake,
Hunting the flamingo or the beast

Go! Granddaughter of Enfak
Under the velvety, violet sky.
Come back! The nights are sly;
Rest your lovely body,
Your eyes deep as wells,
Your feet that tread the sand
On the burning and treacherous path.
As soon as the dawn appears,
You leave for the arid desert,
Disdainful of adorning yourself
Only with a purple garment
And your hair blowing in the wind,
You go to the reddening sky,
You go! As the sun rises.
On a determined steed.
But he will come, the flatterer
To take you from my wretched heart,
Leaving me to suffer alone!

Rachel
He will come, good nurse,
His stallion flies towards us,
Leaps over the precipice,
He will be here, soon, tomorrow!
Sekerdid is the lieutenant
Of Koceïla, the Berber king,
And, this mighty Roman hopes
To marry our only child.

Sarah
Mistress, what are you saying?

Rachel
The sad truth.

Sarah
What! This young barbarian has some nerve!

Rachel
Dark presentiments blacken my dreams
I would give the world for them to be lies:
Know therefore that Tabet, son of Enfak, my husband,
Fears Koceïla and his murderous army
Fears for his tribe; he wishes to avoid his wrath,
And has agreed to give our proud and innocent child.

Sarah
Your words make my blood stop and turn cold!
She starts opening her eyes, windows to her soul.

Rachel
How to warn her without distressing her?

Julie*, she wakes up, sits down, stretches out her arms.*

Julie
This dream was disturbing, mother!

Sarah
She wants you.

Rachel
Go fetch her some milk and come back to the Palace.

Sarah
From your black goat or the grey jenny-ass?

Rachel
Yesterday, the ass' tongue and palate were inflamed.
And I worry her milk would intoxicate us.

Sarah
Very well, mistress.

She goes out.

Scene Two

Rachel – Julie

Rachel
She looks overwhelmed and aged.

Julie
From now on, she mustn't exert herself.
Why, mother, are you sad and pale and pensive?

Rachel
We have to yield to the laws of the most powerful!
Listen to me, my dear child, my pure star.

Julie
Tears in your beautiful eyes and this quivering,
Don't hide anything from me.

Rachel
You want me to reveal exactly
What concerns and torments me?

Julie
Mother, I beg you!

Rachel

Very well, this Roman leader,
Sekerdid, lieutenant of the King of Numidia,
Poses as a pretender and asks for your hand.

Julie

His demand is disturbing, mother, bold!

Rachel

Tabet would like you to marry this heathen.

Julie

That cruel stranger! I'd prefer death!

Rachel

Never say that word again or I will lose my mind!

Julie

Then it was he I saw, he who followed my steps.

Rachel

What are you talking about! Have you seen him?

Julie

It was so unexpected!
Six moons ago
I was leaping into the light
Crossing sand dunes
On Zina my beautiful mare
She was neighing, I was singing!
Suddenly a guttural voice
Vibrated! I was shaking with anxiety,
While these words resonated
And froze me in horror,
These words were, mother, new to me
Their dreadful memory haunts me!
'Daughter of heaven or earth,
Who are you, young beauty?
If I were an eagle, in my grip
I would steal you away
To my unreachable aerie!
But is this dream impossible?'
'Leave!' I said, 'Be gone by tomorrow!
Your fault is unforgivable
My father would be irritated
If he learned that a Roman
Dares approach me on his land.
He would chase him relentlessly
Out of contempt and hatred.'

Rachel

He must have blanched from vexation!
Ah! Why, to be in solitude,
Do you so love to ride off.
And why always disdain
The effect of my concern?

Julie

At these words the proud horseman
Looked troubled. 'Maiden, forgive me.
A Nomad, a vile camel driver
Would have deserved to be beaten,
I would have deserved it myself,
You reap what you sow!
So young and proud under the heavens,
Look at my anxious repentance.'
Bowing rather low, he left,
And his horse, like an arrow,
Spun off, but in the dry breeze
His gallop resounded for a long time.

Rachel

You know that he will reign here after your father
And he'll chase us away if we refuse this.

Julie

I know, at least he believes it, my dear mother,
Great is God, so let's not assume anything on earth,
Am I not loved by all! Listen to me.
This gift that God gave me, this gift of prophecy
Makes people enthusiastic and stirs them up.
What are you afraid of? I was born to rule.
Do you know my name in the Aurès? The Lioness!
If my den one day were to be invaded
Or if the crown was taken from my head,
My followers, then, would have betrayed me!

Rachel

You get your audacity from Tabet, son of Enfak,
And the tenacity, Julie, you get it from your race.
But it is, believe me, provoking the danger
To fight against this stranger, my child,
Your soul is plain to read, it is a pure crystal
And you don't know how cunning is the jackal!
But here's your father approaching us.
If he would want to force this cruel union,
I am ready to face his wrath for you.

Scene Three

Julie – Tabet – Rachel

Julie
Father! what has become of the faithful courier?

Tabet
I put him to rest, but come my dear treasure
Come and support your father in his cruel ordeal
Approach beloved child, with golden hair
Tell and show me how much you love me.

Julie *wraps her arms around his neck.*

Julie
I show it well and you know it.
Come, so I can hold you tenderly as ever.
Why this sadness! Here all is so calm!
Look outside, the breeze envelops a palm
And sends us from afar the bitter smell of hay,
Ignore your worries, chase them away!

Tabet
Julie and you, Rachel, my beloved angels,
Listen, hear the horses in the plain,
They stamp and trample in the fields on golden wheat
And from Koceïla I already feel the chain,
He comes from Kairouan, he, the victor of Ocba
To force on you, my daughter, a husband.

Julie
What impertinence!

Tabet
Bearers of gifts, warriors from far away
Come here on their camels following his trail.

Rachel
What are we going to become; what must be done,
Oh heavens!

Tabet
Don't worry, I'll go to them alone.

Rachel
But they're going to take you!

Julie
Mother, Father is brave.

Tablet
Let's hide nothing, yes, the hour seems serious,
My warriors are absent, the black body is gone.

Rachel
Unhappy coincidence, so what are we going to do?

Tabet
You now only have one move to make.

Rachel
Which?

Tabet
Go and join your brother in his Palace.

Julie
What, among the Nefuças, the tribes that converted!

Tabet
Through me, my child, they are warned;
Their people have returned to the religion,
Since the Berber King reigns in Ifrikia.

Rachel
Will you, my husband, be welcome near them?

Tabet
They will welcome you with a pure and sincere heart
To them, a parent is sacred and respected.

Rachel
Well, we'll follow you, sir, it's agreed.

Tabet
I find it hard to leave you, dear wife and daughter,
But you two must go without me.

Rachel
Tabet, if you would die, I would die with you,
The sources of my tears would dry up.

Tabet
You try, quite in vain, my wife, to soften me
Go both of you, let me die well,
What! Tabet, son of Enfak, would flee from danger!
No! Whatever my fate, I'm staying put,
No, Rachel, my decision cannot be changed;
In doing so, I will follow the example from my race.
I want, I say, to be alone in the palace of my fathers.
My bones and dust to intermingle with theirs,
In the final hour these images will be dear
To my oppressed heart, sweet to my pains.

Rachel (*to* **Tabet** *then to his servants*)
We will stay, both of us! Tangar and you, Sarah,
We are therefore going to leave
Our daughter in your faithful care.
You have to head to the Sahara,
Pass through the region of rebel oasis
And, joining my older brother from Ifrikia,
Return the child you are given.
Come here, Julie, bid us farewell!

Julie
Mother, this plan is foolish!
Father, deign rather, to listen to your daughter.
Didn't you want, so as not to be besieged,
To send me away from the bosom of the family,
And force me to marry this stranger?

Tabet
To this union, yes, I almost forced you
And pushed by my people;

Rachel
As a hostage,
She would have then been sacrificed so casually?

Tabet (*to* **Rachel**)
Revolted, I kept our love's pledge.

Julie
From a heavy sorrow I am freed
My heart is grateful to you
Oh you, parents whom I venerate,
See me with tender eyes
Tell me, would I be beautiful enough
To move Koceïla,
When I shall share the news
That the Lord entrusted to me.

Tabet
What news? Tell us!

Julie
Be patient; I want to avert disaster
By avoiding their proud wrath.

They go out.

Tabet (*before the tabernacle*)
You have enriched us, Lord, by giving us this star
Powerful God, Eloim, and father of Israel,
Protect my child from this cruel leader.

Spare Julie's immaculate purity.
Give the young heathen a compassionate heart.
Hear me, Lord, make my task easy.
Bring to my lips the striking words.
You know, this child was born in our old age.
She was our pride; she is our tenderness;
She makes your name resound from the highest towers,
She is the Kahena, the ardent prophetess.
Protect her flower, her keen intelligence,
Spare her innocence, spare her beauty,
Save me from a bitter failure in my old age,
Which could result from some atrocity.
Whatever you do, God, blessed be your name.
By the Jews and their leaders who infuriate you on earth
Like an immense chain, and link by link,
We tie our hands to love you, oh! My father!

He bows three times, kisses the tabernacle.

To **Tangar**.
Can't you hear, Tangar, sound the trumpet.
Let's walk to them and hold our heads high.

Curtain.

PART TWO

A great square paved with large stones overlooking the palace of Tabet whose architecture recalls that of present-day Sudan – four tall, square tours. Ramparts. We see in the distance, the mountain, the wooded hills, fields of wheat, cedars, palm trees. When the curtain rises, many warriors descend from their mounts and place themselves near her, horses and camels.

Scene One

Koceïla – Tabet – Sekerdid

Koceïla (*to* **Tabet** *who bows*)

Hello, chief of the Aurès! It is you the son of Enfak
Guerao was his father and his ancestor, Isaac.

Tabet
My late ancestors bore these names, Oh King!

Koceïla
I knew Enfak, a reckless warrior!
In battle he was an awe-inspiring tawny.

Tabet
I like to hear you talk about my father
This tribute flatters my respect for him.

Koceïla
I saw this noble and superb chief fight by my side,
The day when, his combat with Ocba proved fatal!

Tabet
I did not leave him, like a red sheaf,
His blood gushed onto me, his last word vibrated,
Glorifying the author of our independence
When Ocba's army finally fell apart.
Among the songs, the cries of happiness and the dance.
We heard this powerful name: 'Koceïla,
Your name, for all of us, Lord, will be remembered forever!

He beats his chest.

We, the chiefs of the Aurès felt our hearts beating
You avenged our bitter wrath onto Ocba,
And finally freed an enslaved race
From the Umayyad tyrant, but how pleasant
Is the surprise to see you now.

Koceïla (*to* **Sekerdid**)
Tell Tabet what you desire!

Tabet
Your emissaries, my King, gave me your messages.

Koceïla
Tell him, Sekerdid, say for whom you sigh,
Who you long for in your dreams, in your cries.

Sekerdid
It was by chance, one day, that I saw her,
I was in the desert looking at the mirage,
When, suddenly, before my enchanted gaze,
The most beautiful maiden, a disturbing image.
On her dove-grey steed
She was off, in a proud gallop,
The sun that was melting in the sky,
Wrapped her in its halo,
Her leonine hair,
Cast golden reflections
Chief, they set my heart on fire,
I fell in love right then with this treasure!

Koceïla
Do you see his ardour, Tabet?

Tabet
But this child, great King, is only a teenager!

Sekerdid
Oh! Prince, son of Enfak, you must yield,
The vision of this maiden haunts my warrior heart.

Tabet
I sacrificed, King, a fair alliance.

Koceïla
Sekerdid will therefore be her blessed husband,
Bring her to us so we can betroth them right away.

Tabet
Here she comes, but great King, have mercy! Leave her to us;
She is my only child, my joy, my light.

Julie *enters veiled, followed by* **Rachel** *and* **Little Gazelle**.

Scene Two

The same – Julie – Rachel – Little Gazelle

Koceïla
Come, Princess. Now. I don't have all day.

Rachel
May I, great King, address my prayer to you?

Koceïla
First of all, I wish and desire to be heard.
What is this? Let the girl take off her veil.

Julie *reveals herself.*

Koceïla
Your daughter, a maiden! Ah, was that warrior lying?
The one that appears before me is a star from the heavens.

Julie
No, King! I'm not the one you've been told about.
The one who can do anything and who commands princes,
Who has given glory to the people, and dispenses
Her most varied gifts so as to be remembered.

Koceïla
Your seriousness makes you look like these idols
That the Romans take with them when they go to the desert.
But why, young maiden, do you say these words
And why this lightning that flashes through the air?

Julie

Listen, and heed well these words, Koceïla,
It is my all-powerful God, it is Him who inspires them.
Mighty King, an attack will take place in five years;
It will be ruthless, decisive, fearsome.
The King of Egypt in the name of the Allah's Prophet
Assembles an excited, frenzied army.
Defend Ifrikia, prepare for battle.
This time, they will want to break your resistance.
Listen, Koceïla, noble victor of Ocba,
And don't be surprised by my insistence.

She gets up and points her index finger at an invisible point.

Koceïla (*troubled*)

Prophetess, tell me, will I still be victorious?

Julie

Ah! what I see makes me shudder with horror!

She veils her face.

In a distant fog, I see an immense circus,
Surrounded on all sides; the enemy advances,
It's the Umayyad Caliphate warriors,
At the front are the Rijal, the Fursan, the Rumat
Carrying long pikes, a large scimitar
Unfolding their banner. They dismount.

Koceïla

Say more.

Julie (*eyes fixed, hands outstretched*)

Against them come the Berbers.
They clash in a disordered battle
In the blood of horses where their bowels swim,
The horsemen slide; you are thrown off!

Koceïla

But can't you say, finally, if he will defeat me?
Look carefully, which of the two of us will be victorious?

Julie

To my eyes, the picture fades into a fog.

Tabet *and* **Rachel** *enter the Palace.*

Koceïla (*worried*)

Don't you think, Sekerdid, that the maiden is tricking us?

Sekerdid

The people here, my lord, call her Kahena
Everything that she foretells, they say, is infallible.

Koceïla

Kahena, come here, you who leads us,
Beautiful seer, to the edges of the invisible.
You have troubled me, I'm going back to Ifrikia.
You must prepare yourself, young maiden, to follow us.
Zobeir the Egyptian once challenged me,
He is the one who wants to avenge Ocba and pursue me.
Here, the undisputed leader among my soldiers,
Sekerdid the venerable, he wants you for his wife.

Julie

I beseech you, King, do not insist.
You cannot mix the green fruit of the garden with the wild flower
Of the desert. You know what I am.

Koceïla

This Roman chief wants to make you a pledge.
That of a powerful, faithful and tender affection.
Slaves, come here!

The slaves put down bundles on the ground, which they open and from which they remove silk and gold fabrics.

Koceïla *opens a small box and takes out splendid heathen jewels encrusted with sparkling emeralds and rubies. He fastens the necklaces around* **Julie**'s *neck, who lets him do it, resigned or absent, and gives her bracelets and earrings, like the ones that are worn today by the Ouled-Nayils.*

Koceïla

Let the bridegroom make his pledge again.

The slaves follow **Koceïla**.

Scene Three

Sekerdid – Julie

Sekerdid

Human and divine Kahena
Refreshing oasis of the great desert,
Pale-coloured butterfly of the hill
Who flies and flutters in the air
I fled, far from the citadel,
Led by the spirit of Love,
Like a bird, I flap my wings hard
To come and offer you a valiant heart.

Julie (*fierce*)

I am not the one for you, Roman,

I cannot, as you know, marry a Christian.
An intelligent leader would abandon this futile venture.
Otherwise, fear that my call will bring forth Azrael.

Sekerdid (*fiery*)
I do not fear, child, the angel of death,
Every day, I expose my chest to danger,
I only fear those eyes of yours and their strange colour
With that glistening gaze which fascinates me.

Loud cries are heard; the servants, their hair over their faces, weep and wring their hands. **Rachel** *on the doorstep holds out her arms towards* **Julie**.

Scene Four

The Same – Rachel – The Crowd

Rachel (*a cry*)
My child!

Julie
What is it?

Rachel
Your father!

Julie
Well, speak!
Answer me, mother.

Rachel
He fell suddenly!

Julie (*wringing her hands*)
My poor father. He is dead. He is dead! We are cursed!

She falls, they surround her, **Koceïla** *appears, the leaders follow him, all shaking their heads with emotion, the slaves go in all directions and beat their drums, it is the rallying sign. From all sides come women, old people, children, warriors; their cries growing louder and louder.*

The Women
Oh! Ah. Ah! Oh! Ah. Ah!

Scene Five

The Same – The Crowd – Rachel

An Old Man
Weep, women, weep and cover your hair

With ashes; may your cries reach the mountains,
Be heard all across the Aurès, to the furthest parts.
Cry, howl again and cast out the demons!

Women
Oh! Ah. Ah! Oh! Ah. Ah!

A Chief
Dead, alas! Our chief, we mourn him,
The earth will cover his corpse, let's bid him farewell
As a time of misfortune follows one of prosperity,
This dark evening follows a bright morning.

A Soldier
Like a young fawn follows its mother
So, Prince, we followed you,
You the just, you the severe,
You spoke and we listened to you,
You were a chief to us, a brother
And the spring that quenches our thirst.
Alas, who will now protect us
When a leader will bring us down.

A Priest (*dressed in white linen*)
We'll all be praying for you
In your silent house
Death has gripped your pious soul
With its thin finger.

Little Gazelle
I'm crying, I'm distraught
How frightening is death!
It is for you I danced, adorned,
With grace, taking my flight.
You laughed at my light leaps
Like a lion cub, I came and went to please you
Or curled into an arch
Oh master! I was a slave,
But you deigned to break my chains.
In heavens, in a sweet garden
May your soul rest well.

Rachel *and* **Julie**, *followed by the slaves, the chiefs and the maids, enter the palace; the soldiers,* **Koceïla***'s leaders go behind the ramparts, night falls slowly.*

Scene Six

Koceïla – Sekerdid

Koceïla
I regret his death.
He was a loyal and strong leader!

Sekerdid
He asked for a favour, a miracle,
From the God of Israel,
He invoked with fervour,
Leaning over the tabernacle.
Suddenly, we heard these words:
'Put an end to my life,
Lord! That is all I desire.'
With these words, his wife
Rushed to his side,
And with great tenderness
Pressed him against her old heart:
But she was only holding a dead man.
His soul had left his body.
Smiling, effortlessly,
Like a flame that dies at the hearth.

Koceïla
When you followed me to the mountainous region
To save our land and our independence,
I promised then that your reward
Would be to become, one day, the Lord of this region.
Your hour has come, at last, and Tabet's great soul
Has simply returned to his god. We should celebrate.
Come, bid me farewell, and respect my wishes.
Protect the kingdom, and its youth – Kahena.

Sekerdid
King, You have my word – you know my loyalty –
I would come running at once as a faithful servant
Every time you give me the signal
For war, for conflict, for battle, for any quarrel.

They enter the Palace.

Scene Eight

Night is falling, the stars are shining in the sky. From the vast house emerge the warriors, pikes in hand. They form a hedgerow. Slaves carrying lighted torches advance slowly, veiled women follow and moan. **Sarah** *and* **Little Gazelle** *support* **Rachel** *and* **Julie**, *both veiled, followed by* **Koceïla** *and* **Sekerdid**. *On a board covered with lion skins is placed the body of* **Tabet**, *son of Enfak. A priest follows, chanting the prayers; the warriors preceded by the torchbearers take the lead of the procession which marches slowly towards the countryside.*

Curtain.

PART THREE

Scene One

Eight days later, at dawn, in the large hall of the first part, eight young girls with dishevelled red or blonde hair, dressed in white woollen clothes or purple fabrics, enter moaning under the jingling of their bracelets and their necklaces. Here comes the **Kahena**.

The Maidens – **Julie** *(hair covered in ash)* – **Sarah** – **Tangar** – **Little Gazelle**

The Maidens
We beg you on our knees
To avenge us from Sekerdid!

First Maiden
We disturb your mourning
Forgive us, beautiful Princess,
We shudder in terror
Save us, time is of the essence!

Second Maiden
Alas! deaf to my pleas,
Not to force himself on me, a virgin,
That shameful man with claws of a vulture
Stole my perfect innocence!

Third Maiden
Seizing me by force, one evening,
Like an animal attacks its prey;
He condemned me to despair,
Now I drown in my own tears.

Fourth Maiden
My mother wanting to defend me
Exasperated by his cruelty.
He killed her, then, ignoring my cries.
Stripped me naked.

Fifth Maiden
Flanked by his cruel soldiers,
Yesterday, he surrounded my home
Plunging me into eternal tears
All my family! I will surely die of grief.

She falls, the others surround her.

Sixth Maiden
I shudder at the thought of a similar fate,
Every night a young virgin

Is brought to his bed, and I whimper,
I pray as hard as I can, I fast!

Seventh Maiden

He tortured the men
Who watched over you.
But alas, what can armour do
Against such a heinous monster?

Eighth Maiden

He wants us all, but only you
Rock his unfulfilled dreams
He calls for you, sighs and; weak,
Cries over his crime!

All

We beg you on our knees
Avenge us from Sekerdid!

Julie

I understand, my sisters, cry no more.
And leave me now. Your Princess
Will save you and will relieve
Your hearts of this distress.

They exit.

Little Gazelle, come here
Go warn the armed men
Say a dream revealed to me
That soon their alarms will cease
Let all my people come here,
Brave, ready to defend me.

Little Gazelle *exit.*

To **Tangar**.

You, old servant, go too
Tell Sekerdid to come,
Without delay, to join me,
That I'm wasting away waiting
And that I quiver with emotion;
Let him prepare his tent
For his tender and submissive wife.

Tangar *exits.*

To **Sarah**.

Bring the old wine that is intoxicating
And put a cup on the table
Almond cakes and milk,

Take honey bread and cut slices.
I must go and prepare myself.

She goes to the back.

Scene Two

Sarah
The evening star has risen eight times
Since our chief Tabet has passed
And sweet Rachel, inconsolable wife
Wants to join her noble husband at the bottom of the sand.
However, Kahena, generous lioness,
Goes near Sekerdid pretending to be in love
Then will avenge her father and her oppressed people.
But here is the tyrant, he arrives in haste,
With his guards in front. Child! You must get down;
But, quick, remove the ashes from your hair.

Scene Three

The **Kahena** *gets down and comes to the fore. She is magnificent and covered in Berber jewels, necklaces, bracelets, rings. She is wearing a white tunic with a golden hem. A purple drape thrown behind her, trailing on the ground, makes her seem imposing. The clicking of weapons can be heard, followed by the sudden stop of horses on the paving of the courtyard.*

Sekerdid – Julie – Sarah

Sekerdid (*to his soldiers*)
Soldiers! Rest near your mounts,
And wait.

He enters, **Sarah** *closes the door.*

Here I am, Princess! And overjoyed.
I have come at your call and bless nature
For having made you beautiful and pure.

Julie
Spare me your words, your Highness!

Sekerdid
Come here, come closer, I like this hairstyle
The rubies on your skin launch their sparkles like fire,
But they are not as bright as those dark eyes.
I would never have believed you'd please me so much,
Julie, but, when far from you, I was pining.

Julie

Your affection, for me, is it without flaws?
I've been told that each day in your tent,
A new maiden, tearful and unwilling,
Eased your sorrow. Are these reports false?

Sekerdid

They are true, Kahena, I tried in their arms
To fill the abyss of our painful separation.
But with no luck, child, you will know it,
Hours, days of waiting passed sad and slow.

Julie

Your words are like honey!
But behind this sweetness
There's a cold, unwavering cruelty, it is said,
Once you're done with this maiden
You make her watch as her mother and her sister
Have their throat slit!

Sekerdid (*laughing*)

The spy who informed you will meet a quick death
Are you really the daughter of a daring warrior
To be so moved by the rightful spoils of war?
But, let's forget about all that, and of my passion,
Julie, hear again its faithful devotion.

Julie (*gets up*)

No! I could not accept the love of an executioner.
When the people compare you to my much-loved father
They mourn his gentle firmness, his integrity.
A monster like you can no longer live!

She thrusts a large dagger into his heart. **Sekerdid** *falls with a gasp.* **Sarah** *approaches, trembling, pale.* **Julie** *is amazed at her own action and stares at the blade.*

Sarah (*taking her in her arms*)

Oh! Second Judith so brave, so strong,
The people will be celebrating their liberation tonight!
Sekerdid has gone! The wild beast is dead
You removed sadness and darkness from our faces!

She looks outside and opens the door wide in front of the crowd that has come to her call. **Julie** *advances, raising her bloody hands. – Murmur).*

Scene Five

Julie – The Crowd – The Maidens – Chiefs – Warriors – Sarah

Julie

Women! Soldiers and you great chiefs, look at my hands!

The Crowd

They are red!

Julie

Red from the blood of the oppressor
Who carried out inhumane acts on you.
I wanted, my people, to be your defender.
By removing the culprit; I invite you to judge me!

The Crowd

Glory to the Kahena who killed the heathen!
May the holy prophetess reign forever!
For us all she was, in the face of danger,
Devoted to the Land, without fear nor weakness.

The Maidens

Oh, superb Kahena, Oh great Kahena.
Great in courage, her heart full of kindness,
You avenged us! Your name will become legend!
It will live on for all eternity!

A Chief

Come women, warriors, people, come in great crowds.

They approach.

Like the southern wind whips the sand into movement,
Your presence inspires the people to rise up.
Be our queen, Kahena, for this moving act.
Now command after Tabet this prosperous land,
We will follow you everywhere and we will obey you.

The Warriors

Queen, you have inspired joy and hope again.
Kahena, if necessary, we would die for you.

Julie

Valiant people, thank you! I want only to be worthy
Of the hopes and dreams you entrust to me,
If you all wish to follow me, know this,
My people, my warriors, soft will be my rule!
Let me, now, have time alone to recover and mourn
And ask forgiveness from my adorable mother
For not having been able to either pray all this time or pick
From the tree of regret that sad and hardy flower
O, my sweet father! If you can read in my heart,
You will know why I avenged your pain.

Shouts in the crowd: Glory to the **Kahena***!*

Curtain.

Act Two

PART ONE

Scene One

A rough terrain on the hill where the Berber horsemen stand. The horses neigh, the camels bray; we hear cries, complaints, shouts of 'Allah, Allah, Muhammad' or 'Listen Israel' or even 'Gursil, God of war' or 'Blessed Virgin Mary', or 'Oh you God of battles' and further groans.

On the front of the stage, on the left, there's a large tent. **Old Sarah**, *hunched with age, comes out, supported by* **Little Gazelle**, *more of a woman than in the first act. Sheep and camels graze in the distance.*

Sarah – Little Gazelle – Tangar

Sarah
Do you hear the heartrending lament of the dying?

Little Gazelle
I hear the hoarse and warlike cry of our soldiers,
The clamours of combat, the delirious crowd.

Tangar
Hidden by the branches of a large mulberry tree
I could see the battle. Hassan the Rhassinid
Overwhelmed by the Bothr and the Numidian warrior
Runs away at full speed with his battalion
A few warriors still face the whirlwind,
Try to resist, but we break their line
We all rally around the red ensign
That the noble Kahena wears in her hair.

Sarah
I would like to see her, but what is our queen doing?

Tangar
She runs singing all around the plain
We can hear up to here the clamouring 'hosanna'
I could see from my tree through the foliage
Seeming much smaller from the distance
Her horse carrying her through the carnage.

Sarah
Alas! what you say adds to my torment!

Tangar

She is the most valiant and the most bold
But this audacity is hereditary for Julie.

Scene Two

A Chief *on the hill addresses the invisible warriors.*

The Same.

The Chief

The Umayyad Caliphate have finally broken the chain
They flee, sinking their spurs into the flanks of the horses.
Here, soldiers, are new times!
Djeraouas go, salute your Queen,
Share her triumph and behold the glory
Given to noble hearts by a noble victory.

The Chief *and the horsemen leave.*

Scene Three

Sarah – Little Gazelle – Tangar

Sarah

She finally knows the superb triumph!
Burst you, my old heart, from joy and from pride!
The child that I fed and who played on the grass
Who I protected from the evil eye,
With whom we went to the sinking sands
To rolled or sleep in her youngest years
Who sucked at my breast, a pure, sweet milk
It was you, Kahena, my admirable warrior!

Little Gazelle

I fed her sons, her two teenagers,
So similar to two flowering shrubs
I can't wait to see them, joyful with us
Relaxing on cushions of gold and silk
To give free rein, nurse, to my happiness;
I want to laugh and dance, sing in their honour,
My body is still supple and I feel light
As at the age when I used to walk, being only a shepherdess
Through the plain or the mounts leading my herd
Only wearing a short tunic on the skin
And sing with a shepherd, to the soft sound of a flute
And dance, then to join my mother in her hut!

Tangar

It was there that one day, Tabet, son of Enfak, found you.
You were weeping over the body of your dying mother,
But he, a pillar of strength, sensitive to your fateful ordeal,
Brought you into the palace as a servant.

Sarah

Yes, but on a festive night, forgetting your condition
and your feet agitated at the sound of the cymbal
You leapt like an antelope in the middle of the room
Since then, from the dance, a demon inhabited you.

Tangar

Princess Rachel took you up next to her,
Offered you veils, tunics and many necklaces
Since then, we called you the little Gazelle
And often by dancing you brought them joy.

Scene Four

Warriors *come down the hill, leave their mounts and enter the scene.*

The Same – Warrior

A Warrior

The Princess for a moment would like to relax
Make sure that no one enters her tent,
Our youngest Prince, also seems harassed
And follows the Kahena at a slower pace.
When after the fight, the eagle returns to its aerie,
It is followed from afar by some young eaglet.

Tangar

We're going to do everything right now to please her,
But I can already see them in the valley.

Sarah *and* **Tangar** *enter the tent.*

Little Gazelle

The end of this great magical day
With a red halo girdle
Her forehead, this magnificent marble
From whence was born her vast design
How upright she is on her saddle
For having watched so many nights!
From her eyes the flame sparkles
The dark anxieties have fled,
Everyone, look how beautiful she is!

The **Kahena** *appears on her mount, followed by the tribal chiefs.*

Scene Five

The Same – Chiefs – Princes – Khaled – Julie

Kahena

Julie, *on her mount.*
Come back, my Berber mare
With my victorious battalion.
I am the warrior Kahena,
I am the fearless Kahena!

To **Khaled**.

Young man in chains,
Remember this conquest,
Am I the hurricane that you can stop
When it is finally unleashed?
You who wanted to take our lands,
To convert us by force,
Return quickly to your mysteries
Let us be free from them!
I fight for your freedom,
Great people who wanted me as queen,
Sun, I run to your light,
Crossing the mountains and the plain,
Leaping like a panther,
I lead my warriors with a great heart,
Gallop, my Berber mare,
I am the fearless Kahena!

She dismounts and comes to the front of the stage, the warrior chiefs follow her; then come the child princes, the prisoner **Khaled**.

The Numidian Chief
Warriors, it is before Meskiana
That our Kahena has vanquished.

Sarah (*presses her to her chest*)

What indescribable joy that you return alive and well,
Oh! How I have shuddered during all these long days.

Julie (*laughing*)
I want everyone around me to dance and sing
To banish memories that are too heavy to our souls.

Sarah
You must first come and rest.

Julie
Sarah! goat skins, to bring here.

Cushions are laid, etc.

I prefer to be here; I feel very brave.
Great chiefs, all approach and come in turn,
After this happy day, this emotional struggle,
To receive from a sister a mark of love.

They come in turn and she places a kiss on their forehead; and they press the bottom of her tunic to their lips.

The Aureba Chief
You will see in Kairouan the fortress again,
I offer you forever, Kahena, my strong arm.
There, bold leader and enchanting woman,
You will live days woven with silk and gold.

The Chief of the Numidians
From now on you will be Queen in Ifrikia,
In the palace that an Umayyad built
In the heart of Kairouan you will live free, happy,
Forgetting with rest the stormy conquest.

An Old Man, Chief Nefouca
Let my moved eyes contemplate a face
That reminds me of my sister when she was your age!

Julie
In her name give me the blessing.

The uncle puts his hands on her head.

Esteemed uncle, my task will seem heavy to me,
But only cowardly-hearted princes can tremble!

The Chief of the Roums
We portrayed as fearful people
All of your race's descendants, Princess,
But I saw that the Jews are also courageous,
Have as much value, virtue, nobility
As a daring Roum or a superb Frank.

Julie
Chief! You seem sincere and frank.
I smile as I listen to you.
All Christians question
The honour, the virtue, the value
Of Israel through the ages.
Overwhelmed with ailments, with pain,
Weakened by dark rages,

However, each time one appealed
To their nobility, to their courage,
In friendship they came!
But, who, ever wants to pay homage
To the oppressed people of Israel!!
Chiefs! In all races
Souls either noble or base can be seen!

The Numidian Chel

In the hearts you will live on, powerful Kahena,
Who knew how to command us and made retreat
A mighty army! Ah! How surprised he was!!
Trembling with despair, Hassan, in his defeat;
To be chased away by you seemed inconsolable;
'A woman,' he said, 'An execrable woman
Has vanquished a famous governor of Egypt!
Tugging his reins, he ran away, sad and ashamed.

The Chief of the Veiled

We pay homage to you, bowing before you,
You led an imposing army as a chief
Queen! I remember, when, trembling with fear,
The couriers in the desert spoke of their horror
And of the famous exploits of Hassan the Rhassinid.
All of us! With the same desire, the Aureba, the Numidian,
The Zenete, the Roum and the Veiled, finally,
Have, under your great wing, followed your path.

Julie

Thanks! the Kahena, warriors, will remember!
For a long time, our leaders' great deeds will be spoken of.

To **Khaled**.

Come closer, come close to us
Without dragging yourself on your knees.
Even closer, cease your complaint,
What is your name? Speak without fear.

Khaled

My name, alas! I don't have one any more,
I at least have that of slave,
Princess, unless it pleases you
To break this chain.

Julie

Yes, but first you have to tell me
What name, what country are yours.

Khaled

Yet I can only curse
The shame of all these ties.

I live in a land where the amethyst sky
Casts its strange glow
In the pure evening; where the artistic nature
Disperses its colour,
Where the curious day, but the more discreet night
Protect the loves,
Where joy is brighter and pain is secret,
Where hearts are less heavy!

Julie

What is your name, fierce, young warrior?

Khaled

I suffer that my name exhales from my mouth.
They call me Khaled: I have the title of Prince.

Julie

By your proud air I recognized your rank.
When were you born and in which province?

Khaled

I was born twenty years ago in the house
Of my father, the Emir,
In royal Damascus where the hour seems short,
Where one dreams at leisure
In my palace of alabaster and red porphyry
Coos the wood-pigeon
And the odalisque sings while touching her lyre
Under a vast palm tree.

Julie

Good! Young prisoner, if you will promise me
Never to betray,
By spoken words, gestures or by letter,
And not to run away;
I will return to you this state, most desirable of all,
The holy freedom.
Near us you will live an unforgettable time
In total bliss!

Khaled

I swear, if you want to admit me into your home,
Never to run away
And, if I betray my oath, may I die
For forgetting your benefaction!

He takes the bottom of her robe and presses it to his lips; the chiefs rise, bow very low and go back up the hill. The chains are removed from **Khaled** *who lays down, while the* **Kahena** *goes with the Princes and her servants into the tent.*

Curtain.

PART TWO

Scene One

In Kairouan. In a beautiful garden overlooked by a Berber palace. Against a basin where a jet of water murmurs, on the cushions placed on the ground **Khaled** *and the* **Princes** *are seated.* **Little Gazelle** *fans them.*

Prince Nefous – Khaled – Temsit – Nefous – Little Gazelle

Prince Nefous (*16 years*)
Before we went to visit this vineyard
With our steward to distant hamlets,
Say again, Khaled, this noble phrase,
Beautiful is the cadence and sweet are the words.

Khaled (*reading*)
'Then, having fulfilled your duty on earth,
Your light souls will escape from your bodies,
And, following the path to the celestial sphere,
To the garden of Allah, they will lunge.'

Temsit (*12 years*)
I am just like you, Khaled, moved, seduced
By the sound of this splendid word.
But my God is might, we only believe in him
And we are not ears for your sheaf.

Khaled
Far be it from me, children, to seduce you
With the infinite charm of my religion.
Your noble spirit is harsh in this region
And could not taste the songs of our lyre.

Nefous
I want to make you love our wild Africa,
Am I not an affectionate brother to you?
It is not necessary, Khaled, to constantly miss
Your magical country – its sweetness and its skies.
If to your people this land is only the Far End.[1]
Your treacherous Caliph ignores our limpid heart.

Khaled
I love your momentum and your freshness of soul,
But isn't she the queen coming!

They stand up.

[1] Ifrikia

Little Gazelle

Yes, she calls for me

She goes to meet **Kahena** *and takes a bowl from her, the nurse follows them.*

Scene Two

The Same – Julie – Sarah

Julie

My sons, this is the day you must come
All three to take from my bosom honey and fine barley.
From Berber usage we cannot abstain,
Be as brothers, come all three on my chest.

Sarah *puts the dough on* **Kahena***'s chest and the three young men bow down together.*

The Kahena

Here then, you are more united than the fingers on a hand,
My dear children! This day is full of charms for me,
The spirit is at rest, we have laid down our arms.
Gazelle! Tell me again the song of the Nefouca.

Little Gazelle

A greedy lion cub suckled milk,
One day, from a goat lying down,
Who was lost in these places,
Peacefully she was asleep,
While the golden beast
At her breasts swooned,
Happy and endlessly thirsty.
Finally, the goat woke up,
But seeing a beast close to her,
Naïve, she marvelled
And pressing him against her side
Exhaled her joy by bleating!
Since then, the Berber Lords
Like the goat to the lion cub
Be as a mother to the foreigner
And their hearts are a cradle to him.

Khaled

Queen, I am sensitive to this kindred
That binds us forever. Your sons with their tender souls
Need support, I will be able to defend them
And with my arm support their inskill.

Nefous

To our eldest, Temsit, we both will obey.

Temsit

He is also our equal, by the heart, the birth,
Against the tree or the wall climbs the bindweed.
He will know how to watch over our adolescence.

Nefous

My mother! With regret we must leave you,
You asked us to watch over the vines.

Julie

Let's all go and let Khaled relax.
But see, the Steward sends you signs

The sound of the horn is heard.

Nefous *and* **Temsit** *leave the garden.*

Sarah

The Chief of the city wants you, mistress.

Julie

I'll follow you.

To **Khaled**.

Chase sadness away from your eyes.

Scene Three

Khaled *sighs and takes a stringed instrument from which he scrapes a few sounds.*

Khaled

How beautiful Kahena is! Her infinite heart
Is as vast as the sea!
I sigh after her and the bitter fate
Has made me miserable!
Come on, think of it no more! Come back to me
Exquisite memories of the beautiful moments
Where I could pluck from the tree of pleasures
The best delights.

He tunes his lyre and resumes.

How far are your palaces, your gardens and marbles,
Oh, beloved Caliph
When will I again smell from flowers of your tall trees,
Their fragrant pistil
Harmonious land! Syrian hill

Under the scorching sun
Lebanese nature, harsh magician
Cedar with blue foliage!
And my city of nacre, refreshing shade,
Lazy Damascus!
How often in the regret of your obsessive heat
You consumed my heart.
Alas, who will return my magnificent steed to me
And whose winged feet
Carried me through the magical countryside
Beneath starry skies
My mare, lustrous and caparisoned
From gemstones and gold,
On which I flew the penultimate year.
Where do you now fling yourself?
I loved you tenderly, much more than your companions;
At the sound of my voice alone
You flew away, demon, climbing the mountains
Quivering with excitement!
I wander and my moved eye, from the mountains of Gilead
Evokes you, brown trees!
My sensitive sense of smell, heavy rose-tress of Baghdad
Inhale your perfumes.
What has become of you, my beloved father?
Like a flexible genie
I would like with a single leap of my animated being
Flee towards the friendly land.

He drops his lyre and falls asleep. A moment passes. **Julie** *returns, contemplates him and sighs.*

Scene Four

Julie – Khaled

Julie

Be silent oh my soul and don't talk to me!
I know; you will plead the law of nature,
Whisper that soon death awaits me
And that the human creature has a right to happiness.
You are too weak Kahena! Are you no longer the priestess
And can't you fight with a serene brow?
Give back to your children the caress of your arms
To forget in their presence your depressing sorrow.

Looking at **Khaled**.

Why so much beauty, what tempting demon
Put him in my way? Why have I not with a chain
Tied, taken, dragged this dark visitor
To a deep dungeon by fear I would be tied!
A devouring fire burns my chest.
I don't know if I can still resist!
Is it you Kahena, is it you the heroine
Who saw death visit you every day!
He wakes up. Oh, cowardly heart, learn to resist
To anxious beats, give me a moment's rest.

To **Khaled** *awakening.*

Do you now feel a little less depressed?
Did sleep take you on the wings of dreams?

Khaled
Your presence is enough for my enchantment.

Julie
You don't know the danger of such a word.

Khaled
Punish me, because I love you with intoxication.

Julie
Listening to you, Khaled, my heart is beating and racing.
Be quiet! It's a mistake to love the Kahena.
Tell me, what nocuous force brought you to me;
I am a warrior and cannot be a woman.

Khaled
Above all, it's madness to restrain our soul!
I followed flagrant slopes in order to love you
They took me through insidious paths
To your domain, where our two lively souls
Will join and know human happiness.

Julie
I am ridden by your disturbing confessions,
I feel alternately frightened or fulfilled.

Khaled
You don't have to look for why we love each other,
Kahena, very short is the moment that passes

He hugs her.

Come into my arms my queen, together let's hold
The emotion stronger than anything, that is beyond us!
Cover my face with your silky veils,

I look through them to your radiant gaze.
The bird sings of love in the surrounding air,
I am your prisoner, happy to be a hostage,
And want to drive away my painful regrets.

Julie
If I could, at least, Khaled, make you happy!

Khaled
Come, think only of us, forget the whole world
I want with your golden arms to make myself a long necklace
And be captive, chained in the deep forest
By your heavy hair, to cherish you, to forget!

They enter the palace.

Scene Five

Sarah – Little Gazelle

They arrive worried.

Sarah
This cursed stranger will bring us bad luck!

Little Gazelle
I don't believe, Sarah, that he tricks the queen,
His heart-broken voice conveys his pain,
I heard him earlier when he was singing his pain

Sarah
Yet I noticed his pallor, Gazelle,
When he gave a donation to the old beggar
The last one seemed like a dangerous prowler

Little Gazelle
Old Sarah! Fear, I believe, will drive you mad!

Sarah
No, not fear, Gazelle, but the dreadful torment
Let us mourn the sad collapse of its pride.

Little Gazelle
Why being so bitter then, good nurse
When they are in each other's arms, bewitched
I see you take pleasure in tormenting yourself,
Aggravating animosities for Khaled
Let's rather watch over the happiness of our queen
Let's avoid that some indiscreet person would come here,

Let's shield her from evils, let's shield her from pain,
Let her be happy and have no regrets.

Sarah

Through your mouth, dancer, a wise old man has spoken
I want to chase away all remnants of bitterness
Help me! Throw away your beautiful pearly laughter
Tell me some tale as usual.

Little Gazelle

In the pink marble palace
That Sidi-Ocba had built
The Slave Princess rests
Then for a moment she frolics
In the basin, where the jet of pure water
Caressing her supple sides
Covers her white breasts with pearls.
In a palm tree, the bird whispers.
But here, brushing with a slow step
Against the fine sand of the Moorish courts,
Then, pressing her burning forehead
Against the wall, decorated with arabesques,
Ocba! The lord of these places,
He sees the daughter of the Berbers!
Staring at her wide eyes
The blood beats hard, in his arteries,
He bends down and says,
Not daring to touch her with an unclean hand.
'Zaïna, I followed your steps
Admiring you naked in the greenery
You come in the morning hour
When no one can yet see you
To moisten your virginal skin!
You must my beauty, this evening,
Come join me in my bed
I want to hold you in my arms
I want to kiss your young mouth!
'I'll be in your arms tonight
Answers the fierce captive
But now go! Leave me!
I don't want to be touched.'
'Never a slave so splendid
Had garnished the couch of a king
Your purity, your candid air
Make me give in to your dread.'
He leaves! Poor sorry child

What dreadful fate you expect!
No one to console the lonely
To stop the hour and time!
Ah! God of fire, God of war
Gursil! Protect your Berber!
The virgin, when night fell
Went to find Sidi-Ocba
Without saying a word, the young slave,
Undressed and laid down
Her face was pure and serious
But suddenly it turned pale and changed
And, when in love, he, the proud
Ocba, came near the captive,
He saw her eyes already glassy
And moaned in a plaintive voice
'Of us two you were the strongest
You who knew how to die at fifteen
To offer yourself to me once dead!'
And, on the beautiful transparent forehead
He placed a kiss with a sigh.

Sarah

How sad is your story today my gazelle
But, Kahena is waiting for me and I'm going to her.

Curtain.

Act Three

PART ONE

The **Kahena** *troops are inside the Thisdruss coliseum (El Djem).*

The Berber queen and her troops are still trying to hold position despite the attacks of **Hassan** *the Rhassinid. For five months the assaults have been relentless. The Berbers resist, but are weakened.* **Hassan** *charges* **Khaled**, *who passed through the Umayyad lines, on a mission for the* **Kahena**. *We see the citadel.*

Scene One

Hassan – Khaled

Hassan

For five months, Khaled, the enemy has resisted us
And despite our violent, repeated attacks,
I do not yet see the hour of their defeat.
Chiefs hide their fear until death.
How then do they live? Does the beautiful Kahena
Believe she is immortal?
What have they done all this time while our mighty army
have been striking the rebel stone?

Khaled

They have strengthened
The walls of their refuge.
Hassan, they will hold out until the end!

Hassan

One thousand defectors,
Ripe for betrayal,
Have passed into our ranks, the others will follow.

Khaled

You are wrong, great leader, all the others will die
And the free Berber tribe
Will still be able to defend the coliseum for a long time.

Hassan

You must therefore, Khaled, speak to the Princess,
Reason her!

Khaled

Alas, my leader! Nobody can force her.
Her iron head is nothing but strength and nobility.
She will refuse, Lord, be sure of that.

Should I sound the horn?

Hassan

Sound the horn! I want it.
Oh! How I hate her! But how I admire her!

Scene Two

Khaled *sounds the horn. A moment passes.* **Khaled** *uses a clear banner. Berber soldiers watch over the citadel; after a moment, a gate opens slowly.* **Khaled** *approaches. The* **Kahena** *comes to meet him.*

Julie – Khaled

Khaled

Dihya![2] you know the deep love I have for you.
I come as a messenger of peace and gentleness
Begging you to surrender and open that gate
To the powerful and victorious Umayyad.

Julie

I listen to you, Khaled, I admire your ease.
Have you forgotten that you were my captive?
Shamelessly, you return flaunting your power,
And you want to actively work against me?

Khaled

Princess, you're mistaken about my feelings.

Julie

We all know here, Khaled, how you lie.

Khaled

On anyone but you I will avenge myself, woman!
My heart belongs to Islam, I am not dishonourable.
It's not against you, Dihya, that I fight,
But between these two duties, I am conflicted.

Julie

No, you are not conflicted.
But, do not bother to veil your heart;
From Hassan, your cursed chief, give me his message.
Without wanting to adorn you to us with a halo.

Khaled

I put you on such a pedestal that I don't hold any grudge from you,
I only tremble to see you bring about your death.

---

[2] Dihya means Queen.

Julie

I don't provoke, but I defend myself well
And I'd rather die than be his prisoner.
Say it well to your chief, he knows I am too proud
To ever accept the shame of a bond?

Khaled

I cannot forget the ineffable tenderness
With which you and your sons surrounded
The prisoner Khaled, when a favourable fate
Helped you defeat that stubborn Hassan!
I want you to live, you, my second mother,
My lover, my sister, and my younger brothers,
I will introduce you to a land of mystery,
A land of happiness . . .

Julie

You believe we have decided!
That you have returned to your people, Khaled,
From the sound dear to your heart, with a warlike march,
I understand it, despite all your old oaths
Never to run away; but that to the haughty Queen,
To Kahena, the chief of my proud cavaliers
You come to propose a disgraceful escape,
Khaled! Never! I want like the tall palm trees,
To only ever be uprooted by a storm.

Khaled

Whatever happens, oh Queen, in me you'll find support
Don't you want from my Prince Hassan the Rhassinid
To hear his words? He reveres you and considers you,
Of all his enemies, to be the most bold.

Julie

Listen, then, Khaled! If your chief is victorious,
I entrust to your care the fruit of my womb.
You know how painful exile would be to their hearts!

Khaled

Oh Kahena! For your sons you tremble,
I swear on Allah, if our weapon will prevail,
To obtain that we let them govern in Aurès.

Julie

Kahena, when that moment comes, will be dead,
But her spirit will fly away light, reassured

She accompanies him and **Khaled** *kisses the bottom of her dress.*

You can tell your chief that I'm waiting for him here.

He goes out.

The time has come, alas, for anguish and fear.
I dreamed the other night of a bitter defeat,
I will not surrender, I will die with my head held high,
I will fight valiantly and alone if necessary.
Their blood will mingle with mine, in my grave!

Scene Three

Hassan – Julie

Hassan
I finally see you, alone in front of me,
Oh, you who conquered us and whose dark rage
Caused terrible destruction in this beautiful land.
After ten years of peace, here I am before you.

Julie
I recognize you well, Hassan, but your face
Shows greater pride! Yes, I caused destruction
So that my citadel would not fall into
This wild hand; and the uprooted plants
Will no longer provide shade to your harnessed mounts.
May these misfortunes fall upon your head, Hassan!
It is you who unleashed massacres and horrors!
Why do you want to conquer this land
Imposing on us a God whom we do not want to know.
Know it! Kahena is not afraid of death.
She wants Berbers to avoid misfortune.

Hassan
You will prevent nothing and your iron head
Will send them sooner to the gates of hell.
Hear me, Kahena, whose audacity I admire.
There is still time, give us this place,
Otherwise, having conquered it, we will pursue you
To the end of the Aurès and there we will defeat you.

Julie
Great is God! I remain subservient to his decrees
And I will bow if your strength breaks me,
You will not be able to treat as a coward nor despise
The one whose goal had been to overcome you.

Hassan
Kahena, your word affirms your nobility.
If I hate you, I respect you, mighty leader.

The hours pass and our time is short.
To war! Farewell then! Defend yourself, Princess!

He goes out.

Scene Four

Julie

Changing destiny, we must follow your curves,
The fight, this time, must be merciless.
They are numerous, powerful and well-armed, the tricksters.
I see in the distance an entire battalion
Arrived recently to reinforce the army!
Their troop is fired by a new ardour
The Roman defectors you stole from me, Hassan!
Unfortunately have weakened my legions
What can valiant but uncontrollable warriors
Do against the perfect order that I see over there.
My generous lions still! What will you do
When they unleash the murderous attack?
I had guided you with jealous care,
Tomorrow, you will close your eyelids forever.
Well, no! Stand up again, sensitive woman,
Become the invincible Kahena again for a moment,
Make hope and faith flow through their veins,
Find words to speak to them with no troubled mind!
My people! I don't want you to come down
From the single pedestal where I had hoisted you.
Die! Weapons in your hand! I want you to defend
A free land, a proud land, a land that your
Confident race has entrusted to you, it requires that your blood,
Will spill drop by drop and until the last
And pour out its riches, before a proud cohort,
With its chief, would surrender to the Arab!

Scene Five

Little Gazelle – Julie

Little Gazelle

They wait, Mistress, astonished, anxious.
The storm roars deep in silent hearts.
Do you hear the shouting of the Umayyad troops?
They come to us and powerful organs chant
'Muhammad, Muhammad, forward!
Muhammad in the night, in the rising sun!'

Julie (*sitting on a stone*)
Let my spirit calm down for a moment.
Tell me about the past; how sweet is, Gazelle,
The memory of the days when, with tender eyes,
We followed the ewe or its kids in the fields.

Little Gazelle
How rare was this game, Mistress. You loved
Your mount especially, and Rachel the Princess
Was waiting for you on the road. When you returned.
She was horrified to learn of the prowess.
To Tabet, son of Enfak, weary, she used to complain.

Julie
To hurt her, believe me, my young heart bled
But! Who can resist the lure of such open space!
Aurès! Blessed land! The men of your race,
The beasts of your mountains defend your corners!
Aurès, with long palm trees, Aurès with strong beings,
Nature varies its audacity for you,
At the edge of your riverbeds, I was trampling tenaciously
And my bow was stretched to aim at the birds
Which fell bloody among the reeds.

Little Gazelle
And when you went, alone, to the desert!

Julie
Pink horizon! Pale horizon! Green horizon!
My eyes opened wide to capture the images
That your precious mirages reproduced in the sky
And, in the light whirlwind of golden sands,
My being flew towards you, joyful and strong!

Little Gazelle
You would have liked to follow the caravans.

Julie
I would have liked, following the camels, the donkeys,
To penetrate further, into the quicksand!
I would have liked to run, to throw myself into the wind!
Oh! My youth! Charming memories!
But I hear the alarm horn blowing again.

Scene Six

The Same – Warrior – Voice of the Imam – Voice of Hassan

The Warrior

Queen, hasten to enter our citadel,
Do you hear their call to battle in the distance?

The Voice of the Imam
Run all at the sound of our Holy Prophet,
Muhammad is his name; Allah is our God.
Forward! And kiss your holy amulet.

Hassan's voice
We must push away this odious people
Chase them forever from this fortress,
Redouble your efforts and show your skill!

Julie
Since the time has come, let's all go to battle,
Let's show them, my warriors, that nothing brings us down.

PART TWO

Scene One

The Mountain Palace of the first act in the Aurès.

The entrance courtyard and the ramparts are guarded by armed Berbers. **Julie** *leaves the palace.*

Julie (*looks beyond the ramparts*)
Here I am in your woods, tormented hills
Where the vulture swooped down on the young birds.
Plain! At the edge of your lake with its enamelled waters,
I will no longer pick flexible reeds!
Take a last look at the calm nature.
Kahena! Here is the hour of renunciation.
God who satisfied you, happy creature,
If he takes back the good from you, give you the torment.
Such is life, and I have no complaints.
But I am quite permitted to exhale regret.
Oh you! That we must love but also fear.
Lord, you fashioned me to your liking.
Kahena! Kahena! See, look inside yourself!
Judge yourself without pity. He, the supreme judge,
Will take your confession. Did not power corrupt you?
And make you seem cold and cruel?
Repressing the faults, did you unwittingly
Oppress the innocent and forgive the outlaw?
My dissatisfied soul is sad and sorry.
But you know it, great God! Only noble sentiment

Can excite me. At this hour, alone,
I feel, from my mistakes, the dark despondency!

Scene Two

Julie – Nefous – Temsit

Julie
Come here my sons, stand close to me.
Let me still contemplate your two dear heads.
You must Nefous, Temsit, submit to the law
Of a mighty God! Children, your souls are nourished
From the lessons of my life. The day has come
Where I see over my head a threatening shadow.
Love each other tenderly, with a brotherly love
And always uphold the honour of your race.

Nefous
We listen to you, mother, and we will obey you.

Temsit
Before your will, we will bow.

Julie
Your father was a Greek, Nefous, yours a Berber,
Temsit, you know, I've often told you.
But I want to recall this accursed memory,
Their death! Koceïla suffers the severe blow
From the Umayyad, when Nefous, in Kairouan,
I married the Greek chief. I was twenty-three.
Koceïla died in front of Mems. My husband
To avenge the great king fought.
Your birth, my eldest, brought us happiness; You were gentle
Like Rachel, my mother. But Alas! your childhood
Did not know, my son, the caresses of a father.
He perished in battle and I fasted for a long time,
I was crying, suffering, a husband who died too young.
My will, alas, was the prey of the people.
It was necessary to obey their silent desire.
Through a second marriage then, I poured joy
Into countless hearts. Your father was killed,
Temsit, three years later, and the cruel duty
Brought to me again the worries of power.
To lead a people was my destiny,
To see them free, happy, I was stubborn.

Nefous

Mother, we owe you a just pride.
All the Aures chiefs and Numidian warriors
By your subtle mind and your will
Have climbed, thanks to you, the splendid mountains
Of triumph and glory.

Temsit

Yes, and managing from all fronts
The struggle and the conquest and your duties as a mother,
Once you made wounded the Arabs.
You, a woman! defeated Hassan, and he has come today
To heal this bitter wound.

Nefous

His hatred for you, which he cannot control,
Made him swear yesterday to your demise and ours.

Julie

If I accept my death, I refuse yours,
My sons! I tell you my ultimate will,
And beg you to accomplish it.
If we are defeated, count on tenderness
From Khaled. Join him; it was he who encouraged me
To surrender, on the advice of Hassan, the fortress
Of Thisdruss. My refusal on our behalf worried him.
He promised, if fate would bring me down,
For you two, my dear sons, to be a father.

Nefous

If you die in combat, we will no longer be able to live
And we will be eager to avenge your blood.
You don't know the strength of our tenderness!

Julie

It moves me to hear you express it,
But to save the Berber, one must nevertheless live.

Temsit

What can the dwarf palm do without the giant palm,
We have always relied on your strength!

Julie

Oh! My upright shrubs! Strong is your bark,
Make this pledge to your mother's wish,
This will be your final show of love for me.

She returns to the palace.

Scene Three

Temsit – Nefous

Temsit
We will go to Khaled for assistance,
Our mother must be assured of this.
This valiant soul has never known fear,
She only fears, Nefous, for us.
Her happiness will be to know that we shall live.

Nefous
What a terrible sacrifice
To the just desire to perish in battle.

Temsit
She sees the superb edifice
Of her work of glory crumble and that is what brings her down.

Nefous
Temsit, we must stand strong, yes, stand until the end
And finally overcome the warriors of Hassan.

Temsit
Chase away this insane hope,
This is the last fight, I feel it, I know it.
They surround us below, we will give in.
The fragmented troop, then, will all perish.

Clink of weapons.

Scene Four

The Same – Chiefs – Warrior – Julie

The Numidian Chief
Princes! Do you hear their battle screams rising?

The Zenete Chief
Neither their warriors nor their screams frighten the Berber.

A Warrior (*comes running*)
The Arabs are at the bottom of the great rampart.

The Numidian Chief
I had planned their manoeuvre, so if he surrounds us
Hassan will break our lines!

Julie (*on horseback, burnous coat thrown back, head girded with a red headband*)

The last departure!
Hear me, brave warriors
And you, children of my womb.
I dreamed of vast mass graves,
Of sad, horrible battles.
Three times, the same night, this dreadful dream
Disturbed my sleep
I have seen, I have seen death and its dreadful tongue
Lick my scarlet blood
She held my detached head in her hands,
That with her cloven feet
And with her hooked fingers, her sharp teeth, she had snatched
From the dark Umayyad
I tried to weld my mutilated head
To my scary trunk
Death repelled it.
In the remote shadow
A grimacing warrior
Looked at the long sabre with which
Hassan, Hassan the Rhassinid
Cut off my head, and, with his sticky finger,
Wiped the damp weapon.

Nefous
Mother! What are you saying! Our terrified souls
Cast away this misfortune which haunts you!

Julie
You, you were under my flag
Jew, Christian, idolatrous Numidian
All gathered together like a herd
Under the baton of a single shepherd.
We have resisted for a long time
Against the Umayyad conquest
But here on earth everything lasts a while
And, over my head the shadow hovers.
Let's go, chiefs! Let's go down for the final fight
Let's create a solid barrier of the bodies,
Come, my proud warriors, in a supreme assault,
And try to break the line of their weapons.

They descend on horseback, trumpets, warriors.

Curtain.

PART THREE

Scene One

A steep path surrounded by groves overlooking a fairly large clearing, we see through the tree branches, the fighters and **Kahena** *on horseback and shouting.*

Julie – Hassan – Khaled – Soldiers

Julie
Gallop my Berber mare
Farewell my big-hearted lions
I am the warrior Kahena
Who runs to death and without fear.

Hassan
This woman is a formidable genius, Khaled!
See how she defies all our battalions
She stands tall and hear the agony of her troop
Her hair is dishevelled, her tunic in rags!

Khaled
Since yesterday, running downhill, uphill,
Trying, but in vain, to break our line,
She leaps on the plain, she climbs a mountain,
And her formidable fury on us is unleashed.

Hassan
The outcome is imminent, we must seize it!
The enemy is broken, but see many we lost.

Khaled
Hassan, my noble leader, I burn with desire
That she may escape, in spite of everything, the grave.

Hassan
That, Khaled, never! Her life is mine!

Khaled
She was a mother; she was my support!

Hassan
I must send her superb head to my Caliph
I vowed to and the weapon is already ready:
'If you are going to fight in Ifrikia again,'
He said, 'may you cut off the head of this woman who defied us, as soon as you can.'

Khaled
See through the wood her fair ride,
She knows she is lost and fights to the end.

Hassan

We will honour her; she will die standing!
I will finally avenge my injured pride
By her triumph, one day, my heart was ripped!
Hate feeds on the hope of revenge.
Seeing her suffer, Khaled, will ease my pain.

Loud screams are heard.

Umayyad Soldiers

Allah! Allah! Muhammad! Muhammad! Allah!
Woman! You are going to die, say your prayers!
Here she is, here is the terrible witch!

Soldiers bring the **Kahena**. *On her bloody horse, dishevelled, in rags, magnificent, she enters the scene.*

Scene Two

The Same – Kahena – Warriors

The Warrior

Chief! We promised to bring her alive!

Hassan

All right, tie it up and get my tent ready.

They bind the hands of the **Kahena**, *dismounted from her horse, the warriors go out.*

Hassan

Is it you, formidable woman?

Julie

It's me! As you can see!

Khaled

Will you allow me, Lord, to remove this chain?

Hassan

Don't do it, I like her hands tied.

Julie

Do I still frighten you?

Hassan

No, I never feared you.

Julie

Liar! For ten years your suffering was terrible
Hassan, vanquished by our allied troops.

Hassan
Woman, how old are you?

Julie
What do you care about my age!
Tell me, did I not live well, Umayyad leader?

Hassan
I will remember from you this insolent image.

Julie
All is vain, glory and beauty, Prince Hassan.

Hassan
Has your God predicted a frightening death for you?

Julie
I fear nothing and I welcome it with a smile.

Hassan
We're going to cut off your iron head!

Julie
But my pride, will you ever be able to remove it?

Hassan
You thought you could defeat us again, arrogant woman?

Julie
My victory over you was the most wonderful,
Chief Hassan! We finally were defeated by your numbers,
But we also fall upon your mass graves!

Hassan (*furious*)
I will punish your rage, bold woman,
I'll stare into your dying eyes
Until their fire is extinguished forever.
The executioner will soon hack at this strong neck,
From your neck, Kahena, blood will flow,
The hyena will laugh tonight as she drinks it!

Julie (*calm*)
Man comes from dust and to dust he shall return!

Hassan
I entrust to your care, Khaled, the prisoner.

He goes out.

Scene Three

Khaled – Julie

Khaled

Kahena! do you want to run away?
Take my horse and go, I will cover you with this large garment!

Julie

A Queen to run away! She must lead by example
With virtue! But, Khaled, it's late
And my time is short. Will you keep your promise?

Khaled

Could you doubt it, admirable Princess!
Could I betray you again without degrading myself?

Julie

You calm my anguished mind with these words.
I entrust to your care my sons, these two lights.
Farewell! Go, leave me! It's time for prayers.

Khaled *exits, moaning.*

Scene Four

Julie

I present, Lord, my naked heart before you,
You know my love for our holy law,
My God, I submit myself to your judgement alone.
I had only one concern, I had only one torment
My sons! if my actions have sometimes pleased you.
On their heads place a salutary hand,
My soul will fly away serenely from my body,
Forgetting my pains both as a woman and as a queen;
But I hear the executioner, it's time to die!
May my strength, Lord, not betray me!

Scene Five

The Shadow of Koceïla – Julie

Shadow of Koceïla

It's me! Koceïla! I have come to help you.
I left the realm of shadows to see you,
Like me, Kahena, you couldn't resist
To the fearsome onslaught of dark-eyed troops.

Julie (*under seizure*)
I salute you, Oh king! noble conqueror of Ocba,
You will see how Kahena knows how to die!

Koceïla
Both of us have made in the enchanted Aurès
Resound the hosanna of glorious hymns;
Like mine, your vast mind was tormented.
You wanted to restore ancient customs.
But, if against force, a noble dream is vain,
It nevertheless deserved a people to remember it.
And, in this harsh country where pure hearts are born,
Our image, believe me, towards the distant azures,
In the green meadow or the wild moors,
Will sometimes appear and beautiful legends
Will be born from our two names, on this blazing ground.

Julie
After the storm, an iridescent arc is born in the sky,
Thus, grows in my soul an ineffable hope.

Scene Six

The Same – Hassan – Khaled – Chief – The Executioner – Warriors – Prisoners

The Prisoners
Kahena! The most admirable of human beings!

A Chief
We want to collect your last breath.

The Prisoners
You will leave this world, oh superb warrior!

Julie
Farewell, last ears of a splendid sheaf!

A Chief
Queen! You knew how to live well and will know how to die well.

Julie
Dying next to you is a sweet pleasure to me.

A Prisoner
See! The Aurès still envelops you in a caress.

Another
Kahena, we want to die with you.

Julie

My heart thanks you, oh! Race of strong men
It is sweet to me to see you, my fellow fighters
Before the executioner's axe kills me.
Look, Kahena, the loyal Berber
Who only dreamed of honour and freedom for you.

Hassan

I punish today, chiefs, her tenacity.

Khaled

You were the noble woman and the bold chief.

Julie

I ask, Khaled, just one favour.

Khaled

Speak, I would like to make your end less bitter.

Julie

I want to sleep near my father and my mother,
My bones and my dust intertwined with theirs.

Khaled (*moved*)

I accede to your wish, Dihya, the hour has come.

Julie

I am ready for my end, it is welcome.

Hassan (*full of hate*)

Oh what! not a regret, not the slightest terror?

Julie

He who fears death does not know its greatness
I welcome her as a friend, she who delivers me,
The prisoner Queen would have regretted to live.

Prisoners

Kahena, our queen! Oh, Kahena the Great,
Great in courage, with a heart full of kindness,
You guided us! your name will be in legend,
Living on every lip and for eternity.

Hassan

Queen, make your last prayers to your God.

Julie

I exalt you, nature, so did my fathers!
Farewell then, to life, to rural sweetness,
To the resplendent day, to the calm of the night,
Farewell beauty of the world, farewell celestial charm,
Farewell beloved country on whom I was the support.

Farewell energetic, ardent and resolute people!
Aurès, farewell! To you goes my last salute.
Listen Israel, the Lord is our God,
The Lord . . .

The executioner raises his axe.

Curtain.

Papa'gina

Hana Vazana Grunvald

Translated by Sivan Battat

The Playwright

Hana Vazana-Grunwald is a director, creator, playwright in Israeli theatre, founder of the Frechot Ensemble, and winner of the Rosenblum Prize for Performing Arts 2022. Her work promotes content and theatrical language that intersect with the cross-gender Sephardi identity status and different forms of femininity. This is an artistic and political commitment to the silenced voices of Israeli society and theatre. Her work underpins a new theatrical genre of poetic-documentary theatre, using community theatre tools that emphasize her personal, social, and historical experience. Works include *Papag'ina*, *Frecha a Beautiful Name*, *Pearl Paper Heart*, *Sof Al Hakatino*, *Maternity*, *Whistle*, *Consensual Murder*.

The Translator

Sivan Battat (she/they) is an Iraqi-Jewish theatre director and community organizer based in New York City. They are the Associate Artistic Director of Noor Theatre, a New York theatre company dedicated to supporting, developing and producing the work of theatre artists of Middle Eastern descent. Sivan creates performance at the intersection of justice and cultural work, across theatre, community, ritual celebration, and beyond. Recent credits include *Layalina* (World Premiere, Goodman Theatre, Chicago), *Heroes of the Fourth Turning* (Studio Theatre, Washington DC), *Brass Knuckles* (Ensemble Studio Theatre, NYC). sivanbattat.com

Synopsis

Jaffa, the end of the seventies. Yemima, an eleven-year old girl, encounters the smells, tastes and sensations of the world outside and the softness within, from open sewage pits to the sticky, sweet insides of a watermelon. Passion, violence, shame, hunger and lust bubble up and tempt the narrator of today to meet the Yemima of her past, forcing her to choose between the Baba Sali and Ben Gurion, between Israelis and Arabs, between reality and imagination. An autobiographical and imaginative theatrical story, 'Papa'gina' is drawn from Moroccan Arabic, referring to dough that hasn't risen.

Production History

Written and Directed: Hana Vazana Grunwald
Set Design: Daniella Mor
Composer: Eyal Weiss
Lighting Design: Uri Weiss
Dramaturgy: Daphna Krone and Irit Rachevsky

Narrator	Hana Vazana Grunwald
Yemima, *eleven-year-old girl*	Moriah Beshari Liphshitz/Tslil Halaf
Mother	Limor Zamir/Eden Uliel
Yemima's classmates, Neighbours	Eden Uliel/Anat Levy/Selly Arkadash
Father	Eyal Salama
Boolbool, Arab Peddler	Eyal Salama

Scene One

Narrator Waking up in the middle of the night was an opportunity. I was willing to give up sleep for the chance. I was willing to part from the warmth of my bed for this chance. My feet were still toasty; they were the first to meet the cold of the floor, a piercing cold. It's impossible to dream now. I rolled out of my bed and trudged over to the closet. I opened the door and fumbled around inside. It turns out that a person's eyes adjust to the dark because in the darkness, they found something to grab on to. The quiet of the house was foreign to me, the rhythmic breath of sleep climbing up a ladder and sliding back down. My hands were swallowed inside the neatly stacked piles of clothing, the feeling of the fabric brushing against my hands over and over again. But the feeling of the familiar fabric refused to reveal itself. (*Urgently.*) They have to be here, I saw them here last night. (*Slyly.*) And just like that, the idea began to nest itself inside me.

Yemima I'll wake up in the middle of the night, get my gym shorts, wet them and put them back in the dirty laundry so I wake up to the smell of rot.

Father *enters. Music with bass.*

Narrator The turn of the key in the lock startles me. I hear it turning, once in the top lock, once in the bottom.

Yemima It's Daddy. He's coming back from work.

Narrator I leap back into bed, holding my breath – trying to give it the steady tempo of sleep, imitating everyone else's breath.

Father *comes in, goes to the chair, takes off his shoes and scratches between his toes.*

Yemima I hear him come into the house like a thief, unzip the zipper of his work bag and (*disgusted*) take out dirty dishes. Then, he puts the newspaper he brought home for Mommy on the table.

Narrator (*remembering*) 'Sha'ar Lematchil'[3] News in Easy Hebrew. September 29, 1978.

Father 'At the Knesset meeting held today, the Minister of Finance submitted the budget proposal for the new neighborhood rehabilitation program. We understand that he stated "Within five years we will see considerable change."'

Yemima Instead of reading this newspaper, Mommy will clean the windows with it.

Narrator Dad opens the door of the bathroom

Yemima lifts the toilet seat, rolls down his gray underwear and patiently waits for his stream of pee. Then, he gets into bed, looks for something and lights a cigarette. (**Father** *lights a cigarette.*)

Music down.

---

[3] 'Gateway for the Beginner' – A weekly Israeli newspaper published in simple Hebrew.

Narrator Royal Cigarettes, made in Israel.

Yemima In the dark, it looks like a lantern.

Narrator I abandon my shorts idea, my thoughts racing, and picture the face of my gym teacher.

Yemima Tal Borshtein.

Narrator Tal Borshtein.

Yemima When she stands, her pelvis tilts back and her butt seems all cramped. I think she feels sorry for me. Every time I pass her I can feel her eyes stabbing me in the back.

Narrator There's a little battle between us that only we know about. She does everything possible to get me to exercise . . .

Yemima And I do everything possible so that she'll never succeed. When I manage to get excused by the nurse, I give her the note triumphantly and she crumples it up, and rolling her eyes, sends me off to sit on the side.

Father *gets up, covers* **Yemina** *and leaves. Calling after him:*

Yemima I never liked gym class.

Narrator I never liked gym class.

Mother *enters with bags from the market, puts them on the table.*

Mother Stop rubbing your eyes. It's late, you need to get up.

Narrator I rub the sleep from my eyes. A strong yellow light blinds me. I keep rubbing. My eyes are filled with morning webs. They block me from seeing what I might otherwise be able to see.

Mother It's morning already, almost seven o'clock. Today's Friday.

Yemima (*sitting up in a panic*) I have gym class today. (*Laying back down, cringing*)

Narrator Mum's making sandwiches in the kitchen. Every now and again she calls out my name. I promise myself that when I'm a mum, I won't yell at my children.

Mother It's 7.30!!

Yemima (*shrinking*) My pillow is so soft and she promises me that if I stay right here with her she will love me forever. I believe her.

Narrator Mum and the alarm clock both announce

Mother It's already a quarter to eight.

Narrator If I don't hurry, I'll be late again.

Yemima My body will not get up.

Mother It's already five to –

Mother *pulls the blanket from* **Yemima**.

Yemima I'm not going today.

Mother And what is that supposed to mean?

Yemima I'm not going.

Mother There's no 'not going', there's nothing for you to do at home. Get up, get dressed and go to school.

Yemima There's nothing important, just gym class.

Mother Gym is important. It wouldn't hurt you to exercise a little.

Yemima But I hate that teacher, she's always yelling at me.

Mother So do what she asks and she won't yell. Teachers don't yell just for fun. Get up, your dad worked all night, I do not want to yell. Today is Friday, it's a short day. Go to school.

Yemima (*an idea*) I don't have gym clothes, my shorts are in the laundry.

Mother Your shorts are on the chair. I took them out last night. Get up, wash your face, I'm bringing them to you. (*Yelling.*) Get up!

Yemima *rolls out of bed.*

Narrator I get up! I drag myself to the bathroom.

Mother *hands* **Yemima** *a pair of blue pants.* **Yemima** *takes them reluctantly, tries to pull them on while lying down.*

Yemima This elastic is squeezing my legs, they're too fat.

Music – Slow theme. The **Narrator** *walks forward, lifts her skirt and glances at her thighs.*

Narrator I'll try a new tactic.

End of slow theme.

Yemima Mummy, mummy. (**Yemima** *crosses to* **Mum***, dropping the pants behind her.*) Can I stay home today? I promise I'll help you, I'll do anything you want. (*Caressing her.*)

Narrator I'm begging.

Yemima Please . . .

Narrator She's almost convinced . . . I see her forehead wrinkle, but she reconsiders and says

Mother No, today is Friday. I have enough work. (**Mum** *gets the backpack, puts it on* **Yemima***'s back.*) Besides, what would I tell your dad? You know he doesn't like it when you miss your classes. Enough. Go to school.

Narrator I take my bag from her and go outside without saying . . .

Mother Goodbye, we say goodbye. Goodbye is for God.

Narrator *crosses left.*

Narrator My nostrils flare with anger. I'm figuring something out for myself . . .

Yemima There are things you just can't tell anyone.

Narrator There are things you just can't tell anyone.

Mother (*shouting*) YEMIMAAAAAA. (*Waving the pants.*)

Music – Dramatic.

Yemima (*and* **Narrator** *step forward*) My name is Yemima. (**Yemima** *and* **Narrator** *step forward.*) If you call me Yemima, I'll answer. (**Yemima** *and* **Narrator** *step forward.*) Behind my back they don't call me Yemima. (**Yemima** *and* **Narrator** *step forward.*) Behind my back, I hear them saying that I'm . . . (*She can't say it.* **Yemima** *and* **Narrator** *step forward.*) I hear them saying that I'm . . . (**Yemima** *and* **Narrator** *step forward.*)

Narrator Papa'gina.[4]

Music down.

Yemima Papa'gina is my second name.

Narrator Dough girl.

Yemima That's what it means, the nickname.

Narrator Dough woman.

Yemima That nickname, I hate it. It reminds me of all the things that I'm not.

Mother (*with compassion*) Not so active, not so responsible, not so alert, not so organized, not so . . .

Yemima When Mommy says

Mother Papa'gina

Yemima I know she means that from this girl, we expect . . .

Yemima and Narrator Nothing.

Mother (*takes* **Yemima** *to a chair, puts the pants on her, and sends her to the left of the stage*) Her arms are dough, her legs are dough, she drops everything you give to her. You forgot your shorts. Hurry up, you're already late for school. And close your shoes, how many times do I have to tell you that if you walk with your shoes open like this you'll fall. Fix your hair. You're late for school. Hurry up. Papa'gina, it's a miracle that your head is still connected to your body.

---

[4] Pronounced like Pap'ah'Jeena with a soft G sound like J.

Scene Two

Narrator On Friday morning, the world is running.

Music – The street. **Mother** *shakes out the blanket.* **Anat** *and* **Evelyn** *enter with bowls of seeds. They step forward.*

Evelyn On Friday morning, the world is running.

Anat Running? The pots on my stove are already boiling for Shabbat.

Evelyn The *bourekas*[5] pans are already cooling on the floor to make room for the pans of sunflower seeds.

Anat The sunflower seeds. Even the best housewives can fail sometimes in their preparation.

Evelyn One minute too long

Anat One minute too long in the oven and they'll be

Evelyn Burnt

Narrator Scorched.

Anat Scorched.

Evelyn And if they come out in time . . .?

Anat Warm and salty enough?

Anat (*tasting a sunflower seed*) May the name of this housewife be blessed and every tongue taste

Evelyn and exalt

Anat and crack one open

Evelyn and praise.

Music – The street, rises and falls.

Narrator On Friday morning the world is running and only Yemima has time to meander. The windows are wide open, the quilts are airing out, and the pillows are resting from the tussle of the night before. Yemima walks the sidestreets. She hears a song in Arabic playing on the radio, spilling out loud enough that everyone can hear it. Bits of the song burst out in spurts, and blend with the noise of Leon the welder, welding the grates. (**Mother** *pounds the mortar and pestle.*) Yemima <u>knows that it's forbidden</u> to look directly at the light that the machine makes. But the <u>sparks</u> that make the <u>fire</u> draw her in. They make her forget what she knows is not allowed. (**Mother** *drops something from the chair.*) The sound of shutters opening pulls her attention. Right behind the shutters stands Aharon the truck driver's wife.

---

[5] Middle Eastern hand pies/baked pastries.

Yemima Penina.

Narrator You can smell Aharon's aftershave from a block away. He doesn't look behind him or side to side, his head is buried in his truck. Penina's hand rests on her mouth peacefully, but her eyes tell a different story. It's a story that began long ago, a story that the adults loved to tell. They roll it around on their tongues like candy, first sweet, then spicy and biting. In the end, it leaves a bitter taste that just won't go away – the sourness of a love that has passed from this world and left behind a heart that's still hurting.

Yemima (*waving, calling*) Penina, Penina . . .

Narrator But Penina didn't notice her, because right then, in that moment, (**Narrator** *stands and the three of them look from left to right*) in a storm, burst onto the street The Alpha Romeo Car belonging to

Penina Avi

Music – Eleanor.

Mother Haviva's son, who everyone knows

Evelyn Was fooling around with Penina before she got set up with Aharon.

Mother The son of the fat pickle guy. Remember? How he and Penina . . . .

Yemima (*holding onto the light switch from from the left*) They were kissing in the stairwell and the light kept coming on again and again. When they couldn't see me, I was holding down the light switch so they could kiss for a little longer. Avi would hold Penina's face and lift her chin and run his fingers through her hair. Like the soap operas that Rachel, their neighbor who had already had three heart surgeries, would buy into every week. Mummy says that

Mother We don't do things like that. Lovers don't separate. Penina's mother Chemda was blinded –

Yemima Rachel says that

Evelyn Money isn't everything in life. He'll never leave her, and she'll never forget him.

Yemima Cause <u>that's</u> how it is with your first love. Sixty years in the grave and you'll still remember.

Music – The Accident. (Everyone stops and looks to the right.)

Penina Aharon what happened? What happened?

Evelyn Avi's Alpha Romeo rear-ended Aharon's truck and knocked the entire bumper off.

Mother Aharon, who parked his truck as usual using the 50–50 method (two of the wheels on the road, and two on the sidewalk), has no idea what happened.

Yemima Wow, what a boom.

Music – Tense.

Evelyn Avi comes out of the car

Yemima But inside the car, Zohar the King continues to sing at full volume about beautiful Eleanor, like an angel, without her –

Evelyn Shhh . . . Aharon, her husband, gets out, grabs Avi by the shirt and pins him against the wall, Aharon grabs him by the throat and starts to choke him.

Narrator In their eyes, there was just one desire. Defeat the opponent, tear down his defenses and wipe the smile off his face.

Evelyn Cold sweat pours across Aharon's face. Avi's Adam's apple sticks out, bobbing up and down, up and down, up and down.

Penina (*shouting*) Leave him alone! Leave him alone! (*She spills water,* **Evelyn** *and* **Mother** *exit.*)

Music – Dramatic.

Narrator (*stands on the side,* **Yemima** *crosses to the puddle and starts kicking the water*) Yemima clings to the peeling wall like a magnet, she wants to escape but fear freezes her in place. She looks at their faces, the look in their eyes scaring her. His face is collapsed and from the side of his mouth you can see some kind of foam, white saliva like the kind that bubbles up with hate between my dad and my mom, the kind that turns my dad into a stranger. When Mum and Dad are fighting, Yemima reads her book, concentrating so intensely on the story that she drowns them out. The blood from Aharon's face mixes with the smell of his aftershave and dribbles down his chin. Yemima escapes from her spot (**Yemima** *runs over the puddle*) and runs into a private alley. Only tenants are allowed to pass through, they even put up a sign:

Yemima Do not enter. Private.

Scene Three

Narrator (*discovering, as if from behind a door*) In one house, you can hear a man and a woman whispering. Yemima stops.

Yemima I hear a man getting closer to a woman, she says something to him, and then they close the door. I hear her heels clicking on the floor. (**Evelyn** *is backstage, walking with heels.*) She walks from place to place closing the windows. After that, they move something heavy. (*Dragging something heavy backstage.*) I think (*standing on her tiptoes*) . . . that it's a table. But the window is so high up, I can't see in even if I stand on my tiptoes. The woman comes closer to my window. (*Kneeling.*)

Narrator The woman's eyes almost catch her. Yemima notices doubt and fear in the woman's eyes.

Yemima But the man who is waiting for her calls her to come and she flies away. I think she's flying because I can't hear her steps anymore after that. A second later, (*surprise*) they kiss loudly, (*disgusted*) their saliva mixing up. (*Quickly.*) Then one long zipper opens slowly, (*slowly*) and then another zipper, shorter this time. Then suddenly, the woman is crying. No . . . she's singing, no . . . she's howling. (**Yemima** *moans.*) It sounds like . . .

Narrator Prayer. (*Moans.*)

We hear **Boolbool**, *over the sound of moaning.*

Boolbool Candy, ahmonds, candy, ahmonds!

Boolbool *enters from the right,* **Mother** *pounds the mortar and pestle and it rings.*

Narrator A familiar voice wakes her up.

Yemima (*secretly and a bit stressed*) Mister Boolbool,[6] the Arab peddler, the one who comes every other day with a cart and brings with him

Boolbool (*during this monologue,* **Boolbool** *approaches* **Yemima** *and she clings to the wall.* **Narrator** *walks to the right and observes them*) Candies, almonds, Turkish delight, Kadaif. Hey, what are you doing here, Yaffa's daughter? Why don't you go to school? (*Concerned.*) How's your mother, how's she doing? (*To himself.*) Really, God, such a good woman, Yaffa. (*Turns to go,* **Yemima** *tries to run away.*) Candies, ahmonds. (*Suspiciously.*) It's late, Yaffa's daughter, are you on vacation from school today?

Narrator He gets closer to where she's standing, looks in the open window and freezes. His eyes widen, his jaw drops, his body draws towards the window. (**Boolbool** *laughs.*)

Yemima (*stuttering*) Mister . . . Boolbool, Mister Boolbool, I have to go, I . . . I'm late for school.

Narrator But he doesn't hear her.

Boolbool (*in Arabic*) *Shu il film il hada?* [*What movie is this?*] *Hahahahahahahah.*

Yemima Mister Boolbool!

Narrator Yemima doesn't understand what he says but the movement of his hand shoos her away and he says again

Boolbool (*Arabic*) *Eev mamnou'a, eev mamnou'a* [*It's forbidden. It's forbidden*].

Yemima Mister Boolbool!

Narrator (*stressed*) But he doesn't hear her!

Yemima MISTER BOOLBOOL!! (**Yemima** *pushes* **Boolbool** *and he turns around. She backs away.*)

---

6 Boolbool in Hebrew slang means 'penis'.

Narrator Yemima backs away. She wants to escape, to erase this morning, to erase Boolbool, to close the shutters, to run to school. She doesn't notice that the shoelace she forgot to tie is caught. And her foot goes right into an open sewage hole. Pain sears across Yemima's foot (**Narrator** *joins in* **Yemima***'s scream.*)

Yemima Ay! I hurt my foot. It's stuck!!!!

Boolbool *goes to* **Yemima***, grabbing her from the back and with his back to the audience, frees her foot.*

Narrator Yemima's shouts spill out of the alley to the main street, strangers gather around her. (**Yemima** *groans in pain.*)

Evelyn Excuse me! Excuse me! (**Boolbool** *moves out of the way.*) What happened to you, girl? You fell? Where does it hurt?

Anat (*pulling* **Evelyn** *aside*) What is an Arab like him doing in an alley with a little girl?

Boolbool (*defensive*) This is Yaffa's daughter.

Evelyn What was that? Do you know him? (**Yemima** *nods.*)

Boolbool I know where her house is, I know her mother, I'll take Yaffa's daughter. (**Boolbool** *picks* **Yemima** *up on his back.*)

Narrator Boolbool's hands lift Yemima and place her gently on his cart of goods. The smell of an unfamiliar body fills her nose, mixing with the smell of the sewage wafting off her leg. Yemima doesn't look at him, she is afraid of what he will tell her mother. He gets on his cart and takes hold of the handlebars, Yemima close to him. The smell of his sweat assaults her, the smells of salt, lemon and honey creep in through her nose and settle into her throat. They ride two blocks in embarrassment. As they enter the yard, Mum is standing by the grates, cleaning the windows.

Yemima Mummy!

Boolbool *takes* **Yemima** *down from the cart.* **Mum** *is cleaning the screens with a rag, and when she notices* **Yemima***, throws the rag.* **Boolbool** *brings* **Yemima** *to a chair.*

Mother What happened? What did you do? I had a bad feeling this morning.

Yemima I fell down.

Mother It's my bad luck, nothing is going right. How did you fall down? How did she fall? You don't have eyes? How many times have I told you that you should walk straight home from school! What am I going to do with you? (**Mother** *tries to take off* **Yemima***'s shoe, a struggle ensues.* **Boolbool** *calms them down and gently takes* **Yemima***'s foot.*) She's always falling down. Her father is sleeping, he worked all night. I can't wake him up now.

Narrator Mum's words are racing out of her, but her tears are even faster and she starts to cry.

Yemima Mummy always cries when she's hurt or when other people are hurt, family or not, people we know or strangers. (**Mother** *goes in front of the table.*) She says it's her

Yemima and Mother damn heart.

Mother My damn heart. It can't take anything. One day it will explode, and then you'll be sorry.

Boolbool Don't worry, Mrs Yaffa, I will help you.

Narrator His hands gently unravel the laces, remove the shoe and roll down the sock.

Yemima (*instructing her mother*) He's asking for a bowl of hot water!

Narrator He goes out and returns with two bottles. He pours some into his hands and a strong smell spreads throughout the kitchen. The smell of olive oil.

Yemima And another sweet smell . . . (**Boolbool** *massages his hands and faces* **Mother**.)

Narrator that Yemima can't quite place. His touch is so gentle, Yemima can barely feel it. He holds her ankle securely, spreading out the pain, dissolving the sting, turning her foot into a hunk of warm dough. Instead of the pain, Yemima starts to feel . . .

Yemima a nice tickle

Narrator that climbs up her spine, the feeling spreading over her belly and below, and creates a new sensation that she doesn't recognize, the kind she gets when she sees

Yemima people kissing on TV.

Narrator The kind that glues her to the couch and tickles her between her legs. Boolbool's hands leave Yemima's foot and start to touch her knee.

Yemima I want him to keep drawing smooth snakes on me that smell like oranges. But he stops. He puts my foot on the sofa, covers it with the leopard print blanket and stands

Yemima (*accusatory*) Next to Mum.

Mother The girl keeps falling, I have to take her to someone who can take away this evil eye.

Boolbool (*promising, drawing closer*) There is one woman in our village, they say.

Mother He wouldn't have it, he doesn't believe in anything . . .

Boolbool Don't worry, Mrs Yaffa. (*Arabic.*) *Allah K'bir* [*God is mighty*]. Come, sit down, Mrs Yaffa.

Mother How can I sit?

Narrator And her hands knead in the bowl, breaking the semolina pieces apart. Boolbool stands behind Mum, putting his warm hand, the one that touched Yemima just a minute ago, on Mum's hand. He caresses her gently, tracing new lines along her hand. Along the veins, towards her nails, he caresses her chipping nail polish, skipping over the golden wedding ring that she never takes off and continuing up her arms.

Yemima And Mummy bites her lip and lets Boolbool's hand tickle her, and it seems to me like their hands are playing a game (**Boolbool** *begins to sing*) and Mummy whispers 'stop' but her voice is as soft as the grains of the couscous she's crumbling. They fall into each other and Boolbool sings into Mummy's ear, Arabic words that Yemima doesn't understand.

Boolbool *and* **Mother** *sing together in Arabic.*

Music – Lev Rahel El Sooti.

Narrator And she closes her eyes and remembers the Arabic movies they show on Fridays, and how the women in those movies move their bodies and how they dance and rock their bellies back and forth.

Music down.

Narrator And Yemima remembers

Yemima that Daddy (*urgently, panicked*) doesn't let Mummy speak Arabic and tells her (*imitating her father*) 'You must speak Hebrew, Yaffa, we are in Israel now' . . . If Daddy were to wake up now to go to the bathroom and see that Mummy is enjoying herself so much . . .

Mother (*longingly, but afraid*) No, Boolbool, I am not that kind of woman.

Narrator And Mum jumps as if a snake bit her, and with a clenched fist says:

Mother (*quietly accusatory*) Aren't you embarrassed? I let you into my home.

Mother *goes to* **Yemima***'s leg,* **Narrator** *pushes* **Boolbool** *out.*

Narrator And Boolbool moves away, his tail between his legs. He steps away, words of apology fumbling in his mouth.

Boolbool (*sighs*) God forbid, I swear! (*Making himself small and moving away from her.*) Mrs Yaffa, I don't mean any harm. I help you, you're a good woman, Mrs Yaffa, by the grace of God, I didn't do anything, come, please I brought you the sunflower seeds you wanted, you can pay me next time, we are all human beings, we all have one God, Jews, Arabs, we are all His children.

He exits. **Mother** *starts chopping furiously.*

Narrator After Boolbool leaves, Mum cleans the floor with lots of water and venom.

Mother (*crossing to the table*) Let him burn in fire in hell, that he won't even be left with his manhood.

Yemima Mummy curses Boolbool. And Mummy says they don't have any honour. Who are 'they'? All men or all Arabs?

Music.

Narrator And Yemima's mum says that today is Friday

Mother And it's already eleven o'clock and I haven't had time to cook anything yet.

Yemima And her hands, that just a few moments ago danced with Boolbool's hands, start to work like a machine. They chop everything they can find: onions, tomatoes, zucchini and beets, and while she chops, she starts to cry, tears slowly rolling down her cheek.

Music down.

Scene Four

Narrator It's 11.00.

Yemima Gym class is about to start.

Narrator Yemima imagines the gymnasium.

Yemima It's a dark hall, the sun can't even sneak a single ray of light in. The high ceilings are covered in spider webs. The spiders stare down on us from above, watching all the fifth graders coming in through the creaky iron door. They wear shorts and white shirts with the school emblem sewn on the right side, far from my heart that skips a beat as the lesson draws near.

Music – Hot chocolate. **Anat** *and* **Evelyn** *enter doing an aerobic dance. As it ends they run forward shouting 'Hot chocolate'. Music out.*

Narrator The children huddle on the bench waiting for the teacher to arrive. She'll bring a rope and choose two strong and skinny girls who will get to choose who is first.

Anat I'm first

Evelyn You're always first, I'm first. (*They start to fight about who will be first.*)

Yemima And they examine the faces.

Narrator And bodies and their status, not their kidneys or their hearts, and their fate will be determined.

The girls point to the audience.

Evelyn Who will come up

Anat And who will give up

Evelyn Who will be humiliated

Anat And who will be glorified

Evelyn Who will sit in the throne

Narrator And who will exact the judgment, to pluck out the useless weed? (*The girls point to* **Yemima**.)

Yemima (*singing*) One, two, jump again, two[7]

The girls join in the singing. **Yemima** *tries to make pushing movements with her legs, but her feet don't leave the ground.*

Narrator Yemima stands in line too. She waits for one . . . and another one . . .

Yemima One . . . and another one . . .

Narrator Her thighs rubbing together in anticipation.

Evelyn But she continues to stand and wait for her turn.

Anat She always gives up at the last moment. She doesn't have the guts!

Evelyn Yemima, Yemima. (*Teasing, and continuing with 'Yemima, Yemima'.*)

Yemima What?

Anat You'd rather spin the rope, right? Come here, take it.

Yemima I spin the rope with all my might. Watching it spin in the air is mesmerizing. I spin it forcefully, forward and back. I don't stop, even when my hands get tired, even when ants start to crawl onto my hands. My hand lets go for one second, right at the moment when Miri Batito comes in.

Evelyn You're out, the rope touched you.

Anat It didn't touch me, I swear on the Torah. I swear by my mother it didn't touch me, I swear by my brother Meir. (*The girls begin to fight. They stop, and walk towards* **Yemima**.)

Evelyn Yemima, right, it touched her? Say it touched her.

Anat It didn't touch me, right? Right? Come on, why are you silent? Answer me, what are you a mute?

Yemima Miri Batito looks at Tikva and she looks back at her. I want to escape, I want to ask

Narrator *stands to the left of* **Yemima** *and interrupts the girls' panic.*

Narrator What happened? What's funny?

Yemima But I'm silent. They must be laughing at the new shoes Daddy bought me.

---

[7] Could use here an English speaking jump rope song such as – 'Teddy bear, Teddy bear, turn around, Teddy bear, Teddy bear, touch the ground'.

Narrator Twice a year they go together to buy shoes. In the fall and in the spring. A silent journey of stations and stops.

Anat and Evelyn The bus that takes you from Jaffa to Ramat Gan is full of people, Yemima is pushed to the heart of the bus and looks for something to hold onto. Dad stands far away but she can see him because he's a head taller than everyone else. Dad doesn't look for Yemima, doesn't speak to her, doesn't ask her questions. One station after Elit he calls

Father Yemima we're getting off

Anat and Elvelyn They meet off the bus. Dad is in a hurry, his steps are huge and Yemima has to run so that she doesn't lose him. Every now and then, he stops and looks back to be sure she's still there.

Yemima When we go into the store, the saleslady is busy and Daddy smokes a cigarette outside, he's looking for something and . . .

Anat and Elvelyn (*circling* **Yemima** *with various movements*) The store is full of pairs of shoes. Shoes with buckles, shoes with zippers, leather shoes, canvas shoes, boat shoes, moccasins, sandals in every colour, and flip flops.

Narrator But Yemima has a prescription from the orthopedist specifically for bowed legs and flat feet. (**Father** *lifts his hand with the document,* **Narrator** *takes it from him.*) Tall shoes made of hard leather with plastic insoles. (**Narrator** *opens the prescription document, sees that she remembers correctly, and wrinkles her brow.*) Yemima eyes the other shoes, making a list of all the shoes she most wants. (**Yemima** *steps forward with a longing look and tries to touch one of* **Evelyn***'s shoes.*) Of all the shoes she wants most, at the top of the list stands a pair of sandals the colour of the sea.

Anat Can I help you? This isn't for you, sweetheart.

Girl B Excuse me, please. (*Pause. She invites* **Father***, who is standing back, embarrassed forward with her hand. He steps forward, with embarrassment.*) Tall shoes made of hard leather with plastic insoles.

Anat And don't be sad, sweetheart, I have something for you.

Evelyn And the saleslady sweetens the bitterness with a blue balloon.

Girl B *brings a blue balloon for* **Yemima**. **Yemima** *stands with the balloon,* **Father** *behind her, and they line up for the bus.*

Yemima When I was a little girl balloons used to make me happy. But now, at age eleven

Narrator But now, at age eleven, the balloon becomes excess baggage. She tries to hide the balloon, but he floats to her level and with all his strength he defies her, gusting through the wind. And it seems to her that . . .

Yemima everyone is looking at me.

Everyone looks at **Yemima**.

Narrator On the way from Ramat Gan to Jaffa on bus 42, Yemima puts her hand out the window and releases it. Dad doesn't see. He sits up front near the driver, listening to the news.

Scene Five

Mother You asleep? Get up. Eat something. How's your foot? Does it hurt? I'm going.

Yemima Where?

Mother To get some air. (**Mother** *exits.*)

Narrator It's already afternoon, the kitchen is buzzing and bubbling to greet the Shabbat. On the stove, we put steaming pots that fill the cramped space with smells. On the table, we arrange the salads that Mum prepared for Shabbat in a row.

Evelyn Orange carrot salad.

Anat Tomato and spicy pepper salad.

Evelyn Fried eggplant salad.

Anat Eggplant in mayonnaise salad.

Evelyn Potato salad.

Anat Red beet salad.

Evelyn Preserved lemon salad.

Anat Fennel and lemon salad.

Narrator Yemima gets off the couch and the smell of food descends upon her. She walks straight to the pots and her eyes blur. She doesn't hear, she just smells and sees and her mouth waters

Yemima Mmmmmm.

Anat To taste

Evelyn To sink her teeth into

Anat To cut

Evelyn To devour without chewing.

Anat And just to swallow

Narrator 'How many times have I told you not to eat standing up?' Mum would say if she were here. Pull back your hair so it doesn't fall into the pot, God forbid, and take a plate with what you want, why are you eating with your fingers? Go wash your hands.

Yemima But Mummy is not here.

Narrator And Yemima stands close, she reaches out her hands and fingers and scoops up

Anat A hot meatball. Right into her mouth.

Evelyn It burns the tip of her tongue, but she can't resist

Anat She wants to eat everything

Evelyn To satisfy her mouth

Anat Her teeth

Evelyn To stuff her stomach to the brim

Anat Until she can't anymore, until it hurts.

Narrator But the food doesn't satisfy her. Yemima's stomach gurgles with painful emptiness and she goes to lie down on the couch. She closes her eyes, covers herself with the leopard print blanket and makes it into a tent. From the outside she can see Baba Sali, Mother's hero and Ben Gurion, Dad's hero looking down on her. Yemima hides from them under the blanket. Inside her tent, images of the day mix with images of the darkness. The light that pours through the blanket turns red. Yemima puts her hand inside her tight pants and touches her belly. She takes them off and throws them outside. She keeps her hands in her underwear and when she touches them she discovers that they're

Yemima Wet.

Narrator Her hands are full of oil.

Yemima They're smooth, just like Boolbool's hands.

Narrator They stroke her stomach

Yemima They move gently towards her leg

Narrator And then to the other leg

Yemima Separating both legs

Narrator Finding a space between them.

Yemima A nice space, a soft space. So, so

Narrator Soft.

Yemima A ticklish space

Narrator Dripping

Yemima A sticky space

Narrator A space that climbs upwards and stops the heart

Yemima And Yemima's fingers get smoother and faster and her mouth opens and her head throbs like . . . . and she gasps and moans . . .

Narrator And Yemima doesn't hear anything, not Dad waking up and getting out of bed in his underwear with bare feet, and she doesn't smell anything, not even the smell of the sunflower seeds burning in the oven. Her cheeks burn as they meet her Dad's eyes.

Yemima Daddy.

Father Where's your mother?

Yemima What . . .?

Father Where is Mum?

Yemima She went . . . Umm, she went to get some air.

Father What are you doing home so early? God will burn your father because of you.[8] Dammit. (**Father** *takes the pan off the heat with the pants.*)

Yemima I went to school, but on the way I fell

Father You fell? Where'd you fall?

Yemima In the street. In La Martin Street. I hurt my foot and it swelled up.

Father How did you fall?

Yemima I didn't see that there was a hole and I fell and Boolbool pulled me out.

Father Boolbool?

Yemima The seller. The one who Mummy buys her sunflower seeds from.

Father I know who Boolbool is.

Yemima The Arab.

Father Where's your mother? Where is she going at this hour?

Mother *enters.*

Mother What happened? What's this smoke?

Father Where were you? You left sunflower seeds in the oven and left.

Mother You were here, how did you not smell it?

Father Was he here?

Mother Who?

Father I told you I don't like you buying from them.

---

[8] Arabic expression that is loosely translated here. Other alternatives might include 'Your father will rot in hell because of you'.

Mother He brings the best merchandise, nobody has the things he has, now move and let me wash up.

Father Don't tell me to move.

Mother Move or I'll take the sunflower seeds and throw them in the trash. I don't need sunflower seeds. I don't need this poison.

Father Sure, why not, throw them in the trash. Did you work hard for them?

Mother I don't do anything . . . all day I just go from hairdresser to hairdresser.

Father You know you're going out, why do you leave things in the oven?

Mother Excuse me? You're coming to me with complaints? I've been on my feet since this morning.

Father You think I partied all night? You don't know how to appreciate anything, what am I even working for?

Mother I'll tell you what for, for your stomach and for this grave you've built for me.

Father The house could have burned down, Yaffa.

Mother For my part, everything can burn down, I'm fed up with you, I'm fed up with your life. I'm fed up.

Father You're fed up. Aren't you ashamed to talk like that? You have the nerve to come to me and complain?!

He throws the sunflower seeds on the floor.

Was he here?

Mother Who?

Father I told you I don't like it when you buy from them.

Mother Doesn't like! But then every Friday it's 'where are the sunflower seeds? Mmmm my wife's sunflower seeds . . .'

Father You could have burned the house down!

Mother Everything can burn, I'm fed up with you and your life. I'm fed up.

Father He was here.

Narrator Dad leaves!

Father *exits.*

Yemima Can I help? Mummy. . . . (**Yemima** *lays her head on the table.*) My foot doesn't hurt anymore.

Mother God help me. You sit still so I can finish. Shabbat starts soon.

Narrator Yemima sits on the bed and picks up her feet. Mother collects the scattered sunflower seeds and finishes cleaning the floors. Time drips like the wax of the candles that Mum lights for Shabbat. Then, she turns on the television and Yemima hears

Yemima The melody of the Arab movie!

Nalga Fatchi

She's getting on the table!

Farid Shawki!

Mother Who?

Yemima The hero who died last week!

Mother Yemima go wake your father up, it's almost Shabbat.

Yemima But I'm watching.

Mother Get up, Papa'gina.

Yemima *walks and shouts backstage.*

Yemima Daddy, Mummy says to get up and come make the blessings.

Yemima *goes back to the movie.*

Yemima You see? He doesn't want to get up.

Mother The food is out on the table, come make the blessings? Do you hear me?

Narrator Mother collapses the length of the tiles between them with three steps.

Mother Don't pretend you're asleep. Food is on the table, don't think you are punishing me if you don't eat, it's your children.

Yemima Nagla Fatchi and Farid Shawki are always so beautiful.

Narrator Yemima and the leopard dive into the movie.

Yemima Their love is so real and there's so much tenderness in their eyes.

Mother I'm working like a donkey for who, huh? For who?

Yemima When she sees him her heart beats and her shirt sticks to her body.

Mother (*knocking on the door*) For who?

Yemima He approaches her, looks at her, lifts her chin.

Mother Do you hear me?

Yemima Their lips meet in a kiss.

Mother Do you hear me?

Narrator Yemima swallows her saliva and wipes away a tear from the corner of her eye. Mum comes in with nothing in her hands.

Yemima No need, if he doesn't want to eat let him starve, whatever. Why are you crying? Stop, Mummy, don't cry. Look, they're kissing.

Narrator And Yemima hides her tears, fighting with them. They well up like hot steam from her stomach to her throat, she can't breathe. Finally, they leave quietly. Her nose runs and tears run down her cheeks towards her chin, into her pajamas.

Mother *exits.*

Narrator When the movie finishes, it's hard to tell who is who, traces of the heroine embed into Yemima's body, and the Arabic words continue to echo in her head. In the bathroom, she looks in the mirror and sees

Yemima Nagla, Nagla Fatchi.

Music.

Yemima *copies the actions and words of the woman in the Arab film. She plays the man and the woman.*

Yemima (*Arabic*) *Ma fee-sh mushkila ya rouh albi, ma fee-sh mushkila. Ana bahibek, ana za'alnah, inta ganab, abadan.*[9]

Music down.

Mother Yemima, come eat.

Yemima WAIT[10]

Yemima My name is Yemima. If you call me Yemima, I'll answer. Behind my back, they call me Papa'gina. My name is Yemima.

Mother YEMIMA . . .

Yemima Wait!!!

Mother What 'wait?' Wait what?

Narrator My name is Yemima and the word I love most is, 'Wait'.

---

[9] Arabic, roughly translated to: 'What's wrong, my heart's soul? What's the matter? I love you, I'm desperate for you, you're angry, nevermind.'

[10] 'Rega' in Hebrew.

a People

(*A Mosaic Play*)

L M Feldman

The Playwright

L M Feldman is a queer, feminist playwright who pens theatrically adventurous, physically kinetic, ensemble-driven plays that are both epic and intimate. An alum of the Yale School of Drama and the New England Center for Circus Arts, L is also a circus dramaturg, a professor, a teaching artist, a Playwrights' Center Core Writer and a Shakespeare's New Contemporaries winner. Her work has been nominated for the Venturous Award, Herb Alpert Award, Wasserstein Prize, Steinberg Award, New York Innovative Theatre Award, Doric Wilson Independent Playwright Award and the Blackburn Prize, among others. Her work can be found at www.laurenfeldman.com or www.newplayexchange.org.

Synopsis

A People is a mosaic of eras and lands; generations and deserts; hats and books; clarinets and bread; people lost and people searching; angry young women; sad old men; angels; history; memory; and imagination. The play gathers a versatile ensemble of eight to ten performers, taking on a spectrum of Old and New World perspectives – across time, space, age and gender – in a kaleidoscopic celebration of humanity that explores and explodes the history and present of the Jewish diaspora. A participatory theatrical experience as intimate as it is epic, *a People* spins a luminous and tenuous tale of (dis) connection and (be)longing, all while wrestling with the question: What is my relationship to those who came before me? And are we – or is anyone – still a people?

Production History

Production: Orbiter 3 – dir. Rebecca Wright (2018)

Readings: Global Jewish Voices (Bush Theatre/London) – dir. Julia Samuels (2022)
YiddishFest NYC & GableStage – dir. Avi Hoffman (2019)

Academic Production: Cornell University – dir. Beth Milles (2011)

Workshop: Jewish Plays Project – dir. David Winitsky (2013)

Residencies: Tofte Lake Center, terraNOVA Collective

Finalist: Terrence McNally Award

Honors: Alliance for Jewish Theatre Conference, Jewish Plays Project Top Plays

THE ENSEMBLE

Actors

A cast of 6–10 performers.
A mix of young and old.
A mix of Jewish and not.
A multiracial, multiethnic cast is vital.
All genders are welcome.

Characters

Many.

Including but not limited to:

Wind
Sand
Klezmer Ensemble
Boy *(Young Boy Hawker)*
Yitzak
Young Woman with Polish Accent *(Judyta)*
Old Woman with New York Accent *(Nan)*
Old Men 1–8
Old Women 1–8
Study Group Leader
Woodchoppers 1, 2, 3, 5
Woodchopper 4 *(father of Pete)*
Tanna
Old Yeshiva Teacher *(Morris)*
Contemporary Woman
Contemporary Man
Bride
Groom
Sister
Anne Frank
Fiddler
Moses
Martin Buber
Jocund Old Rabbi
Zayde
Molly
Daniel
Overwhelmed, Linker, Starter, Wrestler
Anchor, Struggler, Griever, Legacyer
Old World Woman
New World Young Adult(s)
Young Man Hassid (*Moshe*)
National Yiddish Book Center (NYBC) Prez
Yiddishkeits 1 and 2
Abraham Koralnik
Irving
Eliezer
Older Woman Answering Door (*Sarah*)
Younger Woman Knocking on Door
Revelers/Choir
Mother
Daughter (*Sarah Rachel Leah*)
Little Choir Boy (*Noah*)
Heschel
Child (*David*)
Parent 1 (*mother of David*)
Parent 2 (*mother of Molly*)
Polish Parent 3 (*father of Judyta*)
Nontraditional Rabbi
Jacob
Sarah
Rebecca
A Bubbe

Casting

This play lives in the *need* to evoke, or the *effort* to embody, the folx you're connected to. The gap between the *performer's* lived experience

and the *character's* lived experience

is the beating heart (and wrestling-space) of this play.

I recommend that after the Tanna scene, the casting starts to transgress/transcend gender . . .

> *(e.g.:* **Bubbe**, **Bride**, *and* **Sister** *played by men.*
> **Groom**, **Zayde**, **Young Man Hassid**, *and* **Abraham Koralnik** *played by women. Etc.)*

and that with Old Men and Old Women #1–8, the casting starts to transgress/transcend age . . .

Character breakdown/The doublings

There are a great many ways of using the doubling in this play.
Here is a possible layout for 8 actors.
(Drop me a line if you want to collaborate on other iterations tailored to your ensemble.)

Performer 1

Boy, Old Man 3+6, Woodchopper 1, Bride, Starter, Eliezer, Older Woman Answering Door, Reveler, Heschel, Polish Parent 3

Performer 2

Old Woman 1+8, Contemporary Woman, Woodchopper 3, Groom, Molly, Wrestler, Irving, Reveler, Child, Rebecca

Performer 3

Old Man 2+5, Contemporary Man, Woodchopper 4, Daniel, Linker, Yiddishkeit 1, Younger Woman Knocking On Door, Reveler

Performer 4

Old Man 1+7, Study Group Leader, Sister, Griever, Little Choir Boy, Jacob, A Bubbe

Performer 5

Old Woman 3+7, Woodchopper 2, Fiddler, Jocund Old Rabbi, Struggler, Yiddishkeit 2, Daughter, Parent 1

Performer 6

Yitzak, Old Man 4+8, Old Yeshiva Teacher, Moses, Anchor, Young Man Hassid, Mother, Sarah

Performer 7

Old Woman With Accent, Old Woman 4+6, Tanna, Martin Buber, Overwhelmed, Old World Woman, Koralnik, Reveler, Parent 2

Performer 8

Young Woman With Accent, Old Woman 2+5, Woodchopper 5, Anne Frank, Zayde, Legacyer, NYBC Prez, Reveler, Nontraditional Rabbi

Rhythm, pace, sound, space

This play moves fast, boldly, and playfully.
Pace is crucial. Momentum is vital. Find the rhythms.
Characters in this world often talk as if someone's about to interrupt them at any moment.
Even if – *especially* if – they're the only one talking.

The soundscape (natural, musical and otherwise)
may be entirely created by the voices of the ensemble.

The play begins and ends with a bare stage.
The feel of a small group of people in a cavernous space.
Or maybe they're in the middle space, with the audience encircling them.
Minimalism is gorgeous.
This whole play should feel like a true ensemble undertaking.

And finally, a note about ***FORM & CONTENT:***

This is a play, yes, but ideally it should also feel like *an experience*,
like a special event to the watcher.
It should include, embrace, immerse, connect, challenge and delight.

So I've endeavoured to express that sense of event
through the formatting of the script itself, to give the reader a similar experience
of an immersive, fluid, rhythmic, playful, physical, musical, sensorial,
mystical, imagistic and participatory event.

Enjoy

a People

The darkness and stillness of an empty space

of a play about to begin.
of the *world* about to begin.
of . . .

Wind blows through ~~

Whhhhhhhhhhhoooooooooooooooooohhhhhhhhhhhhhhhhhhhsssshh . . .

The wind blows in humanity.

A *wee flourish* of music!

Klezmer!! Trumpets, clarinets, violins, fiddles, a bass?,
a flute, a tambourine, !!!

Rowdy voices offstage!

Celebration!!
Holiday!!
Holy day!!
Kaloo kallay!!

YA-da-dai-dai-dai-DAI-da-DAI
YA-da-da-DAI-da-da-DAI-DAI
YA-da-dai-dai-dai-DAI-da-DAI
ya DAI DAI DAI DAI DAI!

Sand scatters through ~~
Sssssshhhhhhhhhhhhhsssssstttttccccchhhhhhhhhhkkkkhhhhggggghhhhtttssssss . . .

The sand scatters time and music and voices and other things . . . . . .
. . . . scatters them out of sight.

Stillness.
Absence.
Hush.

The Wind picks back up ~~
Hhhhhhhhhhhwwwwwhhhhhoooooooooooooooooosssssshhhhhhhhhsshhhhh

It blows humanity back in.
KLEZMER AGAIN!!!
Offstage HOOPLA!!

*V*oices! *YA-da-dai-dai-dai-DAI-da-DAI*
*M*usic! *YA-da-da-DAI-da-da-DAI-DAI*
*R*evelry! – *YA-da-dai-dai-dai-DAI-da-DAI* –

The Sand scatters in ~~
cccccckkkkkghhhhhhhhgggsssssshhhhhhhhhhhhhttttttttthhhhhhhhhttssss

It rescatters the people,
who disappear.

Stillness.
Absence.
Hush.
And then?

!!!! . . A Storm Of Firmament, Elements, & Human Sound . . !!*!!*

WIND ~~
hhhhhhwwwwhhhoooosssshhhhhhh . . .

Revelry!
Voices!

SAND ~~
ccckkkhhhhttttthhhtchsssss . . .

~~ *wwhhuuoosshhh*

Stomping!
Dancing!

~~ *tschkkhggthchhtsss*

~~ *wwhhuuoosshhh*

~~ *tschkkhgthchtsss* *Instruments!* ~~ *wwhhuuoosshhh*
~~ *tschkkhgthchtsss* *Wailing!* ~~ *wwhhuuoosshhh*
~~ *tschkkhgthchtsss* *Ya-da-dai's!* ~~ *wwhhuuoosshh*

silence

. . .

a match flare.

(pfhffff . . .)

a flame.
a single light in the darkness.
iconic.

the sun crests over the horizon.
it softens the night into morning . . . which brings:

A young boy hawker
on a street corner in Brooklyn.
He is dressed as a Hassid.
Black hat, black trousers, white shirt, black jacket,
black shoes, black belt, white undershirt tunic with the religious tassels, whatretheycalledagain,
black kippah hidden in the black hat,
and a new young beard trying to sprout.

He calls to us (audience & actors both) as passersby.
He's not having much luck getting people to stop.

Boy
Shana Tovah!
Happy New Year!
Have you heard the shofar today?
Have you heard the shofar today?
May you be written in the Book of Life!
Excuse me, are you Jewish? Have you heard the shofar today?
Are you by any chance Jewish?
Excuse me, are you Jewish?
Hag sameach!
Excuse me, are you by any chance Jewish? Yes?!?
Have you heard the shofar today??
It will only take a minute. LESS than a minute. Thirty Seconds. Well, forty. Fifty.
For the New Year.
Here. You can read Hebrew?
That's okay – just say with me,

'Baruch atah Adonai, eloheinu melech ha'olam,
asher kidishanu b'mitzvotav v'tzivanu leshmoa kol shofar.'

(not terribly interested in the English translation)
Uh . . . BlessedareYouHaShemKingoftheuniverse,
whohasblesseduswithcommandmentsandcommandedustoheartheshofar.
Okay, and again, with me,

'Baruch atah Adonai, eloheinu melech ha'olam,
shehechiyanu v'kiyimanu v'higianu la'zman ha'zeh.'

(not terribly interested in the English translation)
Uh . . . BlessedareYouHaShemKingoftheUniverse,

whokeptusalive,sustainedus,andbroughtustoseethisday.

(calling off)

Yitzak. Come over here. We got one!

(to the person he's snagged)

Tonight, before the sun sets, take a bath. Eat some brisket. It's a holy day!

Yitzak (short, rumpled, quiet, the Hardy to the boy's Laurel) comes over with the shofar (ram's horn) and blows into it in the pattern that the Boy calls.

Boy		**Yitzak**
Tekiah	→	(dt-tooooo-*ooh*)
Shevarim-Teruah	→	(dt-too dt-too dt-too, dt-too-too-too-too-too-too-too-too-*tooh*)
Tekiah	→	(dt-tooooo-*ooh*)
Tekiah	→	(dt-tooooo-*ooh*)
Shevarim	→	(dt-too dt-too dt-too)
Tekiah	→	(dt-tooooo-*ooh*)
Tekiah	→	(dt-tooooo-*ooh*)
Teruah	→	(dt-too-too-too-too-too-too-too-too-*tooh*)
Tekiah Gadola	→	(dt-toooooooooooooooooooooooooooooooooooooooo ooooooooooooooooooooooooooooooooooooooooooo ooooooooooooooooooooooooooooooooooooooooooo *ooh*!)

Yitzak is out of breath.
The young boy hawker is smiling.

Boy
Happy new year!!

A SPLASH into water.
A SECOND SPLASH into water.
A flock of geese take off overhead.
Wind through leaves.
A glass smashed underfoot.

LIGHT on a young woman
with accented English.

Young Woman with Polish Accent
Eh . . . khallow?
Eh . . . I look . . . I looking . . . for for for
for . . . man?
Eh, Winiawski? You knaow deese man?
Khe Khe . . . We met . . . on bowt. On bowt.
Khe telled me khis name: Winiawski.
You knaow?
Khe . . . eh, small. (*gestures short*)
Is, eh . . . graey (*gestures coat*),
graey (*gestures vest*),
graey (*gestures trousers*),
white (*gestures shirt*),
black eh shoes,
eh, stick (*gestures cane*) . . .,
. . . khat (*gestures hat*),
eh . . . (*gestures spectacles*),
clean (*gestures shaved face*), . . . byootifull.
Eh, khe telled me . . .
(exhales, exhausted from the effort of speaking in a foreign tongue)

LIGHT on an old woman
in different accented English.
(Their lines interweave, but don't overlap . . .)

Old Woman with New York Accent
Hello-o
It's nan and pop
How are you, bubbeleh Is everything fine?
We miss you

(embarrassed, smiles; struggles on)
Khe telled me . . . khe live
(*points downward, here*). 'New Jersey.'

I, uh, I just spoke with mother and dad,
and they're coming up to see us on Sunday

'Bayonne.'
Khe telled me,

at Wolfie's
for Brunch
Uch.

'Come *find* me!

I don't know why they schlep all the way
up here.

New Jersey. Bayonne. Winiawski. My name.'

'Carol,' I says to your mom,

You knaow khim?

'Why do you insist on driving all the way
up here?

I *love* khim.

On a Sunday?
It's your day off!

Please . . . Where is 'Bayonne?'
Is, is long?

Uh, Stuart works
You work

Ay Gott.

(a thinly veiled opinion)
Even on *Saturdays*
So you must be tired

I am *Nowak.*

Exhausted even

My name.

WHY do you –'

Judyta.

'We WANT to,' she says.

Nowak.

So?

Please, tell khim I *look.*

What can I tell you

Tell khim . . .

You have marvelous parents

. . . Winiawski . . .

The best

. . . tell khim I *close.*

. . .

. . .

And you're marvelous too.
(then grudgingly)
And your brother.
And your sister.
You're all . . .

If you see, tell khim I khere . . .

So? Poppy and I were just wondering
when we're gonna get to see you again

'KHoboken.'

we know that you're busy

I *khere.*

we know your, your work comes first
And we just wanted you to know
that we miss you!
And we're thinking of you.
And praying for you.
Every night
eighty-three years
I say my prayers.

Tell khim I find 'Bayonne.'

And we pray for you,

Thdank you, please.

(then grudgingly)
and your brother,
and your sister,
and mother and dad,
and all our family,
and all our loved ones, . . .
and this is it.

Ay Gott.

Be happy.
Be healthy.
Don't try so hard.
Enjoy.
That's all we ask.
Is that you *enjoy* it.

Okay?
Love you.
G'Bye.

Judyta takes the kerchief off her head and hands it to a young man who, by blowing his nose into it, becomes Old Man 1. He talks to us.

Old Man 1
So you wanna know how your Bubbe (grandmother) and I met?
You want the long version or the short?
The short.
(clears his throat)
I saw her on the boat . . . And I sat on her hat.

Old Man 2
You don't remember how your Savta (grandmother) and I met?
I told ya, Delta Phi Epsilon.
I was the janitor in her sorority.
She was the tall one.
Hair down to her tush.

Old Woman 1
How I met your grandfather?
Uch, I came from his rib.

Old Man 3
Did you ask your grandmother?
Well what did SHE tell you?

Old Man 4
How I met your grandpa?
Well it was Yom Kippur, so I was atoning . . .
on South Beach . . .

Old Woman 2
He was wearing a hat.

Old Woman 3
He had that groovy long hair . . .

Old Man 4
I had hair then.

Old Woman 4
Why I'm your grandma?
King David liked me.

Old Woman 5
My husband died.
And his brother favoured me.

Old Woman 6
We needed the money.

Old Man 5
I needed the money.

Old Man 6
She came from my rib.

Old Woman 7
He sat on my hat.

Old Woman 8
Did I ever tell you how I met your Nana?

Old Man 7
I lived in Bayonne.

Old Man 8
Match-dot-com

Old Woman 8
I sat on her hat.

Old Woman 7
It was lying on the ground.

Old Man 8
Or was it J-date?

Old Woman 7
'Close the flap,' I said,
'you're letting in sand.'

Old Man 8
Match, Match.

Old Woman 7
So he tied down the flap
and the wind whipped outside

and he spat out some sand that had made its way
to his lips
on his tongue
we laughed
and he picked the grains from his tongue with his fingers
and I spilled some soup I was making
I was laughing so hard
I was nervous
he had snuck out to meet me
this wasn't allowed, you know
Unchaperoned?
So he sat down in the sand
and I said, 'No, Elijah ben Yehuda, take the cushion the cushion.'
And I trip!
And the soup goes everywhere the bread is flying
figs and almonds take off like birds in flight
soaring
splatting
'No, I'm not burned,
todah la'el,
but the soup is gone
back into the earth.
Do you like dates?'
– I asked him –
'We can eat dates
sticky, sweet
until we're full
And zahtar and olive oil
(*coy*) Hey, who needs bread when we have fingers?
. . .
Okay but, listen, *b'seder:*
You have walked through the desert,
we have spilt all our soup,
our bread is in crumbles,
our figs are in puddles,
we can't raise our voices,
so will you get off the sand
and sit on a cushion?
. . .
And *where is my hat??'*

And he gets up to move.
And there was my hat, squashed, underneath him.
. . .
It was the happiest I've ever seen that hat.

(A Contemporary Woman (perhaps it's Molly) emerges, wandering amid this forest of grandparents . . .)

Contemporary Woman
An old, old man and an old, old woman speak in strange guttural tones
on a downtown train.
(*as the old, old man*) 'Coney Island?'
I look up.
(*as herself*) 'Yeah, just stay on the train. It'll take a while, but you'll get there.'
The man nods, and there's that old, old smile on his lips.
What's IN that smile?
It beats a drum in my chest.
What NINETY years of life and humans and love and heartbreaks and deaths and great meals and

Old Yeshiva Teacher (or Old Man 8): *amazing sex*
CW: and different eras and cultures and
OYT: *timezones*
CW: and great wars and
OYT: *great depressions*
CW: and big bands and
OYT: *cigars*
CW: and
OYT: *cognac*
CW: and
OYT: *whisky*
CW: and
OYT: *manischewitz*
CW: and
OYT: *firewood*
CW: and workhorses and strong coffee and
OYT: *dirty fingernails*
CW: and old potatoes and
OYT: *dead dogs*
CW: and sudden weather changes and human cruelties and
OYT: *mortar*
CW: and bricks and
OYT: *cobblestones*
CW: and granite and
OYT: *stern paternal hands*
CW: and stern
OYT: *maternal*
CW: hands and ripped
OYT: *old shirts*
CW: and patches
OYT: *and dishtowels*
CW: – how many dishtowels? –

OYT: *and near car crashes and first terrified airplane trips and rock collections and end-of-summer swims*
CW: and colds and flus and almost-didn't-make-its and
OYT: *moments of exhalation*
CW: while
OYT: *looking up at the night sky*
CW: and
BOTH: ***contemplating eternity . . .***

Contemporary Woman
. . . How many things are clenched in those tight imperceptible muscles around the face because you have to contain NINETY OR SO YEARS OF LIFE INSIDE YOUR ONE BODY
and that's NOT A LOT OF SPACE. For so much of Time to fit inside.

(A Contemporary Man (perhaps it's Daniel) emerges too . . .)

(*Throughout:*
Someone starts absentmindedly humming the opening bars of the fiddler's violin solo from 'Fiddler on the Roof' as the ensemble becomes the Woodchoppers.
Contemporary Woman, also becoming a Woodchopper,
absentmindedly follows with the second strain of the fiddler's violin solo.)

<table>
<tr><td>Contemporary Man</td><td></td><td></td></tr>
<tr><td>There's those old, old rabbi dudes
with the like sidelocks curled
or like the furry hats.
And those whitehaired
slumpedover women</td><td>Woodchopper 1
(slowly, softly)
hm-HM-hm-hm-hm-hm,
hm-HM-hm-HM-hm-HM,</td><td></td></tr>
<tr><td>with the sharp gray eyes and the kerchiefs,
clutching plastic Walmart bags,
shuffling their feet forward.</td><td>hm-HM-hm-hm-hm-hm,
hm-HM-hm-HM-HM-HM . . .</td><td></td></tr>
<tr><td></td><td>Woodchopper 1
(continuing)</td><td>Woodchopper 3
(harmonizing)</td></tr>
<tr><td>She deserves a greengrocer in like Yemen.</td><td>hm-HM-hm-hm-hm-hm,</td><td>BA ba-da BA ba,</td></tr>
<tr><td>Or like a tailor in the Ukraine. But instead</td><td>hm-HM-hm-HM-hm-HM,</td><td>BA-da-ba-DA-ba-ba,</td></tr>
<tr><td>she clutches this Walmart bag,
and he clutches his mini-torah</td><td>hm-HM-hm-hm-hm-hm,</td><td>BA-da-da-DA-da-da,</td></tr>
<tr><td>or whatever, rocking back and forth, humming under his breath . . .. . .</td><td>hm-HM-hm-HM-HM-HM</td><td>DA-da-da-DA-da . . .</td></tr>
</table>

And I get jealous.
(beat)
Old people make me wish I were done already.
(beat)

And that I had something super
important
to wear on my head.

(Someone plops a Woodchopper hat on his head.)

Gavel Gavel Gavel.

(Men's voices . . .)

grumblegrumblemurmurmurmurmumblemumblegrumble

(The men assemble and mingle . . .)

Study Group Leader

Attention . . .? *Puzhalsta* . . . ('please' in Russian)
The Society of Woodchoppers for the Study of Mishna in Berditchev is now called to order.
Are we all met?

Woodchopper 4

Pete's not here.

(beat)

Study Group Leader

Well we don't got all day.

Woodchoppers

WC 5: I'm exhausted.
WC 2: I got work tomorrow.
WC 1: Pete's my study partner.
WC 4: We ALL got work tomorrow.
WC 3: Where *is* Pete?
WC 1: (to an audience member) Will you be my study partner?
WC 2: (to WC 4) I'm AGREEING with you.

Study Group Leader

I'll be your study partner.

Woodchoppers

WC 4: (to WC 2) You're KVETCHING.
WC 3: He's not.
WC 5: *I* am.

Study Group Leader

But will someone fill him in?

Woodchoppers

WC 1: Sure.
WC 2: Yes.
WC 5: Who?

WC 1: Pete.
WC 4: Let's get on with it.
WC 5: Hush up.
WC 1: Shhh.
WC 3: Shhh yourself.

Study Group Leader
Okay. So. Where are we up to?

Woodchoppers
WC 1: *Sotah.*
WC 4: Of course.
WC 2: The Fifth Book.
WC 3: Fourth Book.
WC 5: Third.
WC 2: Nikoleyavich that's absurd.
WC 5: I meant Third Volume.
WC 1: Well I just know it's *Sotah.*
WC 4: (mocking the obvious) And the lake is blue.
WC 3: All right . . .
WC 4: And the wind is clear, and the sand is gold, . . .
WC 2: Oy gevalt.
WC 5: Take it easy.

Study Group Leader
Gentleman.

Woodchoppers
WC 4: . . . He makes up in fore*head* what he lacks in fore*skin.*
WC 3: Actually sand is clear. It's shattered glass.
WC 2: Oy oy *oy.*
WC 3: And water is clear; it's the light that makes it blue.
WC 4: Splitting hairs.
WC 2: And he's off.
WC 3: It's not hairs.
WC 1: Let him split hairs.
WC 3: It's not hairs!

Study Group Leader
Gentleman! *Sotah,* the Fifth Tractate
of the Third Volume *Nashim.*

Woodchoppers
WC 5: Someone's here.
WC 4: Is it Pete?

Study Group Leader
Come in, come in!

(A young Tanna enters.)

Woodchoppers

ALL: . . .
WC 2: Nope.
WC 5: Who are you?
WC 1: Tea? Coffee?
WC 4: (to the Tanna) You know the lake is blue?
WC 2: Ok! Ok!
WC 3: Nudnik.
WC 4: Goniff.

Study Group Leader
Gentleman!

(An Old Yeshiva Teacher interrupts, and points to the Tanna . . . .)

Old Yeshiva Teacher
(He's a fast-talker with a sense of humour.)

(to us) Boys! Do you know who this is?
(We, as his students, shake our heads no . . .)
(to the scene behind him) Hold a sec.
(to us again) Have I got a story for you! The Story of Tannas.
Listen up, lads, to become the smart, learned men you're bound to become.

So there's the Torah and the Torah.
'What's the Torah and the Torah?'
Well the Torah is the Written Torah, the one that God gave our Moses,
that prophet with the long beard?
And the Torah is the Oral Torah.
'Oral Torah? Never hearda nothing like it.'
Well the Oral Torah was what God gave to Moses too – verbally.
(Which is a lot better than rectally, I gotta tell ya.)
So now you got two Torahs.
'Two Torahs? Surely that's confusing, Rav Morris.'
It is!
And it's not!
The one unlocks the other. The mouth unlocks the hand. The tongue unlocks the pen.
It's a beauteefull thing. You'll see when you're grown.
So centuries pass, (can you picture them, passing? Like blown sand and bright stars . . .
WHOOSH!),
and we're passing the two scrolls from generation to generation:
the Scroll of the Hand and the Scroll of the Tongue.

And then? Destruction! Diaspora! Dismantling of our Nation!
So? What do you think we do?
We get a bunch of smartypants sages to write it all down,
lest we spread out so much we can't hear the tongue no more.

So Judah-ha-Nasi – Judah the Prince – (a genius who started out as a lad just like you)
he takes all the writings of the many many sages
and he *compiles* the Oral Torah into a text.
A text so holy it came from the teeth of God.
He puts into Chapters, Verses, and Volumes all its secrets and its contradictions.
So now? Our Oral Torah you can pick up and read. We call it the Mishna.
Here, take a copy! You can hold it in your hands!
This book – this! – was chewed around in the mouths of millions of people before you!

(The Woodchoppers are a little touched, impressed . . .)

Study Group Leader

Ok, *spaziba* ('thank you' in Russian), so, we begin with . . .

(The Old Yeshiva Teacher interrupts, continuing . . .)

Old Yeshiva Teacher

But!
Before the masses could *read* this book – there were ***Tannas***.

(He points to the Tanna again . . .)

Old Yeshiva Teacher

Special young men of the past.
Come 'ere, son.

(The Tanna comes . . . .)
(The Woodchoppers grumble.)
(mumblmumblegrumblemurmurgrumblewondermurmur.)

Old Yeshiva Teacher

Geniuses of memory and bearers of contradiction.

(The Woodchoppers fall silent, struck by this.)

Old Yeshiva Teacher

Geniuses of memory and bearers of contradiction.

Woodchopper 4

(to the Tanna, awestruck) That's, uh, that's pretty good.

Old Yeshiva Teacher

A tanna's job was to memorize a piece of the Oral Torah *flawlessly*,
and then to repeat it, and repeat it, whenever called upon by those who longed to study it.
Every Tanna was responsible for memorizing a different piece,
you see what this means?
This means you get all these Tannas in a room together,
and they *contain* the whole of the Oral Torah inside their heads – *collectively*.
It takes a whole people to contain a book.
This, here, now? All you lads with all your thoughts in all your heads?
What do you think we contain, all put together like this?
. . .

(to an audience member) Aw Yehoshua, I don't trust that look on your punim . . .
(to us) Jews like groups. You can't be a Jew on your own.

(beat)

And then when the Oral became Written, the Tannas disappeared . . . .
BUT what if we who learn – the Scholars, the Rabbis, even the Labourers, even the *Woodchoppers in Berditchev*!, look!,
(to the Woodchoppers) you're famous, you know? –

(They didn't know that. They're flattered. They blush.)

Woodchoppers

(*simultaneously*)
WC 1: Wow.
WC 2: Really?
WC 3: Didn't know I was famous, you?
WC 4: Did they spell my name right?
WC 5: I had a feeling . . .

Old Yeshiva Teacher

No, we don't know your names. Just the group.

Woodchoppers

(*simultaneously*)
WC 1: Huh.
WC 2: Well.
WC 3: Yeah . . .
WC 4: Figures.
WC 5: Oh.

Old Yeshiva Teacher

(continuing) – what if we who learn could still call upon the Tannas to tell us by mouth what's written by hand? Eh? (beat)
Because I tell you, boys:
Life, you hear me?, is *discussion*. It's aloud. It's a *wrestle*.
They say you can't learn alone. You learn *along*.
You learn *with*, Yehoshua. With.
(inviting the Woodchoppers to continue) Okay. I gotta make a pish.
(watching what unfolds as he starts to head out . . .)

Study Group Leader

Well . . . OK . . . Sir, will you please . . .
recite *Sotah*, Chapter 1, Mishna 1?

Tanna

(recites from memory)

The Sages used figurative terms for the stages of womanhood:
an undeveloped fig, a ripening fig, or a ripe fig;
an 'undeveloped fig' means 'while she is still a child';
a 'ripening fig' means 'the days of her maidenhood'–

in each of these cases her father is entitled to aught she finds,
and to the produce of her hands, and to disannul her vows;
a 'ripe fig' means 'as soon as she is mature,'
and her father has no more authority over her.

Study Group Leader
That's not the volume we're on . . .

Tanna
Five kinds of blood in a woman are unclean:
the red,
and the black,
and the shade of the bright-coloured saffron,
and the colour like earthy water,
and the colour like red wine mingled with water.

Study Group Leader
Is there a different Tanna?

Tanna
If she is sitting on a couch and handling clean things, and she leaves the couch and
then discovers blood internally,
she is unclean and they are clean.

(The Tanna begins shedding his outer garment . . . .)

Tanna
If a girl of twelve years and one day has attained her menstrual flow,
and she was wed,
she is permitted to copulate the first night.

(The Tanna is wearing a contemporary shirt.
She has breasts.)

A girl that has not grown two hairs is not able to exercise the prerogative of refusal.

(The Tanna takes off her hat.
She has long hair.)

A girl three years and one day old may be bethrothed by sexual connection;
and if the brother of her deceased childless husband consummated
levirate marriage with her,
he has acquired her as his wife.

(The Tanna takes off her spectacles and looks at the Study Group Leader. She's a contemporary woman invading an earlier time.)

(The Study Group Leader lowers his spectacles and looks at her.
The Old Yeshiva Teacher lowers his spectacles and looks at her.)

(She looks at them back.)

(The Woodchoppers are confused, shocked, standing around awkwardly, ...)

Tanna

I am not a fig.

(One of the Woodchoppers takes off his hat. She's a contemporary woman.)

Study Group Leader

I do not understand this Jewish.

Tanna

I am not unclean.

(Another of the Woodchoppers takes off his hat. She's a contemporary woman.)

Study Group Leader

I do not understand this time.

Tanna

This was not written by anyone like me.

(The remaining Woodchoppers and Leader are looking around – angry, betrayed, confused. The two contemporary women look at the third woman still among the Woodchoppers, who looks torn but shakes her head no and remains, pulling her hat down tighter.)

Study Group Leader

I do not understand your God.

Tanna

Your God doesn't know me at all.

(The Tanna tosses her hat and spectacles aside and starts to go.)

Old Yeshiva Teacher

Carla, wait!

Tanna

I refuse to have been born from this, Morris.
I refuse to inherit this.

Old Yeshiva Teacher

(to Study Group Leader, by way of explanation)
Sorry . . .
My, uh, my son's grandaughter . . . .

(The Tanna is gone.
The Woodchoppers look at each other.
The Old Yeshiva Teacher looks at the Woodchopper Women.
The Study Group Leader shakes his head.)

A SPLASH.
A SECOND SPLASH.
A flock of geese take off.

Wind blows in two young women:
a Bride & her Sister! –
old-world, about to be married,
preparing for her pre-wedding mikveh.

((Apart: a young Groom,
donning his old-world finest . . .))

They're excited!
Running!
Holding hands, dancing, pulling, twirling!
They urge us . . .

Sister
Take it off!
Take it all off!

Bride
Let it go!
Start anew!
It's a mikveh! (ritual bath)

Sister
It's a mitzvah! (good deed)

Bride
It's a bath, a holy bath, it's a holy thing to do. We get *points* for doing this!

Sister
Come jump with us!

Bride
But only women!

Sister
Only women. Especially sisters.
The men's lake is somewhere over . . .

Bride
Over there. Through the trees.

Sister
Two natural-lake mikvehs.

Bride
(to an audience member) They say there aren't that many any more.

Sister
(confused) Where's ours?

Bride
(to an audience member) You should jump with us!

Sister

It's a cleansing.
It's a ritual.

Bride

It's to make me holy.

Sister

It's her wedding day.

Bride

It's my wedding day! I'm holy!

Sister

You're a blessing.

Bride

It's true! They said today I can give blessings.
(to someone in the audience) Shall I bless you?
(resting her hands gently on audience member's head) May you get what you want.
May you make yourself proud.
May you find yourself a husband.

Sister

Or a million dollars.

Bride

That's not a blessing.

Sister

Bless me too, cuz it's gonna be freezing.

Bride

Only for a second.

Sister

For *minutes*.
(still confused) Where *is* it?

Bride

I'm not gonna bathe that long. In and out.

Sister

(*looking up*) There they go.

Bride

(*looking up*) I love the geese.

Sister

(*looking up*) I wonder where they go . . .

Bride

(*looking up*) I wonder how they mate . . .
(stillness . . .

looking up . . .
Sister takes Bride's hand . . .)

We'll go in quickly. Okay? We'll just jump. (to us) Okay? And then we'll scream.

Sister
I'm gonna curse.

Bride
And then we'll climb out.
Ready?

Sister
No.

Bride
Coward. One . . .

Sister
Wait, so *where's* our *lake*?

Ancestors appear with dripping buckets of water.
They stand with buckets at the ready.
Aimed at the Bride and Sister,
and at us.

Yep, us.

Dripping buckets.

Sister
Whoa.

These ancestors with the buckets . . .
They are attired iconically as Jews of all kinds.
Hassidim.
Modern orthodox.
Contemporary secular.
Ancient biblical.
A fiddler.
A woodchopper.
Martin Buber.
Moses.
Anne Frank.
All have buckets.
Dripping buckets.

Bride
Whoa.

Sister
Really?

Bride
Um, two . . .

Sister
This isn't how I–

Bride
Come on.

Sister
Does everyone do this?

The reluctant Bride pulls the reluctant Sister with her as they step into the centre of the lake of bucket-holding ancestors.

Bride
. . . Uh . . .

Sister
Two and a half . . .

Bride
I don't want to.

Sister
What is this?

Bride
Who are they?

The ancestors quickly introduce one another, pointing . . .

Anne Frank
Woodchopper.

Martin Buber
Fiddler.

Woodchopper 4
Moses.

Fiddler
Martin Buber.

Sister
(low) Who's Martin Buber?

(continuing, blazing ahead:)

Moses
Anne Frank.

Anne Frank
We're your wedding present!
From your new family!

From this day forward, there is never a moment when you won't exist in relation to all of us.

Bride

But –

And Anne Frank gives the signal.

The buckets drench the Bride and Sister.

SPLASH!

More buckets drench the Groom, standing apart.

SPLASH!

Moses brings the Bride and Groom together. Bride & Groom look at each other. Strangers.

Anne Frank stomps on a glass wrapped in a napkin beneath her foot (the final step in a Jewish wedding).

SMASH!

Anne Frank

Mazel tov!!

POP!
A cork!
Wine! Champagne!
Hurray! Mazel tov!
(An old man rabbi is presiding over a celebration . . .)

The sopping Bride and Groom are swept off by the ancestral masses . . .

(*Quickly, low, mouthed:*
Bride: *I love you . . .*
Sister: *I love you too . . .)*

. . . as the sopping Sister remains and watches.

Jocund Old Rabbi

Okay! eh, Hurray!, yes, *Siman* tov and *Mazel* tov and
All Good Things
to the Happy Bride and Groom!
I hear after this you're getting on a boat. To Egypt? *Wow*. The irony.
May your Lives be filled with *Love*
and
Union
and
and
and
Nachas
and may your *Bed* be filled with –

Oh ho ho! –
Get your *noggins* out of the *drerd* –

may it be Filled
may it be Filled
with **Children**.

The Jocund Old Rabbi passes around challah (reallydeliciouseggbread) to us as wedding guests.

Jocund Old Rabbi
Mit ***kinderlekh***.
Have Some Bread!

The Sister takes some challah; standing, sopping, a bite, watching.

Jocund Old Rabbi
Is everyone getting some bread back there?
Take some more take some more
Pass it pass it
Are you –
You. Did you get some?
Yes, you. Did you –
Yes? No? Yes? Good. Okay.
You –
Wait!!
What is this, you are *eating*?
Already?
Are you *swine*??
Are you *trayf*?
Wait!
The blessing! The Motzi! Uch.
So *hungry*.
Cannot *wait*
a moment
a second
for your – your –
your *GOD* for your
family
for your
Rebbe.
I am only half joking.

(His jocundness fades some.)

You must learn.
No?
To **Wait**.

Patience.

Things take time.

(beginning the blessing of the bread) *'Baruch –*
(he stops)
(he wants to say something further . . .)

(. . . he looks at us, considers us . . .)

(. . . then he shakes his head, changes his mind, decides not to say it.)

(instead he continues, holding up the bread) *'Baruch asah Adonai, eloheinu melech ha'olam, ha'motzi lechem min ha'aretz.'*

He tears the challah into pieces.
He puts a piece in his mouth.
Chews.

The Sister, sopping, sneezes.

Jocund Old Rabbi
Tsum gezunt (Bless you).

A Zayde (a grandfather) is passing through . . .

Zayde
What are you standing?
Why aren't you working?
You sick?

The Sister opens her mouth to speak.

You got kids?

She opens her mouth to speak.

When you gonna have kids?
You got a sweetie?

She opens her mouth to speak.

You love him?

She opens her mouth to speak.

Then you're waiting for what?
You think I got time?
You think <u>you</u> got time?

Her nose is running; she wipes it on the back of her hand.

He hands her the handkerchief from earlier (Judyta, Old Man 1).

Zayde
It's clean.

Is it? She examines it,
wipes her nose in a corner of it. Meanwhile:

Zayde
Uch. You kids today.
The headcolds. The flu shots. The herpes.
In my day, we had one thing: pleurisy.
Maybe some whooping cough. A little dysentery.
Small pox.
Large pox.
But we moved ON! We hacked, we drank, we sang, we slept,
we sweat out the bad blood, the bad spirits,
and we *NEVER STOPPED WORKING!*
Hats. Shoes. Gloves. Watches. Babies. Clocks. Every day.
Except the Sabbath.
You keep the Sabbath?

She opens her mouth to speak.

Zayde
But now?
You got 'sick days.'
Vuss a Sick Day?
The *DAY* – the *SUN* – it's got a runny *shnoz*?

And we, we had JEWISH sicks. The spots. The coughs. Old-world, Ashkenazi ills.
And now?
You got the, the, the ailments with the GOYISHE names.
'Mad cow.' 'Swine flu.' 'Allergies.' '*Anxiety* . . .?'

Try some leeches.
Drink some soup.
And hurry up and make babies.
There's no *time* for sickness; we're a dying race! *Dying* is sick.
You hear what I'm telling you?

She opens her mouth to speak.

Zayde
(about the hankie) Keep it.

Zayde goes and leaves her with the hankie and her silence.

An email/voicemail in the ether . . .
LIGHT on a young woman
writing us a letter.

[In the style of Gertrude Stein – but swift & funny. She's happy, excited, newly in love.]

Molly

Dear Nana,

I am not gay but I am dating a woman
I am not gay but I sometimes date women
I am not gay but I am gay right now and I am dating a woman and I love her and her name is Carla and she's jewish. She's a nice jewish girl, that's the irony.

Another voicemail in the ether . . .
LIGHT on a boy
leaving us a message.

Daniel

Yo, Great-Great-Great-Great? Grandfather,
It's Daniel. Pick up.

Molly

I am not gay but I am gay, and I am gay but not gay, I am gay.
I might be gay for a while yet, and then not, and then again, and then not.
Or maybe always.
Or maybe not.
But I am dating a nice jewish girl named Carla.

Daniel

Are you there? Pick up.
Pick up pick up pick up pick up pick up.

Molly

Dear Mom,
I am gay.
Dad,
I am gay right now.
Sis, Bro, Roxy and Seb,
I'm so gay right now and dating Carla and I love her.

(Molly goes.)

Daniel

Hello?
You're not there.
Well listen, I got a new job!
I'm a short-order cook. I make eggs. At a 24-hour breakfast diner.
I'm working at the library. I check in books, I check out books, I shelve.
I have a bike route; I'm working as a courier.
Dude, I'm working part-time at the local organic farm. I get free milk! Whaaat!
I'm a baker's assistant. I make croissants and pastries.
I make pizzas! I . . .

(Molly returns with a new thought.)

Molly

Dear Zayde,
Remember that day I saw you take your bridge out? And you put it in a cup to soak? And then I forgot and drank water out of that cup? That was so gross. And you were smiling all toothless at me? I was just thinking about that today. And the sound of your laugh.
(beat)
Well Zayde, I miss you and I've got a girlfriend named Carla.
And I may not have children.
And you may not have greatgrandkids, and greatgreatgrandkinderlen.
. . . Sorry.

(Molly goes.)

Daniel

So Great-Great-Great-Great? Grandpa, I've got this new job – and it made me think of you 'cuz,
you know, my hands. It's, like, so much better than all the friggin academia –
anthropology, ornithology, epistemology, postmodern art . . .
Like, I'm of WORTH now, you know? ALL of me. Like, my BODY matters now.
My muscles – my arms – my fingers – and fingertips – my BONES, you know?
MY JOB? Finally NEEDS FEET.
I feel so, like, Connected to you, you know? In a way I didn't before.
Because I didn't, like, SEW. Or TAILOR. Or like, HABERDASHER and shit.
I wrote, like, essays. And I made, like, conceptual art. And, like, important, yeah, but transitory. Evanescent. Gone.
And, like, that hat you made your son?,
it's still, like, in Mom's CLOSET. You know? It LASTED. It *exists*.

(Molly returns with a new thought.)

Molly

You know, Dear Nana,
I want you to know me while you're still here.
What my world looks like, how my street sounds,
what we eat for breakfast, what I like to read,
how I always wanted to do field hockey and never learned how
cuz I know it's kinda goyish.
I want you to see me paired like an animal boarding the ark –
paired with someone like-minded,
someone like me, I want you to know that *there are people like me*,
and I'm not even talking about being gay, though that's part of it,
though I'm *not* gay but I *am* with Carla,
and all of this because although you think I am *one of us*, one of 'our family,' I am *not* 'one of you,' I am distinct.

(Molly goes.)

Daniel

I really want the shit I make to *exist*.

I want to end up in my, like, progeny's closet someday.
I don't know, I mean if I have a progeny.
I don't know, you know?
(unconvinced it's a good fit for himself) I don't know.

Sister
(who's been watching all of this)
Hey Grandma Bea and Grandpa Lou,
Listen, I'm a little (*gestures freaking out*), you know?
Because if all you want is for me to be happy and to enjoy things and to make my life worth your sacrifice,
that's *a really tall order.*
I think I might be failing you.

(Sister goes.)
(Molly returns, with a new thought.)

Molly
Actually: Dear Nana, maybe *you're* not one of us either!
Maybe you're more different from us than you realize!
Or maybe you *used* to be different and then you just . . . (*gestures melded* . . .).
But how can I know you, how can *you* know you, separate from this family
if this family is what defines you and you chose it to be as such
such as it was it is and you chose it and it was and so and such, it was, you were, it is, you.
Maybe you could've been gay but not gay, childless and fine,
unmarried and happy, jewish and goyish, related to but completely distinct.

(Sister returns.)

Sister
Plus, I extremely miss my sister.

(Sister goes, and gives the hankie to someone.)

Daniel
Anyway. I called to tell you that, like, somewhere in my, like, (*gestures bones*),
your hands are still making hats.
They just look like eggs in a short-order cook line.

Molly
Okay: Mom, Dad, I'm gay but not and this is Carla.
Say hello.
Please be kind.
Roxy and Seb, call me. I miss you. Where are you?
What, you have no time for your middle sister?
We are *all* middle children . . .

Daniel
I love ya.

Molly

Love to you all,
Molly.

(Griever emerges, calling for his grandmother . . . .)

Griever

Grandma?

(. . . he's listening, looking . . .)

Grandma?

(. . . he's listening, looking . . .)

Bub?

(audience cough)

Is that . . .?
Oh.

(silence)

. . . She passed yesterday,
but I thought, maybe if I asked, she might make a special appearance.

(He really looks & listens.)

Bub??

(silence
He concludes she really is unreachable from now on.)

Would, um, . . .
Would someone adopt me? Just for today?
I'd really like to be someone's grandson right now.

(He waits, or he bargains, until he gets a grandparent.)

(surprised and moved . . .) Really? You'd do that?
Hey thanks – that's, that's like, . . .
Thank you.

(More young adults emerge . . .)

Overwhelmed

It worked? You got a grandma?

Griever

Yeah, this super nice stranger.

Struggler
(to the audience)
Could someone adopt me too?
Could I have a grandmother?

Legacyer
(emerging)
Could I have a Zayde?
Mine died before I was born . . .

Overwhelmed
(emerging)
A bubbe?
I know I'm [*age*], but I still want a bubbe . . .

(While some continue to solicit the audience to be their grandparents & other relations, others seem to be searching in the audience & calling beyond, looking for their lost kin.)

[Performers may also call out the names of their own lost kin. Feel free to add, overlap, repeat, . . .]

Anchor
Dad?

Overwhelmed
Bubbe?

Legacyer
Zayde?

Linker
Mom?

Wrestler
Abuela?

Pop-Pop?

Mom?

Starter
Sharon?

Mom?

Aunt Sharon?

Anchor
Dad?

Uncle Saul?
Cousin David?

Wrestler
Cousin Louis?

Abuela?

Overwhelmed
Nanny?

Struggler
Nana?

Wrestler
Grandpa Pete?

Abuelita??

Great Uncle Dan?

Overwhelmed
Nan?

(An older woman arrives.
Another voicemail in the ether.
LIGHT on somebody's Nana.)
(She dons the spectacles that the Tanna or Study Group Leader were wearing.)

Old World Woman
Oh my loves.
You think of me, and you think of my life, and you think it sounded like:
[she hums a maudlin snatch of a Yiddish/klezmer song]
But no, my loves, my youth sounded like:
[she hums a buoyant snatch of a Yiddish/klezmer song]

And in Brooklyn it became:

[she hums 'Take me out to the ballgame' or the like]

How old was I then? I was ten. My sister was twelve and my brother fifteen.
Our parents stayed in Lithuania.
You cannot know.
Our Rebbe back in Vilna, he sounded like: *[she hums]*.
And that's how the Torah sounded to me. I never read it – I never was taught to – but I always imagined it sang to you as you read it.
That the ink of the scribes would sing to you its notes over hundreds and thousands of years,
if you could just unfurl it.
Like a rolled up piano.
My mother and father we never heard from again.
There is no sound for that.

I'll tell you this: Lithuanian chimes different from Polish,
and Polish tastes different from Russian,
and Russian fills the mouth more than English,
which likes to lie heavy on the tongue.

There is so much more I could tell you,
of what sounds like what, each on its own, –
but for me,
the whole chorus of Time, . . .
it sings, oh, it sings in Yiddish.

(She sings a bit of a Yiddish tune.
Something like *Oyfn Pripetchik* by Mark M. Warshavsky.
Maybe an Old World couple dances to it.)

Old World Woman

Oyfn pripetchik brent a fayerl
un in shtub is heys.
Un der rebbe lernt kleyne kinderlekh
dem alef-beyz;
Un der rebbe lernt kleyne kinderlekh
dem alef-beyz.

(Starter is moved.)

Old World Woman

Do you have anything like that?

(Starter thinks . . . .
What he comes up with is *Don't Think Twice, It's All Right* by Bob Dylan.)

Starter

Well there ain't no use to sit and wonder why, babe
If'n you don't know by now
And there ain't no use to sit and wonder why, babe
It'll never do somehow.

(Even *more* New World young adults join . . .)

Starter, Et Al.
When the rooster crows at the break o' dawn
Look out your window and I'll be gone
You're the reason I'm travelin' on
Don't think–

Old World Woman
(underwhelmed) Meh.

(The lost young-adult children who were just searching for their ancestors begin asking Old World Woman and us their questions . . .)

Griever
(to us, or to the audience member that they want to connect with or be adopted by)
. . . Tell me who my people are?

Legacyer
(to us, or to the audience member that they want to connect with or be adopted by)
Tell me things are as hard now as they were then,
even if there aren't chicken feet to boil and menstruation laws to keep?

Overwhelmed
(to us, or to the audience member that they want to connect with or be adopted by)
Tell me if we're still a people?

Linker
(to each other now)
Even if everyone's getting divorced and moving away and converting to Buddhism and secularism and veganism and agnosticism?

Struggler
Even if there aren't any tribes, or figs, or sand?

Wrestler
Even if in cities you can't see the stars?

Anchor
Even if no one listens to klezmer or remembers Yiddish or reads the Torah or gives a hot shit about Martin Buber?

Starter
What's klezmer?

Overwhelmed
Who's Martin Buber?

Starter
Kidding.

Overwhelmed
Not kidding.

Legacyer
Philosopher.

Linker
Genius.

Wrestler
Depends on who you ask.

Starter
Really, you don't know Buber? He's big in the tribe, dude.

Struggler
What tribe?

Griever
Right? Okay, like, . . .

(Griever dons Anchor with spectacles & a black hat,
– the same as the Young Boy Hawker at the start –
and she plays a Young Man Hassid.)

Griever
. . . . like, you and I. Are we still a people?

Young Man Hassid
. . . Of course.

Overwhelmed
. . . Why?

Young Man Hassid
. . . Because. . . . Once you're in, you're in.

Struggler
What does that mean?

Young Man Hassid
Same Torah.

Linker
I don't read the Torah.

Young Man Hassid
Same God.

Overwhelmed
I don't believe in God.

Wrestler
I believe in a Higher Power, but I've never read the Torah.

Young Man Hassid
Same homeland.

Starter
I believe in the two-state solution.

(Everyone opens their mouth to *ardently* concur or conflict.)

Overwhelmed
(to all, with dread)
Can we not?
(They look at her.)
Please?
(They relent.)

Starter
Just sayin'.

Struggler
My homeland is Kansas City, Missouri.

Legacyer
Mine's Colorado. The mountains.

Young Man Hassid
Same origin.

Linker
I have two moms.

Struggler
Adopted. Raised Jewish.

Linker
What do you have to say about that?

Starter
My parents came here from Addis Ababa.

Wrestler
Havana.

Overwhelmed
Marseilles.

Struggler
Lodz.

Young Man Hassid
I mean same traditions, same forefathers, . . .

Legacyer
I totally turn on the lights on Shabbat.

Starter
We eat figs for Hanukkah.

Wrestler
I hate the forefathers.

Young Man Hassid
Same *trauma* then.

Struggler
We do *not* have the same trauma.

Starter
You think the Holocaust *unites* us?

Overwhelmed
Oh no . . .

Wrestler
I reject that as a defining identity.

Linker
So if you're not a Jew from Europe, you don't count?

Overwhelmed
Do we have to talk about it?

Griever: Wait, we're united by trauma?
Legacyer: Isn't every group?
Overwhelmed: No?
Griever: I guess so.
Overwhelmed: Yes?

Struggler
It blinds us from talking about everything else –
other parts of ourselves, other narratives, / other peoples –

Legacyer
(interrupting) There *are* no other narratives.
Trauma seeps into every narrative forever, / before and after.

Overwhelmed
(interrupting) My family never makes it through / this conversation intact . . .

Starter
(interrupting) Aaaand this is why I believe in the two-state solution.

Linker
This is exactly why we need a homeland.

Overwhelmed
This is why I don't want to have this conversation.

Young Man Hassid
Look, we are where we came from! All the way back. EVERYONE has a tribe–

Struggler
That's not actually true.
Half my tribe got erased, so . . .

Young Man Hassid
– And we're all yours, if you want us.

Wrestler
Yeah, on *your* terms . . .

Young Man Hassid
And if you don't? You know what? That's fine.
Leave us. We don't need you!

Linker
I'm sorry, but like . . .

Young Man Hassid
I don't need you!

Overwhelmed
Sorry, it's just –

Young Man Hassid
What? I gotta be a Jew for all of you, so you can ditch where you came from
but trust it'll still exist?
It's a tall order, man. It's WORK, you know? The peyes, the study, the slacks
and long-sleeves all summer, the strict kashrut, the looks on subways,
the laws and mitzvahs, the davening, the loyalty, the hierarchy,
I don't know if I *want* to have children,
but the tribe is gonna disappear, man,
it's gonna *UN-EXIST* without me and my family –
(*gesturing to a performer who dons something and becomes CHILD,*
the Young Man Hassid's kid sibling . . .)
– holding down the fort while you contemplate atheism and what kind of cheese you want
on your pork croissant or whatever.

Legacyer
Pork croissant?

Young Man Hassid
So leave if you want to – but don't come crawling back and expect us to still be here!

Griever
Well . . . what if I'm okay with that?

Overwhelmed
Whoa.

(Upset, the Young Man Hassid starts to go . . .)

Starter
(calling after him) Sorry, dude. But seventy faces to the Torah, am I right?

(The Young Man Hassid keeps going, mumbles 'Whatever.'
A child runs in.)

Child
(calling) Matt-matt, come back!

Young Man Hassid
(calling) I told you, the name's Moshe!
Go home, Davey. I'm outta here.

(Everyone watches Young Man Hassid go . . . .)

The president of the National Yiddish Book Center is here,
– where did he come from? when did he come in? –
Maybe he thrusts empty envelopes at the congregation before him . . . .

NYBC Prez
(shaking our hands, thrusting envelopes at us)
Sholem-aleykhem! Peace be upon you!
Thank you for having me, it's a beautiful space.
I'm here on behalf of the *Natsionale Yidishe Bikher Tsentrale.*
You don't even know what that means, eh?
You cling to *one another*, but what about our texts?
Our tongue! There's no replacing a tongue. A language dies, it leaves a hole in the mouth of history.
No words, no thoughts, the rest is silence.
We had a Yiddish Shakespeare. Several. You didn't know that, did ya?
So today I'm here to find 18 new members – sponsors – *heroes*! –
to rescue our literature!

NYBC Prez retrieves a dusty, orphaned Yiddish book. Opens it and out pours:

Yiddishkeit 1
– Brecht zich a ring, tsefalt di gantseh kait.

NYBC Prez
And every moment you hesitate, another Yiddish book dies.

NYBC Prez stoops to retrieve another dusty, orphaned Yiddish book. Opens it and out pours:

Yiddishkeit 2
– Alts drait zich arum broit un toit.

NYBC Prez
Endangered Yiddish books – all over the world!:
crouching in corners in Dublin and Capetown . . .,

Yiddishkeit 1
– Az du kukst oif hoicheh zachen, halt zikh tsu dos hitl.

NYBC Prez
. . . a whole flock of treatises found in Taipei.

Yiddishkeit 2
– Altsding lozt zich ois mit a gevain.

NYBC Prez
(*waving the two books emphatically!*)
Literary refugees. Bring them home!

Yiddishkeit 1
– Me ken nit foren oif alleh yariden oif ain mol.

Starter
What are you doing about *real* refugees?

NYBC Prez
These *are* real refugees!

Starter
I'm talking about *human beings*.

NYBC Prez
So am I!

Starter
Who need *help*!

NYBC Prez
(to all of us, pressing on)
And I'm not talking *khaloymes*; these are real, achievable dreams!
–With your support.

Yiddishkeit 2
– Der gleichster veg iz ful mit shtainer.

NYBC Prez
(gesturing re: what Yiddishkeit 2 just said)
You see?

Frustrated, Starter goes.
NYBC Prez waves the envelopes with increased fervour, stuffs a few in our hands.

NYBC Prez

Punim-zu-punim I ask you, appeal to you, Save our Species!
Save our History!
Save YOUR Grandparents!

Yiddishkeit 1

– *Takhrikhim hobn nit keyn keshenes.*

NYBC Prez

I know you don't know your *mameloshn*, you never learned it, were never taught.
On Yom Kippur you beat your breast – I should have learned it, I should have learned it,
Am I right? –
I wish I knew the tongue of my ancestors,
I dropped the ball,
I dropped their *loshn* (tongue),
their *tseyn*, their TEETH,
they got DENTURES now because of me.
They gotta eat JELLO.
BLUE.

Yiddishkeit 2

— *Men ken nit tantzen mit ein tuchus oif tsvei chossenehs.*

Yiddishkeit 1

Emes gezogt! Emes gezogt.

Yiddishkeit 2

Yeh.

NYBC Prez

To thine own self be true, *nu*?
So – 18 new members, lucky number, *chai* on life –
Lay your guilt to rest and fill an envelope,
like a real *geboyrner yidish-reder* –
like you were born to.

Yiddishkeit 2

– *Nit kain entfer iz oich an entfer.*

NYBC Prez

And we'll throw in a *tshatshke*. (he touches his heart) *Mit a hartsikn dank.*
Thank you for having me. Good *shabbas*, good night, you can find me near the *rugelach*.

NYBC Prez spots another orphaned book and sweeps it up.

NYBC Prez
(a final appeal) *Please. Hurry.*

And then Abraham Koralnik walks in,
accompanied by two academics,
Irving and Eliezer.

On his way out, the NYBC Prez thrusts this final rescued book at the two academics, who take it.

Yiddishkeit 2 would leave, but Yiddishkeit 1 lingers to tell us:

Yiddishkeit 1
You know, uh, . . .
(excited to practice a little Vaudeville stand-up with us)
It's not the cough that carries you off;
It's the coffin they carry you off in.
Badum-bum.
Nu? Nu?

Yiddishkeit 2 tries to usher off Yiddishkeit 1 . . .

Yiddishkeit 1
Wait. Wait.
A Jewish mother gives her son two neckties for his birthday.
The next time they meet, he shows up wearing one of the neckties.
And what do you think she says?
(pause)
What, you didn't like the *other* tie?
Badum-bum.
Nu? Nu?

Yiddishkeit 2 tries to usher off Yiddishkeit 1 again . . .

Yiddishkeit 1
Wait. *Wait!*
A Jewish daughter comes home from school – a Catholic day school –
and she tells her father,
Did you know that God is really *three*: a Father, a Son, and a Holy Ghost?
Her zikh gut tsu! he tells his daughter, *Es iz do nor eyn Got,*
un mir gloyben nisht in im!
(Now listen good! There is only one God, and we don't believe in him!)

Badum-bum.
(silence)
What, you heard it already?

Yiddishkeit 2 finally ushers off Yiddishkeit 1, who's smiling.

(The academics who came in with Koralnik open the book that was thrust to them. They introduce him – and one of the book's contents – to us.)

Irving

Mazl

Eliezer

By Abraham Koralnik.

(Koralnik continues, addressing us, the American Jews of 1928. He speaks energetically, with a thick Ukrainian Yiddish accent.)

(What he says to us here comes from an essay he wrote called Without Mazl that I stumbled upon in translation and have semi-adapted, with creative licenses taken.)

Abraham Koralnik

(Yiddish essayist & poet with a sense of humour)

Mazl.
You know what this is?
Luck. And destiny.

Everything needs mazl. Even our Torah needs mazl. Perhaps our Torah most of all, since everything depends on who handles her, who explains her, who translates, ...

Suppose you get rich?
(beat, smiles – He's tricked us.)
That's not mazl. That's an accident.
No, mazl is something deeper – it's the destiny at the crux of our being.

Some people have it; others don't.
(pointing) You might. (pointing) You might not.
(pointing) You might even know it. (pointing) But you might even not.

Here we are, in 1928, and it's clear some *peoples* have mazl.
The English have it; the Germans, however . . .

We also have, right now, growing up with us, two literatures.
Hebrew and Yiddish.
Two languages; one people.

Hebrew has mazl.
The tongue of a small people in a small cranny of Asia,
Hebrew became the holy language of the world!
It was the only kingly language we had,
the only one that tied together past and present.

But the ragamuffin Yiddish . . .
Yiddish has no mazl.
We like antiquity. The new doesn't please us.
This can't be fought; it runs in the blood.

(Koralnik's accent fades away until he's speaking in crystalline American English, unbeknownst to him.)

You and I, we're lucky. I can imagine a time
when our people will regret that they have behaved condescendingly to the Yiddish word.
It will be a time when Yiddish will have disappeared.
It will have become old and dead . . . And interesting.
The Jews of that time will grow nostalgic –
the Hebrew-speaking ones, the English-speaking ones –
for the tones born in the Middle Ages and strengthened on the Slavic steppes.
For the sounds of intimacy and human loneliness.
They will regret it, those who follow us, no?
They will *yearn.*

(Koralnik's thick Yiddish accent returns.)

Abraham Koralnik. Palestine, 1928.

Irving

(apologetically; in clear unaccented American English)
Translated from the Yiddish
by Irving Howe –

(Eliezer hands the book to Koralnik to see.)

Eliezer

(apologetically; in clear unaccented American English)
–and Eliezer Greenberg.
Michigan, 1972.

(Koralnik is surprised, and saddened, to hear and see this. He turns to the two.)

Abraham Koralnik

Bin ikh shoyn vider gerekht? Moishe zukh mikh? (So I was right? It's gone?)

Eliezer

Almost but not yet.

Irving

(overlapping) It's mostly gone.

Abraham Koralnik

Shoyn vider?? (Already??)
(to us) *Vosi? Keyner fun aykh redt nish kayn mame-loshn?* (Do none of you speak Yiddish?)

(We blink at him.
Maybe there's someone among the audience who does speak Yiddish and calls out.
If so, Koralnik answers something like: *Bloyz ikh mit dir, khevre(s).* (Just you and me, my friend(s).)
If not, Koralnik sadly nods.)

Yiddishkeits 1 & 2 reappear, and by necessity translate for us what they had shared:

Yiddishkeit 1
– One link snaps and the whole chain falls apart.

Yiddishkeit 2
– Everything revolves around bread and death.

Yiddishkeit 1
— When you look to the heights, hold on to your hats.

Yiddishkeit 2
– And everything ends in weeping.

Yiddishkeit 1
– You can't ride to all markets at one time.

Yiddishkeit 2
– The smoothest way is full of stones.

Yiddishkeit 1
– Shrouds don't have pockets.

Yiddishkeit 2
– With one tuchus, you can't dance at two weddings.

Yiddishkeit 1
It's true! It's true.

Yiddishkeit 2
Yeh.
– No answer is also an answer.

And Yiddishkeit 1 sneaks to us with a quick recap . . .

Yiddishkeit 1
The coffin.
The other tie.
. . . *Un mir gloyben nisht in im!*
Badum-bum.

Yiddishkeit 2 comforts Koralnik,
who is crushed that his essay has had to be translated.

Yiddishkeit 2

(patting Koralnik on the back)

You know, it is said: 'You don't speak Yiddish. It speaks itself.'

And with that, the Yiddish world dissolves.

. . .

(A youngster arrives and knocks on an invisible door.
The door opens.
An older person is on the other side.)

Older Woman Answering Door
Yes?

Younger Woman Knocking on Door
Hi. Is this the Rabinowitz household? I'm looking for Greatgreatgrandma Sarah, who begat Greatgrandma Molly, Grandma Ruth, Uncle Saul, Uncle Teddy, and Cousin Pete?

Older Woman Answering Door
. . . I'm Sarah . . . .

Younger Woman Knocking on Door
Holyshit, hi!!! I'm your granddaughter's granddaughter!

Older Woman Answering Door
. . . (underwhelmed) Hi . . . .

Younger Woman Knocking on Door
(overwhelmed) Hi*!*

(silence)

Younger Woman Knocking on Door
I came back! (beat) Here! (beat) I came back to see where I'm from!

Older Woman Answering Door
. . . *Why?* . . .

(The Younger Woman is puzzled.)
(The Older Woman turns to us.)

Older Woman Answering Door
(to us) Baddum-bum.

(And she closes the invisible door.)

Younger Woman Knocking on Door
But – wait! – you're the only one who survived the –

(A few contemporary young adults cross through, still arguing . . .
Younger Woman Knocking on Door and Older Woman Answering Door watch on.)

Wrestler
Why do we have to talk about it?
Why can't we talk about *THE PRESENT?*

Legacyer
Because the present *is* the past!

(Older Woman Answering Door 'feh's her hands and leaves.)

Struggler
Is the *future*!

Legacyer
Everyone who remembers is dying; we're already forgetting.

Struggler
What about remembering who else we are, *beyond* persecution?

Legacyer
When it hits your family, you're never done with it. It's always still happening.

Struggler
But when it's used as an excuse for modern Israeli politics—

Legacyer
Antizionists are anti-Semites.

Struggler
Anti-Semites are anti-Semites.

Legacyer
If you've never *been* there, you don't understand.

Overwhelmed
It's an impossible
conversation!

Wrestler
I want to talk about Walls!
Rallies! Refugees! ICE!
The U.N.! Climate catastrophe!
Privilege! Racism! Poverty!
Palestinian Liberation! Restorative justice!
Human rights!
Today! Today! Today!

Overwhelmed
It's cursed.
It's *literally* impossible
to have this
conversation
without damage . . .

(And so: a sudden swirl of MUSIC!

It's *Christmas*!)

(Assimilated Jews stream in, Santa hats and yamis (yarmulkes), singing and celebrating! They toss us candy canes, or stockings filled with dreidels & gelt!)

Revelers

There must have been some magic in that old silk hat they found.
For when they placed it on his head, he began to dance around. Oh . . .
Merry Christmakwanzukkah!!

(The revelers gather into a choir.
They carol, rehearse, or perform:)

Choir

O come all ye faithful
Joyful and triumphant
O come ye o co-ome ye
To Be-e-thlehem.

(Mother storms in and sees her Jewish daughter among the Choir.)

Mother

Sarah Rachel Leah,
What are you doing???

Daughter

I'm looking for God!!

Mother

I already gave you a God!

Daughter

I can't find him!!

(The Choir continues . . .)

(A little boy, the other Jewish member in the Choir,
having seen this, slinks a little, stops singing?, ashamed . . .)

(The Daughter rejoins the Choir FULL VOICE! – in search of Divinity.)

(Mother, at a loss, stands there.
Then,
at a loss,
she turns to the Jewish choir boy,
points her finger and glowers:)

Mother

Noah Cohen, just wait
until I tell your father!

(The little choir boy shrinks more.)

Mother

(to her Daughter)

Not yours!

(Mother, at a loss, storms out.)

(The Choir rises to climax! It soars! Singing in exultation and joy!)

(Trembling small boy.)

(After a moment sitting there,
at a loss,
the little boy ducks out, little candy cane gripped in his little fist,
and he escapes to an empty part of the stage.
He's wearing old-fashioned leather boots,
wool knickers, high wool socks,
a little shirt,
an old-fashioned hat is stuffed in his pocket,
he's carrying books strapped together with a belt.
He sits on a cement stoop.
He looks at the little candy cane, unwraps it, and puts it in his mouth.)

(Heschel, 77, approaches.)

Heschel

I hope you're studying Torah, Talmud, because I'm seventy-seven and you know what I wanted to do when I was your age, hell, when I was LESS THAN your age?, I wanted to STUDY, I wanted to learn Torah and STUDY, I wanted to go to Yeshiva, like YENTL, you've seen 'Yentl?', . . . well she wanted to go to Yeshiva, but she was a girl, and I'm a boy, and she lived in the 1800s and I was born in 1931, and so she couldn't get what she wanted then and that makes sense it's too bad but it makes sense, too bad she couldn't live now, but I, I could get to study, it was 1940!, I could study, I was a boy!, but do you know what happened I was born in Poland, I was born in Poland in 1931, and so by the time I was your age a bunch of soldiers eighteen times your height with feet eighty times louder than yours came into the town in a tank with lit torches and barbed wire and erect peckers and the houses went up in flames and the books came down in ashes and the *school went backwards* – back into the pile of stones it was before it existed; and the Torah in the temple WAS SHREDDED – strips of animal hide parchment with Hebrew letters like stripes – and I stuffed them in my pocket, in my fat little fist I grabbed them and stuffed this holy confetti in my pocket – and someone yelled RUN! and it was probably my mother but really we'll never know for sure will we and I ran until I got to my cousins in Siberia who stopped me from running and said what are you gripping in your fist I said parchment and they said why and I said I eat it when I'm hungry, and I dug potatoes for five years but it felt like twenty-six-hundred and I cleaned toilets in the POW camp in Czechoslafuckingvakiashithole when I was fourteen and I could trade two cigarettes each day for bread and then I crawled through three different countries' borders until I reached a DISPLACED PERSONS Camp that shipped me to your country and when I arrived they gave me a woman I was seventeen they gave me a woman with a pen who said what's your story I said I want to learn Torah and she said what kind of job do you want I said I want to learn Torah she said but what kind of work can you do I said I want to please lady please I would like that I should go to Yeshiva and learn Torah and she said AMERICA IS NOT YOUR WEALTHY FATHER WITH DEEP POCKETS IT WILL NOT BUY YOU BOOKS YOU CANNOT LEAN ON OUR COUNTRY AMERICA DOESN'T TAKE CARE OF YOU WE TAKE CARE OF IT SO WHAT KIND OF WORK CAN YOU DO???

And I learned,
not Talmud,
I learned to make hats.
Like that one.

(Heschel points to the hat in the boy's pocket.)

Heschel
SO I HOPE YOU ARE STUDYING TORAH!

(Heschel pulls a weathered dollar bill out of his pocket and thrusts it to the boy.)

Heschel
Here! Start now.

(Heschel would leave, but he sees the candy cane.)

Heschel
What is that . . .?

(Heschel takes the candy cane, tries it.)

Heschel
Mint??
Huh.

(Heschel breaks off half, hands the rest back to the boy, and walks off sucking on candy cane . . .

The boy sits with this.
Breathes.
(It's tough being 8 or 10, then and now,
or whenever.))

(A Child and Parent who are struggling to hold onto their family. Parent comes over to her Child.)

Parent 1
When you are grown enough to wonder and ask,
I will tell you:
'Your mother and I met when we were just kids – twenty-two and twenty-eight – and I thought,
(*the sound you make when you meet a soulmate*),
"Her. I want her.
Now this is someone I can stick with."
From the moment we met and talked,
I was in. And from the moment I saw her,
I saw you
And here you are.'

(For a moment the Child is comforted.
Then:)

Child
(to us, from their older perspective) I don't know it yet, but in the coming years my brother will 'make *aliyah'* (immigrate) to Israel, my parents will explode in divorce, and my adopted sister will relocate to Beijing, quote, Where she always belonged.
(to Parent 1, from their current perspective) I'm running away!

Parent 1
(She knows; she's tried.)
You can't run away from your past.

Child
I'm running away from my *future*.

Parent 1
You can't run away from your future.

Child
Well can I run away from my present?

Parent 1
Not that I know of.

Child
Why!?

Nontraditional Rabbi
(emerging)
And yet, you have to admit it's ironic . . .
I mean, the nation of Israel was basically founded by children who left their homes.
(beat)
Three thousand years . . . Oy. We are descended
from a race of fierce, tenacious, glorious, chronic self-pitiers.

You've come from *300 generations* of kinfolk with PTSD.
It stays in the blood, I think. I'm no chemist but . . .

Child
What are you?

Parent 1
(low) David . . .

Nontraditional Rabbi
Well that's the heart of everything, isn't it? 'What are you.'

Child
(low, re: the rabbi) Crazy?

Parent 1
(low) Hey . . .

Nontraditional Rabbi
A bissl crazy. K'tzat meshugganah. Scrambled in the noggin. Noodled in the navel. *Kaputzed* in the kugel. *Farblunget* in the forehead. Baked in the cod. Gefilted in the fish.

(Child starts to go off to be by himself.)

Nontraditional Rabbi
Fried in the – wait for it – herring. I'm a rabbi. Are you hungry?
(beat, he is)
Here.

(Nontraditional Rabbi extends a cloth-napkin-wrapped bundle of food. Child takes it from her.)

Nontraditional Rabbi
It's ham.
(beat)
No it's not, it's matzoh.
(reassuring)
It's matzoh.

Child
You're not like the rabbi I know.

Nontraditional Rabbi
The rabbi you know isn't of the leftist queer feminist reconstructionist persuasion?
Hm. How 'bout that. 'Seventy faces to the Torah.'

Child
And yours is one of them?

Parent 1
David.
(to Rabbi) Sorry. It's a tricky time.

Nontraditional Rabbi
(to Child) You and me both then.
I haven't seen you in tutorial.
Are you gonna be a bar-mitzvah?

Child
No.

Parent 1
He's nine . . .

Nontraditional Rabbi
Well, maybe mazel tov in maybe four years. Maybe we'll meet again.
(beat)
Or we won't.
(beat)
In the meantime, do you know what I like to do?

Child
. . .

Nontraditional Rabbi
(low) Hide the *afikomen* in my own jacket pocket.

Child
. . .

Nontraditional Rabbi
(low) So in order to find *it*, someone has to find *me*.
(*gestures mind-blown*)
My older brother taught me that.
And our cousin taught him.
And our uncle taught our cousin. And our grandfather taught our uncle.
That's the thing about ritual.
It reminds us of who we are.

(The Child, battling all sortsa things inside, goes off to be alone.)

Parent 1
David, I'll meet you at home okay?

(Child doesn't answer, keeps leaving . . ., is gone.)

Nontraditional Rabbi

(to the Parent)
I have to believe the cure to the diaspora can live in how you hide the afikomen (a matzoh ritual on Passover).

(Parent 1 calls out again to her child: *David?*)

Nontraditional Rabbi

Mine left too.

(Polish Parent 3 enters, calling out to his leaving child: *Judyta?*)

Nontraditional Rabbi

They all do.

(Parent 2 enters, calling out to her leaving child: *Molly?*
Jacob enters, calling out to his leaving child: *Joseph?*
Rebecca enters, calling out to her leaving child: *Esau? Shit. Esau?*
Woodchopper 4 enters, calling out to his leaving child: *Pete?*)

Nontraditional Rabbi

But sometimes, they come back.

(Sarah enters, very pregnant, and considers this moment of so many Parents calling for their leaving children . . .)

(Silence . . . Everyone seems to be waiting . . . to see if their child is coming back . . . . .

A moment of suspension.

Parents (and Rabbi) searching/waiting for lost children . . .

for wayward progeny . . .

. . . .)

(The Waiting Parents begin to talk to each other . . .
Maybe sometimes with us, but mostly with each other.
They're yearning, hurting, hungry, confused, urgently trying to connect and to figure things out. They talk at a pace.)

Parent 1

(to Nontraditional Rabbi) Tell me if we're still a family?

Parent 2

(to Nontraditional Rabbi) Tell me things are as hard now as they've always been?

Woodchopper 4
(to Nontraditional Rabbi) Tell me it gets easier.

Jacob
(to Nontraditional Rabbi) Tell me we'll get closer.

Polish Parent 3
(to Nontraditional Rabbi) Tell me my kid's gonna come back home.

Rebecca
(to Nontraditional Rabbi) Tell me I didn't fuck 'em up.

Nontraditional Rabbi
It's unavoidable.

Sarah
Your parents fucked up and *you're* okay.

Parent 2
– Ish.

Rebecca
(to Sarah) Speak for yourself.

Parent 1
Tell me they'll remember where they came from . . .

Jacob
Tell me they'll still be Jewish.

Polish Parent 3
Even if they got on a boat to America and married the first schmo to sit on their hat?

Woodchopper 4
Even if he's stopped coming to study Mishna with the woodchoppers?

Jacob
Even if the twelve of them split, and each started his own *tribe*?
Tell me they'll remember what I taught them.

Rebecca
Even if one cheated the other out of his birthright?
(off of Jacob & Nontraditional Rabbi's look)
(lying) I mean I told him not to.

Parent 2
Please tell me they won't go religious.

Parent 1
Even if they change their name and join the Orthodox and talk about moving to Israel?

Parent 2
(i.e. sounds like bad news) Oooff.

Nontraditional Rabbi
Tell me I'll be welcome in their home.

Rebecca
Tell me I'll get through this.

Sarah
Tell me childbirth won't kill me.

Parent 1
It's not fun.

Nontraditional Rabbi
Tell me I'll still be around.

All
. . .

Parent 2
Tell me she'll be happy. Even if she's dating a nice jewish girl named Carla?
Tell me the world will be kind to them.
Tell me the world will still *be habitable* for them.
Tell me they'll stay out of harm's way.
Tell me they'll *be happy*.

Polish Parent 3
Even if they don't keep kosher.

Nontraditional Rabbi
Even if they don't keep the Sabbath.

Jacob
They'd better keep kosher.

Woodchopper 4
Please tell me they'll keep the Sabbath.

Sarah
(wavering) Tell me it's still worth it?

Woodchopper 4
Yeah, yeah, oh yeah.

Rebecca
(nope) It's sometimes worth it . . .

Sarah
Because it took me 91 years to conceive.
And now I'm eight months pregnant.
And what if I've created a person
Who will blame me for the rest of my life?

Rebecca
I think you just have to laugh.

Parent 2
You couldn't pay me to have another kid.

Jacob
When I think back to my parents, everything makes more sense.

Polish Parent 3
Lucky you.

Rebecca
I barely knew my mother.

Sarah
I never knew my mother.

Polish Parent 3
When I met my father I was fifteen.

Sarah
I was three. He was wearing a hat.

Polish Parent 3
I'm starting a new family. Starting over. Clean slate.

Parent 1
There are no clean slates.

Parent 2
So how do you inherit what you never met?

Woodchopper 4
Does anybody know where Pete is?

Jacob
And how do you handle what's missing when what's here is already too much?

Rebecca
You learn to live with incompletion and move on.

Polish Parent 3
You do what you can?

Parent 1
But it's never enough.

Nontraditional Rabbi
Of course it isn't.

Sarah
Aint no use to sit and wonder why, babe . . .

Polish Parent 3
How does that help?

Parent 2
It's an impossible role.

Parent 1
The leaver and the left . . .

Nontraditional Rabbi
Every child is left in a world they will never understand.
And every parent is a child.
Therefore –

Woodchopper 4
Our Torah begins with the second letter for just that very reason.
It could have started with the first letter, but it doesn't – it starts with the second.

Polish Parent 3
Why?

Parent 2
Cuz our memory has a way of compressing time?

Sarah
The sun is getting low . . .

Parent 2
Where *are* they?

Rebecca
(calling) Esau?

Jacob
(calling) Joseph?

Parent 2
(calling) Molly?

Parent 1
How is there never enough time?

Nontraditional Rabbi
(to Polish Parent 3) The second letter?, it's because—well, they say it's because
even in the beginning, there is something that came before.
Something you can only imagine.
And wrestle with.

Woodchopper 4
Like Jacob wrestling the angel of history.

Jacob
Oooff that was intense.

Woodchopper 4
Everyone who lives is a wrestler of before.

Parent 2
Two Jews, three opinions.
Seventy faces.
Seven days.
Forty nights.
Four questions.
Six hundred and thirteen mitzvot.
Three thousand years of . . .

(Parent 2 has become Overwhelmed;
everything has built to this quiet avalanche of everything they're holding . . .)

Overwhelmed
Feed the chickens
Chop the wood
Milk the goats
Find the eggs
Check the latkes
Start the tsimmes
Marry Misha
Pick up milk
Mezuzah fell
Hang it back up
But kiss it first
And daven

Legacyer
Daven

Griever
Daven

Overwhelmed
Horse needs hay
Car needs gas
And don't forget to

Legacyer & Griever
Daven

Legacyer & Griever & Anchor & Starter
Daven

Legacyer & Griever & Anchor & Starter & Linker
Daven

Anchor & Griever
(breast-beating on Yom Kippur)
Ah ya yai yai yai, Ah ya ya YAI yai yai . . .

(Overwhelmed continues in the background
– an ongoing outpouring, low –
driving, inspiring, underscoring the conversation of the others . . .)

Overwhelmed
Beat your breast
Don't touch ANYthing
Polish the candlesticks in the étagère Buy more candles
Shit, the prayers
I forgot the prayers
. . . bless the bread
. . . bless the candles
. . . bless the wine
Call your grandma
Bless your heart
Grampa needs you
Dad's out back
Help your mother
Where's your sister
Fix your brother
Have kids
When you gonna have kids?
How you gonna feed five kids?
Kena hora
Zai gezunt
Learn the Torah
Hebrew school
Which yeshiva?
Do chavruta
Do not talk back to your Rebbe
WHERE'S PETE?
Drink the soup
Pluck the feathers
Where's the liver
Where's the feet
Honey where'd you put the feet
Keep the Sabbath holy
Don't lie with man as woman
Or with woman as man
WHAT THE FUCK?
You have only one God
10 commandments
1 God
People the earth
Like stars
Like sands
Multiply

Starter Aaaand this is why
I start my own rituals.

Linker But I feel like I still want
a context.
I don't want to be random.
I want to be located here,
at the intersection of you and you,
of then and now.
I want to mean something.
I want to link something together.
I don't know, you know?
I don't know.

Wrestler But I mean, I *really*
don't like the patriarchy, so . . .
Like, what options do I have
for context? Because like,
you can't talk about this stuff
without contending with
where it came from.
. . .
And that's, just, always, like,
crazy hard to do.

Legacyer Hey, who becomes
the patriarch when the
patriarch dies?
I mean, like, *me?*

Linker OK, like, sure,
we resent it and distrust it
and feel oppressed by it,
but I'm also *descended*
from that. Messed up though
it is, that *means* something,
doesn't it?

Multiply
Bathe if she's on the rag
WOMEN ARE LIKE FIGS
BATHE IF YOU SAT ON THE
CHAIR SHE SAT
ON WHEN SHE WAS ON THE RAG
Burn a stone in the oven
Keep milk from meat
It's counterintuitive but fish counts as milk
Cover your head
Don't bow down
Cover your eyes
Go on Birthright
Cover your eyes
Learn Hebrew
Take away vowels
Open your ears
But cover your eyes
Teach me Yiddish
WHY DID NO ONE TEACH ME YIDDISH?
SAVE YIDDISH
Seek forgiveness
Atone
Wash
Walk
Stoop
Give tzedukah
Honour your mother
Honour your father
Honour the lord your only God With
all your soul
With all your might
Bind these words upon your head
Upon your heart
Upon your forearms
Wrap once around the bicep
Thrice around the middle finger
Seven times along the arm
Loop, hold, pull, cross over
Mazel tov!

What's the name
Keep the covenant
Call a mohel
We're circumcizing?
Times have changed!

I mean, it can, right?
Cuz, like, otherwise,
you lose everything before.

Starter Unless you start anew.
Wrestler Good riddance.
Linker/Struggler/Legacyer . . .

Griever Do you think you're still part of something once you're gone?

Linker I don't think we make any sense when we're single.
Maybe that makes me codependent, but.
Anchor That's not codependence.
That's connection.
Wrestler Or internalized –
Starter Totally.
Wrestler Right?
Struggler But, okay, I confess it: Sometimes I just want to be held by the people I came from.
I don't care how grown-up you get, there is just something about old people singing you lullabies in their

East west north south
Start east
Face east
Jerusalem and God are east
Don't say His name
Don't write His name
Use a dash to pitch the paper
There's a bin for sacred trash
BURN IT
BATHE
LIGHT
DRINK
EAT
TASTE
DIP
DIP TWICE
RECLINE
RECITE
RETELL
REMEMBER
ASK
READ
STUDY
REST
On the seventh day He rested
Don't carry
Don't create
Don't destroy
Do nothing
Keep it holy
Just be
Is the kasha done?
JUST BE!
Are you happy?
Be happy!
WHY THE HELL AREN'T YOU HAPPY?
(beat)
Warm the hot plate
Pass the spices
Bless His name
Blessed be He
Shake the lulav with the etrog
Hold the chuppah
Break the glass
Have more children!
Teach them well

mothertongue that just, like, does it for me, you know?
It cuts through all the bullshit.
It CALMS me. You know?
It feels like: this is a real moment that's happening right now; I'm being sung to by an artifact preserved from another time.

. . .

Griever (to Overwhelmed)
. . . Are you OK?
. . .
. . .
. . .
Starter She's *in* it.
Anchor Amen.

(beat)

Legacyer Why does everyone seem to die before you're old enough to really remember them?

Griever I'm afraid of becoming one of the Old Ones.
Disappear before I'm known.
I don't want to be an artifact.

Listen up
HEAR O ISRAEL!
Make a sermon
Bake a challah
Break the matzoh
Make a Kiddush
Plant a tree
Join a temple
Reconstruct
But don't start a fight
Build an ark
Find the dove
Escape the whale
WHERE'S OUR CHILD?
Strike the rock
Lead the people
Consider the lilies
That's not your religion!
Melt the calf
Give her gelt
Buy a bond
Be a mensch
Where's the kugel?
Potato or noodle?!
Does it matter?!
EVERYTHING MATTERS!!!!

Struggler Amen.

Starter I do.
Linker Amen.
Wrestler I don't understand
why we should *have* to
become Old Ones.

Anchor Or how to go through it well.

Legacyer Which, of course, you can't.

. . .
I mean, nobody does.
. . .

A SPLASH!

A SMASH OF GLASS!

A POP!

A FLARE OF MATCH!

A FLOCK OF GEESE IN FRENZIED FLIGHT . . .

(*flapping, honking, flying . . .*

. . . growing faint)

(Griever has a thought.
He decides to follow the impulse.
Using whatever he finds lying around, he makeshiftly dresses himself up as a Bubbe.
Maybe as his was. Maybe not.
He clears his throat, tries to create her in voice and shape . . .
He's not very deft at being her – at least not at the start –
but he's trying to feel a connection, build a community, or fill a void.)

A Bubbe

Awwwwwh. Bubbelehhhhs. Mmmmmnn.

Overwhelmed

(*soft*) Bubbe?

A Bubbe

Shhhhhh. Shahhh. Mmmmnn.

All

(*simultaneous*)
Anchor No way.
Linker Nana?
Starter Grandma?
Struggler Grams?
Wrestler Abuela?
Legacyer Awesome.

A Bubbe

So *heavy*.
Your shoulders.
Your . . .? (*taps her forehead*)

Legacyer

Keppes.

A Bubbe

They hang to your shins, your foreheads, they drag to the floors.
Bent over backs, on such young people.

(A few sit up.)

A Bubbe

Why *so heavy so young*?

Struggler

It's a good question, Grams.

A Bubbe

Eh? What have you got to be heavy for now?

All

[. . . *naming All The Things they're heavy about* . . .]

A Bubbe

(overlapping) No no no no no,
your poppy and I, we *did* the heavy.
We did the labour and the journey and the dying and the saving.
We *wore* all the heavy clothes – gray and wool, scratchy, mended – so that you can wear satin!

No, not satin.

Legacyer: Flannel pajamas.
Wrestler: Neckties.
Anchor: Lycra . . .

A Bubbe

(overlapping) Cotton! Polyester!
Light clothes, light shoulders, light foreheads . . .
If you are heavy, what was it all for?
Eh?

(to Overwhelmed)
You have a very sweet face, you know that? A handsome punim.
Your grandmother cherished you.
(explaining) She wanted to come. She couldn't come. . . . So I came.

(to Starter)
You look a pretty thing. Strong. Smart. In-dependent . . .

(to us all)
Look at me, bubbelehs. In my eyes.

Legacyer

De oigen!

A Bubbe

My ancient yellow oigens.
What do you see?

Starter

Got a little goo in the corner there . . .

A Bubbe

No, besides the schumutz. The gray spots. What else?
Can you see yourself in me?
Can you see me young and sexy and wearing wool but handsomely?

Struggler

Yes, Grams.

A Bubbe

Can you see *my* bubbe before me? And her bubbe? And her bubbe?
All the way back to Rebecca and Sarah and Eve?

Wrestler

And Lilith. Everyone leaves out Lilith.

A Bubbe

You come from there.
From as far back as you can see,
and farther than that – as you can imagine –

and farther than that – as you can guess –
and farther than that – farther than that.
Go back to Abraham and Sarah.
They are your grandparents.
Yes. It's true. You are related.
They're very famous, you know.
There's a book written about them.
Well, they're in the first part.
You didn't know you had famous grandparents, did you?

And strong, did you know that?
I knew them. They were strong.
Strong people.
Old.
Old people.
And strong through the end.
Chutzpah.
And mazel.
Guts and luck.
You come from two old people who had guts and luck.
. . .
Mostly guts.
So you are blessed!
(to us)
All of you, you know.
And now you are here.
Lest you doubt, for even a moment, that you–
just remember: you come from strength.
You are their direct descendants.

What a family.
We're crazy, yes. You're nuts. Sorry.
But you're strong nuts.
Brazil nuts.
Or such.

Linker

Which are Brazil nuts?

A Bubbe

Those long ones, with the shell?, hard to crack, rough like tree bark?
Oy. Bitter.

They're good for you.

Here.

(This Bubbe hands Overwhelmed, and them all, and us, a small beaded bag full of brazil nuts.

Or such.)

(Bubbe disappears.)

The setting sun . . .
Blinding.
Gold.
Sinking.
The sky goes vibrant . . . and then pale . . . and then dusk.

A star appears.

One more.

A third.

It's officially night.

(The Young Boy Hawker reenters,
or maybe he's been crouching and watching the stars come out,
and we heard him whisper-counting: *One . . . – Two. . . – Three. Okay.*
Now that it's nightfall, he calls out for anyone to join him for:)

Boy

Havdalah? Havdalah?
How 'bout a Havdalah?
(by way of explanation)
Uh, it's a ritual,
to help ease the transition from sacred time back to, uh, ordinary time.
It's like a balm for separation.
But for the Ma'ariv prayers we'll need 10 people.
Anyone? Anyone?

Oh, you don't have to *do* anything. Just stand with me.
Metaphorically.
And bear witness. I mean, you have to be willing to *count*.
Metaphorically.
Yes? Anyone? Anyone?

(He waits till he gets enough performers and audience members,
or the audience as a whole, to agree to join as part of the 10.)

Boy

Okay! Wonderful! Wow!
(calling for him) Yitzak, we got a minyan! (required group of 10 in order to do religious things)
Uh, it is said, when ten persons come together in a room, the holy can happen:
weddings, funerals, prayers, benedictions, reading from the Torah, . . .
. . . I dunno why.
I guess ten is what it takes to make a—
(calling) Yitzak . . .!

(Yitzak trots in.)

(So the Young Boy Hawker and Yitzak facilitate our shared Havdalah, in which:)

Wine cups are passed around to be raised . . .

Boy

Uh . . . BlessedareYouHaShemwho made the fruit of the vine.

Yitzak

Amen.

The wine is drunk . . .

Boy

BlessedareYouHaShemwho made loads of spices.

Yitzak

Amen.

Spices are passed around for the smelling . . .

Boy

BlessedareYouHaShemwho made the light of fire.

Yitzak

Amen.

A braided candle is lit and raised . . .

Boy

Okay, wanna finish it up, Yitzak?

(Yitzak lights up.)

Yitzak

(sings) *Baruch atah Adonai—*

Boy

(interrupts) You know how prayer started?

(Yitzak is miffed.
He shakes his head.)

Boy

It started, what do you think, with food.

Yitzak

Bagels?

Boy

No, not bagels. –

Yitzak

Lox?

Boy

No, but . . . bread? Olive oil?
Point is: the ancestors at first didn't gather to pray; they just gathered to EAT.
And then, over time, their gatherings felt more and more sacred.
(considers) Maybe that's the way of the world, Yitzak?

Yitzak

What is?

Boy

Life gets harder. We grow up and feel more alone. And so, in the chaos of the world – coming together starts to take on a . . . a *significance*.
And maybe our old ancestors, they start to think: 'You know what?, we're not gonna get to do this too often.
Yes I WANNA see you on Wednesday, but there's seeds to plant, lambs to salt, water to draw, hats to make,

Torah to learn, parents to bury, children to bear, it's tough times. So you know what? You're here. I'm here. So here: take some meat. Pull some bread. Pour some oil. Shake some salt. –'

Yitzak

Shake a leg.

(making himself laugh)

Boy

'– And sprinkle a little hyssop – it's a special occasion! – special needs spices! – and say a blessing for the holy fact that we're here. May we be here again soon.
And when certainly we're not –

(to Yitzak, who looks concerned/anguished)

we can pretend that's not true, but . . .

(to us)

– when certainly we're not, we'll regard this day as a holy day. A sacred moment of being.'

Yitzak

Our ancestors said all that?

Boy

And then prayer was born.
A blessing of thanks, for being together, in the same time.

(beat)

Yitzak

That's a good story.

Boy

(touched, maybe blushing)

Thanks, buddy.

(Yitzak takes a breath to resume the prayer, then halts and looks to Boy.)

Boy

Yeah, go for it.

(So Yitzak does.)

Yitzak

(sings) *Baruch atah Adonai*
hamav'dil bein kodesh l'chol.

Boy

Uh . . . A blessing for everything holy and common.

Yitzak

Amen.

The candle is extinguished.

A hand-washing pitcher, bowl, and towel
appear for the performers (or us) to wash hands . . .

(The Jocund Old Rabbi reenters.)

Jocund Old Rabbi
(to us)
What is this??
(to the performers with the pitcher, bowl, and towel)
What is this?!?
(to us)
For hand-washing?!
Oyoyoy – you haven't??!?
At the beginning it should have been!
At the beginning you wash!
At the end, what's the point??
You've eaten already with dirty paws!
Trayf with the, the, the fingernails. Eh?

(The Jocund Old Rabbi watches . . .
. . . sighs . . .
. . . and finally aids in passing the pitcher, bowl, and towel around.)

Jocund Old Rabbi
Ooooooyyyyyy . . . Here. Take it take it.

Don't tell the Big One.
(*looks up*)
Shhh. He likes very clean hands.

So.

The prayer for washing away.

Baruch asa Adonai, elohaynu melech ha'olam,
asher kid'shanu b'mitzvosav v'tzivanu
al netilas yadai'im.

(He looks around at all of us . . . . . .
He resigns himself with an old, sad smile.
Maybe he's absolving us of unwanted guilt, responsibility, debt, or devotion.)

Jocund Old Rabbi
There.

(. . . silence . . .)

All clean.

(*. . . silence . . .*)

Not a trace.

(*. . . silence . . .*)

(Having cleaned up all evidence of the Old World, of the Jewish, of the ancestors,
of the lost,
he starts exiting . . . .)

(. . . Stops.

Turns.)

Well, maybe a *trace*.

(And, with that, the Jocund Old Rabbi fades into the darkness.)

Wind . . .

whhhhhhhhhhhoooooooooooooooooohhhhhhhhhhhhhhhhhhsssshh

. . . . . . A strain from a fiddle . . . . . .

Sand . . .

sssssshhhhhhhhhhhhsssssstttttccccccchhhhhhhhhhkkkkhhhhgggggghhhh

. . . End of play.

. . .

Bibliography of Inspirations and Influential Works

Plays

The Dybbuk (S. Anski)
The Golem (H. Leivick)
God of Vengeance (Sholom Asch)
2 Samuels 11, etc. (David Greenspan)
Insurrection: Holding History (Robert O'Hara)
Annulla (Emily Mann)
Still Life (Emily Mann)
Out of My Father's House (Eve Merriam)
Angels in America, Parts I and II (Tony Kushner)

Essays/critical writings (excerpts)

I and Thou – a treatise (Martin Buber)
Voices from the Yiddish: Essays, Memoirs, Diaries (I. L. Peretz, Abraham Koralnik and others)
The Book of J (Harold Bloom and David Rosenberg)
The Vanishing American Jew (Alan Dershowitz)
The Origin of German Tragic Drama: Theses on the Philosophy of History (Walter Benjamin)
Vagabond Stars: A World History of Yiddish Theater (Nahma Sandrow)
Plays (Gertrude Stein)
'They Watch Me as They Watch This': Gertrude Stein's Metadrama (Jane Palatini Bowers)

Religious texts

The Mishna – Tractates Niddah, Nedarim, and Sotah
A Prayerbook (*A Book of Songs and Blessings*)

Other literature

Dear Lizzie: *A Memoir of A Jewish Immigrant Woman* (Leona Tamarkin)
The Poems of Yehuda Amichai
The Stories of Sholom Aleichem
Yiddishe Chochma – A collection of Yiddish wisdom

Films

Yentl, 1983 (dir. Barbra Streisand)
Fiddler on the Roof, 1971 (dir. Norman Jewison)

Other media

'Jewish immigrants from Arab lands found reguge in Greater Miami, too'. *The Miami Herald*. November 28, 2002: https://www.miamiherald.com/opinion/op-ed/article269310082.html
Lilith Magazine: 'Independent, Jewish, & Frankly Feminist'
Wikipedia

Music

'Oyfn Pripetchik' (Mark M. Warshavsky)
'Don't Think Twice, It's All Right' (Bob Dylan)
Klezmer, and tons more

And many conversations

Including the 2009 Slifka Center 'Deliberation On Family'